*(Continued)*

*Early Childhood Education Series titles, continued*

Understanding Young Children's Behavior:
A Guide for Early Childhood Professionals

JILLIAN RODD

Understanding Quantitative and Qualitative Research
in Early Childhood Education

WILLIAM L. GOODWIN & LAURA D. GOODWIN

Diversity in the Classroom: New Approaches to the
Education of Young Children, 2nd Edition

FRANCES E. KENDALL

Developmentally Appropriate Practice in "Real Life"

CAROL ANNE WIEN

Experimenting with the World:
John Dewey and the Early Childhood Classroom

HARRIET K. CUFFARO

Quality in Family Child Care and Relative Care

SUSAN KONTOS, CAROLLEE HOWES,
MARYBETH SHINN, & ELLEN GALINSKY

Using the Supportive Play Model: Individualized
Intervention in Early Childhood Practice

MARGARET K. SHERIDAN,
GILBERT M. FOLEY, & SARA H. RADLINSKI

The Full-Day Kindergarten:
A Dynamic Themes Curriculum, 2nd Edition

DORIS PRONIN FROMBERG

Assessment Methods for Infants and Toddlers:
Transdisciplinary Team Approaches

DORIS BERGEN

Young Children Continue to Reinvent Arithmetic—
3rd Grade: Implications of Piaget's Theory

CONSTANCE KAMII with SALLY JONES LIVINGSTON

Moral Classrooms, Moral Children: Creating a
Constructivist Atmosphere in Early Education

RHETA DeVRIES & BETTY ZAN

Diversity and Developmentally Appropriate Practices

BRUCE L. MALLORY &
REBECCA S. NEW, Eds.

Understanding Assessment and Evaluation in Early
Childhood Education

DOMINIC F. GULLO

Changing Teaching, Changing Schools:
Bringing Early Childhood Practice into Public
Education—Case Studies from the Kindergarten

FRANCES O'CONNELL RUST

Physical Knowledge in Preschool Education:
Implications of Piaget's Theory

CONSTANCE KAMII & RHETA DeVRIES

Ways of Assessing Children and Curriculum:
Stories of Early Childhood Practice

CELIA GENISHI, Ed.

The Play's the Thing: Teachers' Roles in Children's Play

ELIZABETH JONES & GRETCHEN REYNOLDS

Scenes from Day Care

ELIZABETH BALLIETT PLATT

Making Friends in School:
Promoting Peer Relationships in Early Childhood

PATRICIA G. RAMSEY

The Whole Language Kindergarten

SHIRLEY RAINES & ROBERT CANADY

Multiple Worlds of Child Writers:
Friends Learning to Write

ANNE HAAS DYSON

The Good Preschool Teacher

WILLIAM AYERS

The War Play Dilemma

NANCY CARLSSON-PAIGE &
DIANE E. LEVIN

The Piaget Handbook for Teachers and Parents

ROSEMARY PETERSON & VICTORIA FELTON-COLLINS

Visions of Childhood

JOHN CLEVERLEY & D. C. PHILLIPS

Starting School

NANCY BALABAN

Ideas Influencing Early Childhood Education

EVELYN WEBER

The Joy of Movement in Early Childhood

SANDRA R. CURTIS

# TEACHING AND LEARNING IN A DIVERSE WORLD

*Multicultural Education for Young Children*

**THIRD EDITION**

## Patricia G. Ramsey
*Foreword by Sonia Nieto*

Teachers College, Columbia University
New York and London

Published by Teachers College Press, 1234 Amsterdam Avenue, New York, NY 10027

*Library of Congress Cataloging-in-Publication Data*

Ramsey, Patricia G.
    Teaching and learning in a diverse world : multicultural education for young children / Patricia G. Ramsey ; foreword by Sonia Nieto.—3rd ed.
        p. cm. — (Early childhood education series)
    Includes bibliographical references and index.
    ISBN 0-8077-4505-7 (cloth : alk. paper) — ISBN 0-8077-4504-9 (pbk. : alk. paper)
        1. Multicultural education—United States.  2. Multiculturalism—Study and teaching (Early childhood)—United States.  3. Early childhood education—United States.  4. Educational sociology—United States.  5. Teaching—United States.  I. Title.  II. Early childhood education series (Teachers College Press)
    LC1099.3.R36   2004
    370.117′0973—dc22                                    2004051733

ISBN 0–8077–4504–9 (paper)
ISBN 0–8077–4505–7 (cloth)

Printed on acid-free paper
Manufactured in the United States of America

11   10   09   08   07   06   05   04       8   7   6   5   4   3   2   1

In Memory of
Susan Kontos
Friend and Colleague

# Contents

Contents ix

## PART III: A VISION OF THE FUTURE

# Foreword

Patricia Ramsey and I met in 1975 when we were graduate students together. Although we were studying distinct specializations—she early childhood education, and I curriculum—a course taught by Professor Bob Suzuki that autumn became a magnet for us both. It was the first course on multicultural education that had ever been taught on our campus. Patty (as she is known to her friends) and I were electrified by the ideas, questions, and challenges that were at the core of that and subsequent courses. Bob Suzuki became a valued mentor to us both, always impressing upon us that multicultural education was far more than adding ethnic content to the curriculum. In those invigorating days when multicultural education was in its infancy, Patty and I spent numerous hours talking about diversity, racism, social justice, and many other issues that we studied and lived with every day. A central question for us concerned what our roles might be in helping to move education in a direction that would be more just, equitable, and affirming.

Consequently, when Patricia Ramsey's *Teaching and Learning in a Diverse World* was first published nearly two decades ago, I welcomed it both as the first book of a dear friend and colleague, and as a significant contribution to the field that we both loved. Before this, few books had considered what it meant to include a multicultural perspective in the places where our very youngest children are educated, preschools and daycare centers. Some early childhood educators and parents went so far as to suggest that a multicultural approach was too "serious," too "solemn," too "dangerous" for very young children. Others limited their concerns to what has come to be called a "holidays and heroes approach": it was fine to celebrate Chinese New Year, Chanukah, and Cinco de Mayo, and it was acceptable to invite parents to school to cook spaghetti or to teach the polka, but for the most part, racism and sexism, and other concerns about social justice, were not associated with early childhood education. These matters were thought to be best left at the preschool door. Patricia Ramsey's book became one of the first to fill a conspicuous void by directly addressing these issues, and addressing them in an appropriate and developmentally-sensitive ways, in early childhood settings.

It was also true at the time that traditional human development texts rarely examined race, ethnicity, social class, gender, or other aspects of diversity. Yet most human development theories were presented as universal in spite of the fact that they consistently drew their examples only from the lives of middle-class European American children. Consequently, there was a wide divide between those few educators who advocated using a multicultural approach with young children, and most developmentalists, who seldom ventured into discussions of diversity.

Fortunately, Patricia Ramsey came along and wrote her now-classic text to address both of these crucial issues, in addition to numerous others. She honestly and directly confronted racism, sexism, and other institutional forms of discrimination as they might affect the education of young children, and she critically analyzed theories of child development that paid little attention to the cultural, social, and political contexts of children's lives. Further, hers was one of the first multicultural education texts to take language differences seriously by including a substantial discussion on language development and bilingual education. In the following edition, she introduced a number of other themes to the multicultural conversation, issues such as moral development, economic diversity, environmental concerns, and consumerism. In doing so, she challenged us to recognize that multicultural education is not just about racial and ethnic diversity, but about diversity in its many manifestations. On the other hand, she has not lost sight of the original goal of multicultural education: to make education equitable for those children who have historically been most miseducated by our schools, specifically poor children and children of color. The synthesis of issues of diversity with concerns about the economy, the environment, and consumerism makes *Teaching and Learning in a Diverse World* a unique contribution to the field.

In this third edition, Patty has made even more changes. She has wisely combined theoretical issues with practical applications, presenting an impressive model of what it means to put theory to work in real settings, an approach certain to be appreciated by the many practitioners who want to know "what it will look like" in their classrooms. The numerous vignettes and activities she has woven throughout the text in this edition will also help define what multicultural education means in concrete settings of all kinds, from rural to urban, from multicultural to more homogeneous settings. As in the first two editions, she has taken on the most daunting of tasks: guiding teachers to help our very youngest children make sense of this complex world by becoming curious, critical, and compassionate learners.

Patricia Ramsey has written a text without easy answers. Instead, in these pages she questions, coaxes, and motivates readers to be reflective and critical teachers so that education can become liberating, fulfilling, and

meaningful for even our youngest children. She reminds us that teaching is
not a technical activity, but rather that it is fundamentally a decision-making
and political process that can forever change the lives of all those who experience it, be they children, educators, or parents.

Sonia Nieto
University of Massachusetts

# Preface

The three editions of *Teaching and Learning in a Diverse World* in some ways mirror my life and the times in which we live. The first edition, written in the 1980s, reflected the optimism of the early days of the multicultural movement. Buoyed by the successes of the civil rights movement, many of us believed that if we and our children understood the complexities of race and culture, we would be able to work together to erase decades of discrimination and inequity.

The second edition was written in the mid-1990s, when my children, Daniel and Andrés, both adopted from Chile, were in preschool and primary grades in a small town in Mexico, where we lived for 2 years. I was watching with delight as they immersed themselves eagerly into a new life and, on occasion, eloquently raised and argued about social justice issues. At the same time, my joy for them was tempered by the realization that, despite two decades of multicultural education and many other reforms, discrimination and economic inequities still divided our society and would define the futures of all children, including my own.

Now, as I write this third edition, Daniel (age 15) and Andrés (age 12) are valiantly trying to weave together their adolescent identities from the many strands of their lives. The fissures that divide and wound our society are becoming even clearer to me. I worry about whether my sons will be able to negotiate the gap between their White middle-class parents' expectations and popular images of Latino males. As some of their friends become alienated from school, the distance between family and peers widens, and the threads that connect them are stretched to the breaking point. Which parts of their lives will they have to lop off? As these struggles intensify, I am also confronting at deeper levels how my privilege as a White, middle-class, heterosexual, and able-bodied woman has shaped my expectations and worldview. As I see how my sons experience the world, I am painfully aware of how deeply racism is rooted in my own heart and in our society.

As international adoptees, my children face particular challenges, but their struggles are not unique. Many of their friends, from a wide range of backgrounds, are torn between idealism and the media and peer cultures that glorify racism, sexism, homophobia, violence, and greed. As they spin their dreams of the future, they see their prospects diminish as our national leaders roll back decades of legislation and financial support for civil rights, affirmative action, education, job opportunities, and environmental protections. They struggle to define their values while they watch rich White CEOs get away with fraudulent practices, while poor drug dealers of color get locked up for life. In the face of these inequities and contradictions, too many young people are yielding to cynicism and self-destructive behaviors.

Yet as I watch my own children and their friends valiantly navigating through the contradictions of our society—with pain, joy, anger, and laughter—I see reason to hope. As the true effects of our inequitable economic and political systems are unmasked, more people, young people in particular, are recognizing the need for a profound reorientation of our society—from one based on individualism and materialism to one that is equitable and sustainable; from one that is wounded by divisions and discrimination to one that is healed with respect and caring.

I write this book believing that we can work together to create a world where children can be whole, where they do not feel that they have to choose between conflicting identities and loyalties, and where they can reject cynicism for hope and joy.

For the past three decades, multicultural education has been a constant, yet flexible, force for creating such a world. The path has not been easy; in many communities multiculturalism has been scorned, ridiculed, and outright forbidden. In others, it has been diluted to the point where its implementation has been superficial and fleeting. Still, when I talk with young people who have grown up with at least some exposure to multicultural principles, I am impressed at their critical perspectives and their heartfelt commitment to work for social justice. For many, the seeds of multiculturalism have taken root and flourished in the enthusiasm and idealism of youth.

The specific challenge for the readers of this book is how to sow these seeds in early childhood classrooms. How do we deal with these complex issues honestly yet optimistically with young children? I hope that this book will create a space where teachers and parents can join together to scrutinize their own lives and our society and to develop ways of encouraging children to envision and work for a more just world.

The book is divided into three parts. Part I contains three chapters that review different aspects of multicultural education and general guidelines for its implementation. Part II has five chapters. Each chapter explores how a specific point of division in our society (race, economics, culture, gender, and abilities/disabilities) affects children's lives and worldviews and how we can encourage children to challenge inequities related to it. Part III is a story—a vision—of how families and schools, using the insights and skills described in the previous chapters, can critically and compassionately collaborate to make their communities and the world more just and caring places.

# Acknowledgments

Many people have supported and enabled me to write this edition of *Teaching and Learning in a Diverse World*. First, many thanks to my colleagues at Mount Holyoke College, especially those in the Department of Psychology and Education, for making it possible for me to take a sabbatical, during which time I wrote this book. The current and past staff at Gorse Child Study Center—Janna Aldrich, Jean Guarda, Susannah Heard, Helen Johnson, Mary Ellen Marion, Valerie Sawka, Leela Sundquist, and Barbara Sweeney—have been a continuing source of inspiration; many of the ideas in this book are based on their insights about children and their creative curricula. Many friends and colleagues have had the patience to hear me talk through the ideas and issues in this book, as well as the compassion and integrity to push me to see some of my blind spots and contradictions. Thank you especially to Andrea Ayvezian, Chet Bowers, Virginia Casper, Louise Derman-Sparks, Sandra Lawrence, Sonia Nieto, Beverly Tatum, Edwina Battle Vold, and Leslie Williams.

I learned a great deal about the connections between environmental and economic injustices and the human side of resistance from the people of Tepoztlán, the town in Mexico where we lived from 1995 to 1997. Their successful struggle against international pressures to construct a luxury golf club adjacent to the town has remained an inspiring example of how grassroots movements can be organized and succeed. I am particularly grateful to the teachers, parents, and children of Cetiliztli, the school that our sons attended in Mexico.

Many ideas for this third edition were stimulated by a month I spent as a visiting scholar at the Center for Equity and Innovation in Early Childhood, a wonderful group of teachers and researchers at the University of Melbourne in Australia. I am especially grateful to Glenda MacNaughton, director of the Center and my host. Many thanks to other members of the Center—Heather Lawrence, Merlyne Cruz, Jane Page, and Patrick Hughes—for wonderful conversations and new insights. I also had wonderful conversations with colleagues in Adelaide, Australia, in particular Lynn Hall, Judith Jones, and Anne Glover.

I am very grateful to all the people at Teachers College Press who encouraged me to do this project and expedited its completion. A special thanks to Susan Liddicoat, who patiently supported me through several drafts.

My sons, Daniel and Andrés, are my primary teachers these days—shaking me from my complacency, challenging my expectations, and inspiring me to push myself because I want them to live in a better world. My husband, Fred Moseley, continues to be my main supporter and encourager, and I could not have completed this project without him.

# PART I

# Multicultural Schools and Classrooms

The first part of this book provides an overview of different aspects of multicultural learning. Chapter 1 reviews the dilemmas of raising children in a world of contradictions and inequities and discusses how different approaches and goals of multicultural education address these issues. Chapter 2 demonstrates how all of us, adults and children, learn concepts and attitudes about the world and how we can challenge our assumptions and broaden our perspectives through discussions and classroom activities and materials. Chapter 3 makes a case for creating caring, cooperative, and critical communities and describes the roles that adults and children play in this process.

# CHAPTER 1

# Growing Up in a World of Contradictions and Injustices: A Multicultural Response

Alison and Stephanie (both European American 3-year-olds) are busily feeding their (light-skinned) baby dolls and bustling about the kitchen of the housekeeping corner, chatting about how their babies won't sleep. Sofía (Mexican American 3-year-old) bounces up, holding a darker-skinned baby doll. She grins broadly at Alison and Stephanie and announces, "We came to visit!" Alison and Stephanie stop what they are doing and stare at Sofía. Then Stephanie says (in an adult-like voice), "I'm sorry; we *have* to go shopping." Alison and Stephanie toss their babies into a stroller and head out of the area. They walk across the classroom, their high heels clacking on the floor as they go. Sofía stares after them, a small frown on her face. Then she enters the area, plops her doll in a high chair, and lifts the spoon to her baby's mouth a few times, all the while looking at Alison and Stephanie as they stroll around the classroom.

Terrance (biracial child adopted by a European American family), Jeremy, and Sam (both European American) are building a highway in the block corner. All three boys are 6 years old; Terrance and Jeremy live in a relatively affluent neighborhood; Sam lives with his mother in a subsidized apartment complex. As they begin to move cars along their highway, Terrance says, "We're getting a new car!!! It's gonna have a TV and everything!" Jeremy says, "We got a TV in our car, but my sister and I fight over it, so my parents are going to get another one, so we can each have our own." As this conversations goes on, Sam looks down, his shoulders slumped. He starts sorting through the blocks on the floor and picks up a triangle piece. "Look," he says, "we can use this for the gate to keep the robbers off of the highway!" As he goes to put the piece on, he (accidentally) knocks off a few pieces already in place. Both Jeremy and Terrance yell, "Hey! Stop

3

that!" Jeremy then hisses to Sam, "You stupid retard!" Sam frowns and hisses back, "You faggot!" A teacher approaches the area and asks if anything is wrong. All three boys look down and silently and industriously start adding blocks to their construction.

These events that I observed in a preschool and a K–1 classroom are similar to ones that occur dozens of times a day in early childhood settings. Each lasted less than 3 minutes, and neither was particularly dramatic or remarkable: Two close friends "politely" rejected the entry of a third child; two boys expressed annoyance at a third who knocked down part of their construction. The overt disputes were fleeting, and the children did not request adult help. In fact, the boys pointedly ignored the teacher. To be honest, had I been a teacher rather than an observer, I would probably not have noticed these momentary conflicts. I would have been too busy—replenishing paint cups, attending to a crying child, helping a child record a story, or working with a reading group.

Yet these short episodes reveal how young children absorb and express attitudes and values that pervade our society. As I reflect on these observations, many questions come to mind. Was it coincidence that the children I observed were playing in gender-segregated groups, or is that a pervasive pattern in these classrooms? Were Stephanie and Alison simply protecting their time together? Or were they reacting to Sofía's darker skin? Or did the manner of her arrival make them uncomfortable, possibly reflecting cultural differences? Does Sofía, who is the only Latina in the classroom, get a lot of similar rejections from other European American classmates? If so, what is she learning and feeling about herself and her family? What gender roles are all three girls enacting? What early economic views are children expressing when they enact "shopping"?

How did Sam (whose mother does not own a car) feel when his friends were describing their fancy cars with televisions? How conscious are these three children of the economic disparities among them? What role does competitive consumerism play in their relationships? What are children learning when family conflicts are resolved by purchasing additional equipment? What values about the environment and land use are all three boys expressing as they build a bigger and better highway, filled with cars and trucks? Do the boys know what "retard" and "faggot" really mean? How do these insults reflect and influence their developing attitudes about people with disabilities or about gender roles and sexual orientation?

Our children are growing up in a world of contradictions. On one hand, they are learning that all people are "created equal" (Declaration of Independence) and that we as a nation are united to provide for the common good (the Constitution). Yet, as these observations illustrate, children, in their daily experiences, are learning that some groups are valued more than others and that it is acceptable to exclude people and exploit natural resources in order to gain and maintain individual status and material wealth.

One somewhat simplistic but useful way of thinking about these issues is to consider the two meanings of the word *race*. In one sense we are all running in a race, whether it is to get the newest toys in the neighborhood, the best grades, or the highest wage among our co-workers. Even collaborative activities such as sports teams or cooperative work groups function in a competitive context that can undermine teamwork. For example, groups of teachers who have worked hard at developing cooperative working relationships sometimes are dismayed at the friction that arises in the face of merit pay raises or pressures to improve test scores.

As competitors in this race, we can win only as much as others lose; to ensure that there will always be someone behind us, we divide humanity by *race* and accord some groups more power than others. In biological terms, race is a meaningless concept. There are more genetic differences within different "racial groups" (a slippery concept that has been defined and disputed repeatedly) than across them. However, for much of human history and throughout the world, people have created "racial" divisions (often based on virtually no visible physical differences) to justify exclusion, slavery, and genocide (e.g., the Romans enslaved the Britons; the British subjugated the Irish; the European Americans kidnapped and enslaved the Africans; the Nazis killed millions of Jewish people).

Race has been an intractable division in our country since the arrival of the European settlers in the 17th century. Many of the men who wrote and signed the Declaration of Independence and the Constitution, which extol liberty and the equality of all people, took for granted their right to kill and cheat the American Indians in order to obtain their lands; and few questioned the practice of buying, owning, and selling slaves. By accepting and codifying these contradictions, our forefathers established the precedent that private ownership, material wealth, and profits take precedence over the ideals of liberty and equality. As Frederick Douglass said in his famous Fourth of July speech in 1852, "What to the American slave is your Fourth of July? . . . To him your celebration is a sham; your boasted liberty an unholy license; your national greatness, swelling vanity . . . your shouts of liberty and equality, hollow mockery" (quoted in Meltzer, 1996, p. 5). Before and since that time, race has been an indelible and impenetrable boundary that divides our society.

As immigrants arrived, those who could quickly learned to identify themselves as White in order to distinguish themselves from the lower-status African Americans and, in some areas, American Indians or Mexicans. The racism that lies at the core of our national identity has established a pattern of exploitation and marginalization that has been played out with varying levels of intensity against immigrants, women, poor people, the elderly, children, gay men and lesbians, and people with disabilities.

All of us have a number of identities and are often caught in the complicated cross-currents of advantage and disadvantage. For example, a poor White woman is racially privileged but may resent the economic advantage of the middle-class Black woman next to her in the checkout line at the supermarket. Generally in our society, males enjoy more power and privilege than women, but African American men are more vulnerable than African American women to unemployment, school failure, police harassment, and early and violent deaths. Some White middle-class gay men have more buying power than their heterosexual peers because their households include two highly paid male professionals. At the same time, they live with the constant threat of harassment and violence. A child born with cerebral palsy is clearly at a disadvantage in many respects. However, if she is from an affluent family, her access to services may mean that her prospects for a good education and gainful employment are better than those of an able-bodied child from a poor family.

We are also living in a time of rapid social change and are seeing shifts in what it means to belong to particular groups. For example, gender roles have expanded and changed over the past few decades. Likewise, language, traditions, and values of specific ethnic groups evolve as their members absorb and/or resist the influences of other cultures. In the 1950s and 1960s, civil rights laws ended the legal separation of Whites and Blacks but introduced more subtle forms of racism that now shape identities and interpersonal and intergroup relationships. Finally, as groups come into contact, intermarriage increases, and more children have multicultural and multiracial backgrounds that incorporate many traditions and values. Thus, with the exception of a few groups that deliberately seal themselves off from other groups (e.g., the Amish), few people can identify themselves as a member of a single cultural or racial group.

## PURPOSE, TRENDS, AND SCOPE
## OF MULTICULTURAL EDUCATION

The purpose of multicultural education is to help children learn how to navigate these contradictions and ambiguities and to challenge the injustices that divide and diminish their world. Goals include the development of identities, solidarity with others, critical thinking, and liberatory action (Banks, 1999; Derman-Sparks & the A.B.C. Task Force, 1989; Gay, 2000; Gollnick & Chin, 1998; Kendall, 1996; Nieto, 2004; Sleeter & Grant, 1988; see Banks,

1995, and Banks & Banks, 1995, for a comprehensive review of the many dimensions and interpretations of multicultural education).

Over the past three decades, multicultural education has incorporated many different strands. In 1988, Sleeter and Grant identified five different approaches. This typology, which still reflects the major trends in the field, includes the following:

1. *Educating the culturally different*—adapting standard curricula to meet the needs of learners from different cultural backgrounds
2. *Single-group studies*—designing curricula to teach about specific underrepresented groups
3. *Human relations*—focusing on interpersonal and intergroup relationships
4. *Multicultural education*—recognizing and celebrating a wide range of racial and cultural similarities and differences
5. *Education that is multicultural and social-reconstructivist*—focusing on discrimination and power differentials in many areas and encouraging critical thinking and social change

As it has evolved, multicultural education has shifted from surface portrayals of cultural diversity to deeper analyses of power and oppression and the need for radical social and economic change. In this book, I use *multicultural education* more broadly than Sleeter and Grant do in their typology. To me it includes *all* of the strands that they identify, with a particular emphasis on the final one, which also most closely resembles the *Anti-Bias Curriculum* (Derman-Sparks et al., 1989).

The scope of multicultural education has also broadened since the movement began in the 1970s. In the early days, the focus was primarily on race and culture. However, it quickly became apparent that we could not discuss race and culture without examining the effects of social class and economic discrimination. Then, with the rise of the feminist movement, writers began to see that gender, too, was a source of power differentiation that cut across race, culture, and class and needed to be part of the conversation. During the 1970s people with disabilities and their families began to protest their educational and occupational marginalization, and these issues were also woven into the multicultural conversation. In the 1990s, the wider recognition of the hate crimes targeting gay men and lesbians led to sexual orientation becoming a theme in multicultural education.

Most recently we have become more aware of the connections between the exploitation of people and the destruction of the natural environment (Bowers, 2001; Gruenewald, 2003; Running-Grass, 1994). Because this dimension of multicultural education is a relatively new one, I will discuss it in some detail at this point.

Environmentalists, who have traditionally been middle- and upper-class Whites, have often focused their efforts on preserving pristine wilderness areas for the relatively affluent to enjoy and have ignored the environmental issues in cities and poor rural areas (Running-Grass, 1994). However, more and more people are seeing the connections among environmental concerns, economic disparities, and racial and cultural discrimination. As is evident in the ongoing protests at World Trade Organization (WTO) meetings, people all over the world are concerned that global capitalism is "paving over" not only the rain forest but also workers' rights and the traditional livelihoods and cultures of many groups.

A conflict in Tepoztlán, the small town in Mexico where our family lived from 1995 to 1997, illustrates these dynamics. During the time we were there, the Tepoztecos, the indigenous people in the area, were engaged in a long and difficult struggle against a golf club and luxury condominium development that the government and foreign investors were determined to build on the outskirts of the town. The townspeople realized that their water supply and way of life would be jeopardized by this project and eventually were successful in preventing its construction. This conflict generated many discussions at both the local and national levels in Mexico about what is meant by "progress." Is it progress to displace local farmers so that a few wealthy families (mostly from the United States) can live in luxurious condominiums and play golf? Are the service jobs generated by such a project adequate compensation for the loss of self-sufficient communities and cultural traditions? Are supermarkets and malls inherently better than open-air markets where local families sell their produce and crafts? How can people take advantage of technological innovations (such as cleaner water and sewage systems) that improve the quality of life and still maintain their community and traditions?

By integrating multicultural and environmental perspectives, we can look at these world changes in a more holistic way. Moreover, the multicultural focus on learning about diverse values and ways of life may inspire us to come up with alternatives to the "conquering nature" mentality that drives globalization and has created widespread environmental degradation. For example, Rigoberta Menchu, Nobel Peace Prize winner in 1992, describes how her people, the Quiche (Mayan) Indians, respect and love all living things and pray to the Earth asking permission to cultivate the soil before planting their seeds. This perspective provides a good counterbalance to the popular assumption that "progress" and the "good life" mean bigger cars and houses and more roads and parking lots.

Another convergence between the multicultural and ecological perspectives is the disparity between the environmental degradation in poor and affluent communities. Toxic waste dumps, polluted water, and smog are more common in areas where poor people live. Ironically, environmentalists often contribute to this injustice by organizing middle-class citizens to protest against polluting industries that then are located in poorer communities that have less political clout. Given the link between social class and race, people of color inevitably bear the greatest brunt of environmental degradation. For example, 36.7% of African American children in the United States show evidence of low-level lead exposure, while only 6.1% of European American children do (Jackson, 1999). Three of the five largest hazardous waste facilities in the United States are located in African American and Latino American communities. Moreover, in areas inhabited by Whites, the Environmental Protection Agency levies fines for hazardous waste that are 500% higher than the penalties charged for the same violations in communities of color (Fruchter, 1999).

As these examples illustrate, environmental and multicultural issues are connected on a number of levels. By seeing the links between these issues we can also develop more powerful ways of resisting inequitable environmental degradation. A good example of this convergence is PODER, which means "power" in Spanish but is also the acronym for People Organized for the Defense of Earth and Her Resources (Snell, 2003). Two Mexican American women co-founded this Austin, Texas grassroots organization in 1991 to force polluting industries out of their neighborhood (a working-class Latino American community) and to change the laws that allowed them to be there in the first place. They have since taken up zoning issues and have fought "redevelopment" plans that threaten their community.

Fully understanding and addressing issues of power and exploitation require a broad view. To avoid a competition of the "isms" (e.g., arguing about whether racism or sexism is more debilitating), we need to focus on how different inequities connect and interact with each other. Most of us work on issues that are most immediate to our lives, but we need to constantly push ourselves to see the broader context. For example, advocates for more services for children with disabilities should also monitor and, if necessary, challenge the racial and gender patterns of children being referred for special services.

In this book I use the term *multiculturalism* in a broad sense and include issues related to race, social class, consumerism, culture, language, gender, sexual orientation, disabilities, and our relationship to the natural world. To me the term implies personal awareness and strengthening; critical analysis of the existing social, political, and economic structures; and participation in liberatory movements.

Throughout its history, multicultural education has been interpreted in many different ways and has been the site of many controversies both within the field and outside it (see Ramsey & Williams, 2003, for a review). However, it is the most comprehensive approach we have for helping our children understand their world and to work toward greater equity. At the same time, we must be realistic and acknowledge that multiculturalism alone will not change the basic inequities of our society. Rather, it is a tool to prepare ourselves and our children to participate in that effort.

## MULTICULTURAL GOALS FOR CHILDREN

The heavy and controversial issues of oppression, exploitation, and social justice may seem to be a world away from young children. However, as we saw in the observations that opened this chapter, children are constantly learning about power, privilege, and exploitation—in families, schools, and communities. We need to help them critically understand and, when appropriate, challenge these forces.

The following working goals provide a framework for this book. I use the term *working goals* for two reasons. First, as I learn more about the world, my goals and priorities change, and I hope that they will continue to evolve in years to come. The second reason is to encourage readers to use them as a base to develop goals that are most appropriate to the priorities and experiences of their particular children, families, and communities.

What will children need to navigate the contradictions of our society and to challenge its inequities? *First, children need to develop strong identities—as individuals, as members of communities, and as living beings on this planet.* Rather than learn about "how I am special" (a common theme in some self-esteem curricula) or learn that "I am what I own" (the message from commercially driven media), children should explore and develop their interests and gain a confident yet realistic awareness of what they can contribute to their immediate and larger communities. Children need to feel deeply rooted in our society, with strong attachments to family, friends, and whatever groups and combinations of groups they belong to and to the society as a whole. They also need to feel deeply attached to the natural world—to the rhythms of days and seasons that define our lives—and to see themselves as inhabitants, not conquerors, of their environment.

*Second, children need to develop a sense of solidarity with all people and with the natural world.* By learning that human similarities and differences are continua, not polarities, they will be more comfortable meeting and working with people who at first glance may seem "different." They must also develop the emotional capacity to recognize and manage their own feelings; to understand and empathize with others' emotions; and to care for others, particularly those people who are victims of injustice. Children also need to understand that, despite our many differences, we all live on the same planet, breathe the same air, drink the same water, feel the same sun, and live off the same soil. Ultimately, we share an interest in conserving our resources. By learning about different beliefs, traditions, and practices related to land and water use, children can become more attuned to their natural surroundings and question the "conquer the earth" philosophy that prevails in the United States and drives many environmentally destructive projects.

*Third, children need to become critical thinkers.* Rather than passively accepting the status quo, they need to ask good, hard questions. While understanding broad issues of exploitation and inequality may be beyond the capacity of most young children, they are able to cast a critical eye at stereotyped messages in books, materials, and electronic media. They can also identify and challenge classroom, school, and community policies and practices that seem unfair and/or environmentally destructive.

*Fourth, children need to be confident and persistent problem solvers so that they see themselves as activists rather than simply feeling overwhelmed by the challenges of the world.* They need to understand that we all can contribute to making the world a better place, whether we work with people, animals, plants, words, paints, musical instruments, or machines. As they are growing up, children should have many opportunities to work with different disciplines and media, to brainstorm solutions to problems, and to see projects through to completion. They need to learn how to approach and solve problems in solidarity with others and to be creative and eclectic in their strategies. Learning about the beliefs, tools, and technologies from many cultures potentially enables them to expand their thinking about conserving cultural diversity and natural resources and improving the quality of life for everyone. Children are often inspired by stories of people who have fought oppression in its many forms.

*Fifth, we absolutely must ensure that* all *children gain the academic skills that will give them access to the knowledge of our society and the power to make a difference.* In particular, we need to push for excellent schools in all communities, especially those with high rates of poverty. Moreover, we must help those children who feel that academic work has no relevance to their lives to see how these skills are a source of power and how they can acquire them without giving up their identities and criticisms. Rigoberta Menchu (1983) describes how, as an adult, she learned Spanish, the despised language of the *ladinos* who conquered and still oppress her people, because she realized that without it, she could not speak for her people, who were struggling for their rights with the landowners and government. Lisa Delpit (1995) points out that "the language of the master has [often] been used for liberatory ends" (p. 165).

*Finally, we must create spaces for children to imagine hopeful futures in which individual material wealth, privilege, and power are no longer the dominant forces of our society.* With stories, puppet shows, and role playing, children and adults can imagine and create new societies in which people collaborate to guarantee adequate food and housing and meaningful work for everyone and develop sustainable and equitable ways of living on the Earth.

## FAMILIES AND SCHOOLS WORKING TOGETHER

Multicultural and environmental issues are wide-ranging and complex and can be adequately addressed only if families and schools work together. All of us must collaborate to tackle these deep and intransigent problems. Throughout this book I use the word *parents* to signify the adults who care for children in their homes—be they biological, adoptive, step-, or foster mothers or fathers; grandparents, aunts, uncles, older siblings, or close family friends. Likewise, children have many teachers—parents, relatives, neighbors, and other children. However, for clarity's sake, I use the term *teachers* to refer to professionals employed in early childhood settings.

Parents potentially have an intimate, lifelong relationship with their children. They bathe them, put them to sleep, and take care of them when they are sick. Together, parents and children can explore and develop ideas over years, revisit favorite stories and construct new meanings.

Parents define the basic parameters and orientations of children's lives. They decide, within their financial constraints and often with their children in mind, where to live and where to go on family outings. Their social life determines the presence and role of other people in their children's lives. Parents who are part of interdependent families and communities provide their children with close connections with a broad group of people. Others, by choice or by circumstances, may live a more independent and contained lifestyle, so their children have fewer ongoing relationships with other families. Children develop their basic social orientations by observing how their parents interact with people inside and outside the family. They learn values by participating in conversations and outings that reflect their parents' attitudes toward people, institutions, material goods, and the natural environment.

Teachers, in contrast, have a short-term but intense impact on children's lives. They provide stimulation with activities, materials, books, and conversations and facilitate interactions among the children in the classroom. At school children may hear and see things that surprise, intrigue, and even trouble them because they may not mesh with messages and experiences at home.

Children often become very attached to teachers, but teacher–child relationships do not have the long-term intimacy of parent–child ones. Instead, children and teachers form working partnerships in which they together teach and master new skills, and discover, absorb, and challenge new information and perspectives. Teachers enjoy and support individual children, but they focus more on helping children find a comfortable role in the group than on developing intense individual relationships. Unlike parents, who have opportunities to have long, open-ended conversations that can go on for years, teachers are more likely to start conversations and create spaces where children can compare their views with those of their peers.

Thus, teachers and parents, homes and schools have complementary roles and can mutually support each other within their respective limits and possibilities, as we will be exploring throughout this book.

## HOW DO WE TALK ABOUT MULTICULTURAL ISSUES?

The ambiguities and contradictions in our society echo in the imprecise and clumsy terms we use to talk about different groups and dynamics. For example, the confusing labels we use to designate racial groups reflect the difficulty of defining categories that do not exist in reality but play an enormous role in people's lives. Color labels—black, brown, red, yellow, and white— are the most succinct but do not accurately describe the range of physical attributes and backgrounds of individuals from different groups. Moreover, because color terms distinguish individuals on the basis of a single physical dimension, they also objectify and polarize the groups and are associated with evaluative and stereotyped images.

Current usage favors names that refer to the continent of origin, such as African American, European American, and Asian American. Although these terms are more precise and neutral, they exclude many groups whose immigration history does not fit these categories. We also do not have adequate terms to describe people native to this land. While clearly *Indian* is a misnomer, is *Native American* an accurate description of people whose residence here long predated the arrival of the explorer Amerigo Vespucci? In short, terms for different groups reflect the confusion that characterizes efforts to make distinctions among people.

In this book, I have primarily used names that refer to the continent of origin, but I have also used color labels when the former seemed inaccurate or too cumbersome. One exception is that I consistently use the term *White* to reflect the power and privilege accorded people who are identified as White, regardless of their continent of origin.

I have also tried to be as precise as possible and have avoided describing groups by what they are *not,* such as *non-English-speaking* or *non-White* and as much as possible have used specific group names (e.g., *Puerto Rican* instead of *Latino,* or *Algonquin* rather than *Native American*). However, much of the literature on diversity lumps groups together so that we often have to use broad terms that do not give us much useful information. For example, the term *Asian Americans* is commonly used; but, because it embodies a huge range of cultures, languages, and histories, it does not tell us much about a particular person's culture and history. For a more complete discussion, see Sonia Nieto's (2004) chapter in which she discusses these issues at length and traces the history of particular labels.

In the chapter on culture, I include material about the relationships between people and nature, which also poses problems with terminology. All of the terms that I could think of emphasized the separateness of humans from their natural world. I have used *ecology, nature, natural world,* and *environment* because those are the most commonly used terms. However, none of them conveys the sense of unity and the potential integration and harmony between the human and "natural" world that I am trying to express.

I have also struggled with how to refer to people of different sexual orientations. In many contemporary writings, gay, lesbian, bisexual, and transgendered people are collectively referred to as *queer*. However, I find that I have too many vivid memories of hearing that word hurled across playgrounds and hissed in school corridors to use it comfortably at this point. Another common term, *homosexual*, has been tainted because for many years it was included in lists of mental illnesses. For these reasons, I have used the more cumbersome phrase *gay, lesbian, bisexual, and transgendered people*. Referring to heterosexual people is also a dilemma. The term *straight* is often used, but as one of my lesbian friends said, "So does that make the rest of us—crooked?" For these reasons, I have primarily used the term *heterosexual*, even though it feels awkward because I do not use the equivalent term *homosexual*.

We also lack appropriate terms for people with disabilities. Identifying people by a specific disability (e.g., autism) obscures the wide range of strengths and limitations of individuals who share the same diagnosis. Moreover, the terms *ability* and *disability* represent a polarized way of categorizing people—*all* of whom have some abilities and disabilities. In the early 1990s the term *differently abled* was used. It was a useful term because it implied a continuum that is closer to reality, but many people felt that it was too euphemistic, cumbersome, and "politically correct," and it is rarely used now. In this book, I use *people (or children) with disabilities* rather than *disabled people* (or *children*) to avoid making the disability the first and only definition of a person. However, the term is awkward and still incorrectly implies that people with and without disabilities are fundamentally different.

Another dilemma is how to characterize the status and power differentials among particular groups. Terms such as *oppressed, excluded,* or *mar-*

*ginalized* overemphasize the victimization of people and fail to convey their resilience and resistance. How do we acknowledge the power and abuses of one group without presenting others as passive and powerless? In this book, I have tried to point out how groups have resisted oppression as well as suffered from it. However, the results are imperfect and the phrases are often awkward and cumbersome.

As social values and the relationships among groups change, names and descriptions continue to evolve. The terms used in this book will probably become obsolete at some point. Readers are encouraged to continue to be sensitive to what messages are implied by specific labels and to modify their language to reflect the changing identities and relationships and in particular names favored by groups themselves.

These complex issues of terminology illustrate the challenge of bringing these issues into classrooms, yet they also underscore the necessity of doing so. Even as children learn to speak, they are absorbing the values, ideals, and questions that swirl around them in their homes and communities, in classrooms, and in the media. We need to engage them in exploring these complex and troubling issues and in creating a more just world.

# CHAPTER 2

# We Are All Learning

All of us—children *and* adults—are influenced by our social, political, and economic contexts. As we grow up, we absorb our communities' values and beliefs, which, in turn, form our expectations and guide our decisions and behaviors. At the same time, we all share many developing physiological and psychological needs.

Which aspects of development are universal? Which ones are individual? Which ones are environmental? According to Bowman and Stott (1994), children from all backgrounds establish mutually satisfying social relationships and ways of organizing and integrating their perceptions and categorizing new information. They also learn how to speak and perhaps to write a particular language and how to think, imagine, and create. Individual differences, such as sensitivity to pain, distractibility, timing of onset of puberty, and body build, play a formative role in children's development. However, Bowman and Stott point out that all developmental phases and individual traits become meaningful *only* in the context of the child's social life. Children learn how to express their emerging needs and skills in ways that fit the values and expectations of their group. What information they learn, how and to whom they express their emotions, and what language they use are influenced by their immediate and more distant material and social world. These patterns carry through into their adult years.

Bronfenbrenner's (1979, 1986) framework for analyzing the developmental context is a useful tool for analyzing how the environment defines children's experiences and prospects as adults. He identified the following four concentric circles:

1. The *microsystems* of the family, school, and neighborhood
2. The *mesosystems,* which include the relationships between elements in the microsystem, such as those between the family and school, neighborhood and school, home and neighborhood
3. The *exosystems,* which are institutions that have power to affect the child's life but in which the child does not participate, such as parent workplaces, school and planning boards, and systems of social support

4. The *macrosystems,* which include cultural values, the ideology of
the social group, and prevailing attitudes

If we compare the after-school activities of two children living in the
same city, we can concretely see how these factors influence the details
of children's lives and potentially frame their attitudes and expectations as
adults.

> Elisa, age 7, lives in a primarily African American and Latino
> low-income community in a large city. Each day her mother comes to
> pick her up from school. As they walk home, they make a brief stop
> at a small corner store to buy milk, which costs twice as much as it
> would at the supermarket, but they do not have a car and only go to
> the supermarket once every 2 weeks. Then they walk quickly back to
> their apartment in a large housing project. There is a community cen-
> ter in the housing project, but it has fallen into disrepair and the fund-
> ing for the recreation programs that were supposed to be there has
> long since disappeared, as has the playground equipment. The church
> half a mile away has art classes and a Scout program, but Elisa's
> mother, who has to catch a 5:00 P.M. bus to her job as a night custo-
> dian, does not want her daughter walking home alone after she has
> left. Elisa and her 13-year-old sister Lani spend the afternoon in the
> apartment, doing their homework, talking on the phone, watching TV,
> and helping their mother with the housework. After their mother
> leaves for work, they eat the dinner she has prepared for them and
> then do their homework. Lani helps out with Elisa's homework as
> much as she can, but there are a few questions that neither of them
> can quite figure out. During the evening their mother calls them a cou-
> ple of times, and their aunt, who lives downstairs, comes by to check
> on them. The two girls go to bed long before their mother returns
> from work.

> Katie, also age 7, who lives 3 miles away in a leafy, primarily
> White upper middle-class neighborhood, is dropped off at her corner
> by the school bus. She runs home, where her mother urges her to
> change quickly into her leotard so that she will not be late to her
> dance class. Katie grabs a snack to eat in the car and also takes her
> soccer clothes, because she does not have time to go home between
> her dance class and soccer practice. During the 15-minute drive to the
> dance class, her mother uses her cell phone to call another mother to
> firm up car-pool plans for getting her older daughter to a play re-
> hearsal later that afternoon. She then calls the middle school to leave

a message about these plans for her daughter. Both girls will arrive back home around 7:00 P.M., about the same time their father, a corporate lawyer, comes home from work. The family then eats together and the girls work on their homework, often getting help and advice from their parents as they do it.

For Elisa, a member of a group disadvantaged by discrimination and limited job possibilities (macrosystem), the poverty of her community and lack of funding for activities and transportation (exosystems) limit the ability of the school and community to provide extracurricular activities (mesosystem) and therefore determine how she spends her time and what skills she is learning (microsystem). In contrast, Katie is a member of an advantaged group (macrosystem) that is reaping the benefits of the system (exosystem). She has lots of advantages and opportunities to choose from (mesosystem), but she also feels pressured to "keep up" with her classmates (microsystem) by taking part in lots of activities. Both Elisa and Katie are developing skills and ideas about how the world works and expectations about their future roles. What they are learning, however, is profoundly affected by their backgrounds and position in society.

Projecting forward, we can speculate how these two girls might grow up and respond to the challenges of social and economic inequities as parents or as teachers. As an adult, Elisa is likely to have a pretty clear understanding of the effects of discrimination and poverty and how the lines of advantage and disadvantage are drawn. Potentially these insights prepare her to assume leadership positions in educational and social services and in social justice movements. However, the poor quality of her schools and lack of extracurricular activities may limit her educational, employment, and leadership opportunities. Moreover, she may feel disenfranchised and/or overwhelmed by the daily demands of living in a poor community. She may need a lot of encouragement and support to gain confidence that she can participate in social change and make a difference. Katie, on the other hand, is likely to attend a good college and graduate school and be well positioned for a successful professional career and positions of community leadership. However, she may go through her life with only a peripheral awareness of the racial discrimination and economic disparities that touch but do not intrude on her world. Alternatively, she might begin to see these inequities and become an advocate for social change. However, her depth and range of understanding will be limited by her privileged status in society. She will have to critically examine her history, beliefs, and expectations in order to collaborate with people from less advantaged backgrounds and to participate fully in social justice movements.

When engaging children and adults in multicultural work, we need to recognize that each individual's involvement reflects his or her unique experiences, knowledge, and patterns of behavior. As discussed above, some will need to work through their privilege, others their disenfranchisement.

Regardless of their starting points, adults and children can all learn to scrutinize their assumptions and to expand their awareness and knowledge about the world. In this process we all—children and adults—learn from each other. For example, one day, when my son Daniel was 4 years old, he asked if an elderly visitor (fortunately after she had left!) was a "mean old witch." His comment, which of course horrified me, made me aware of one of my blind spots. I realized that, despite our efforts to raise him in a diverse community, we as a family had not had much direct contact with elderly people.

In this chapter, I will first describe how adults can use personal reflections and group discussions to identify and challenge their attitudes and blind spots. The second part of the chapter will focus on how children learn about themselves and other people and how teachers can provide activities and materials to challenge stereotypes and assumptions that children are absorbing. Although adults and children will be discussed separately, we need to keep in mind that there is constant interaction between and among them.

## HOW ADULTS CAN IDENTIFY AND CHALLENGE THEIR ASSUMPTIONS

To teach children to be aware of their world, we, as adults, need to develop a critical consciousness, "an ability to step back from the world as we are accustomed to perceiving it and to see the ways our perception is constructed through linguistic codes, cultural signs, and embedded power . . . [to] ask penetrating questions" (Kincheloe, 1993, p. 109). We each have our unique history of experiences, and throughout our lives we construct lenses through which we view the world. Our lenses have many different facets; some are clear, others are blurred, and still others are completely opaque. They profoundly affect the way we perceive and interpret the world, yet they are usually invisible to us; and we often assume that we are seeing absolute truths. Thus the task of "stepping back" and "asking penetrating questions" requires a great deal of emotional and cognitive effort.

Many people resist acknowledging the effects of racism and other forms of discrimination because they want to believe in the American Dream—the notion that if people work hard enough they will succeed and that their own success is due to hard work, not to their privileged status (Sleeter, 1992). In this spirit of individualism, many of us were taught to not "see" racial, class, and cultural distinctions but to see only individuals. "Kids are just kids, the same the world over."

However, it is virtually impossible to grow up in this country (and probably in most countries) without absorbing prevalent stereotypes and attitudes. Rather than hiding and denying these feelings behind a veneer of tolerance, we need to recognize and analyze them (Tatum, 1997). We also cannot ignore how profoundly the social and economic environment affects children's lives. To assume that the life experiences and prospects of children who live in poor urban neighborhoods or isolated rural communities are the same as those of children raised in affluent suburbs is to distort reality. We need to recognize the content and sources of our own expectations in order to see clearly how each child is adapting to the limits, possibilities, and priorities of his or her particular social and physical environment.

### Personal Reflections

We need to know ourselves—to honestly see our reactions to other individuals and the larger world and to analyze our underlying assumptions. Contemporary prejudice is usually more subtle than the overt racial discrimination and violence that was commonplace prior to the civil rights movement. Many people, even those who profess egalitarian values, find that stereotypes automatically and sometimes unconsciously flash into their minds (Devine, Plant, & Buswell, 2000; Dovidio, Kawakami, & Gaertner, 2000). We may feel ashamed and tempted to deny them. However, it is much more productive to confront them and to analyze how we learned them and how they influence our current perceptions and relationships.

One way to engage in this process is to keep journals that are records of reactions to other people and incidents. A particular advantage of journals is that they provide a space to express and explore feelings that we might be afraid or embarrassed to voice in front of others. Because they are a record of reactions and thoughts over time, they also provide a way to see how our assumptions are changing. In some college courses (e.g., multicultural education, psychology of racism), students keep detailed journals in which they record their reactions to class sessions and readings and analyze their attitudes (for examples of students' journal entries, see Derman-Sparks & Phillips, 1997; Tatum, 1992).

By monitoring our responses to the world, we can make better use of experiences to analyze our limited perspectives. After we adopted our son Daniel, I was struck by how "biological-child-oriented" our culture is *and* how I had not noticed it before. I vividly recall completing a developmental profile for Daniel to attend our lab school and feeling angry and excluded by the endless questions about pregnancy, birth, and breast-feeding and the absence of questions that offered a space to write about adoption experiences. In a moment of pure irony, I realized that *I* had helped to design the form a few years earlier. People who have had the experience of being temporarily disabled with sprains or broken bones suddenly see the world as a maze of high curbs and heavy doors and get a glimpse of the daily life of people who use wheelchairs and crutches. Traveling or living in a new country or community can make us more aware of the frustrations and anxieties of being an outsider. However, we must never assume that a few weeks on crutches or a year living in an unfamiliar community means that we really understand others' daily, lifelong experience. There is not only much that we do not know but also much that we will never know.

Reading books and articles by authors from a wide range of life experiences and perspectives is another way to see beyond our own limited experiences and to understand more clearly how the inequities of this society affect specific groups and individuals. Reading about others' lives also enables us to see our own lives and assumptions more clearly. In her critique of White feminist theory, A. Thompson (1998) suggests:

> White theorists and educators [must] immerse themselves in Black literature and other forms of culture; once one has learned how to read Black folklore or Black women novelists without simply assimilating them to White cultural experience, it becomes possible to begin to fill in the theoretical frameworks with nuanced understanding. (p. 544)

As we read books, write in journals, and reflect on our experiences in the social realm, we can also think about how we have learned to respond to the physical world along several continua such as the following:

- Are we drawn to "scientific" information or to intuitive or spiritual insights?
- In our homes and work, do we rely more on intergenerational knowledge and community traditions or innovative technologies?
- Do we judge materials and experiences in terms of their monetary value or of their personal meaning to our lives and communities?
- How conscious are we of our natural surroundings? Are we primarily concerned with controlling nature, or do we take time to notice and savor daily and seasonal changes?

## Group Discussions

Personal reflection needs to be balanced by conversations in which people can compare experiences, point out each other's misperceptions, and find and give support for personal changes and political actions. These discussions can occur among school staffs, among parents, in parent–teacher meetings, in college classes, and in religious or community groups.

*Guidelines for Supportive Group Discussions.* Hearing and understanding each others' points of view is a monumentally challenging process, especially when discussing sensitive issues related to race, culture, class, gender, sexual orientation, and abilities. Most people approach these discussions with considerable apprehension and anxiety (Tatum, 1997).

It is crucial to provide a mutually honest and supportive environment. Chang, Muckelroy, Pulido-Tobiassen, and Dowell (2000) suggest that teachers share life stories and classroom examples to generate discussion. They also advocate developing ground rules and designating facilitators.

The following guidelines, used by Tatum (1992) in her class on the Psychology of Racism, can be adapted to different settings to create a safe environment in which people can speak freely:

1. The blame game must be deflected by establishing the assumptions that everyone growing up in this society has absorbed prejudicial attitudes and that racism hurts everyone.
2. People cannot be blamed for what they learned as children, but as adults they *are* responsible for identifying and interrupting the cycle of oppression.
3. Participants must honor the confidentiality of the group.
4. Participants must refrain from using overt or covert put-downs, even as an effort to provide comic relief.
5. Participants should speak from their own experience rather than assuming that they know what other individuals or a group of people have experienced.

A designated trained facilitator at each meeting is necessary to keep the environment safe, to protect people who are taking risks, and to ensure that everyone has an equal chance to participate. In workshops and in courses, the trainers or instructors are usually the facilitators. In staff meetings, principals, directors, and teachers often play this role. In parent–teacher meetings staff members and parents can co-facilitate discussions. If there are a lot of tensions among participants, then an outside facilitator would be appropriate.

Regardless of how well planned and facilitated these discussions are, participants will at times feel uncomfortable and may be resistant. We need to be able to hear criticisms and respond openly, recognizing that even our best intentions are limited by our own perspectives and experiences. Cochran-Smith (2000) describes how difficult it was for her, as a White woman, to grasp why students of color felt alienated in her multicultural course. Her struggles to understand their concerns and her own limitations and to modify the course illustrates the need to be open to criticisms and willing to question and change our beliefs and practices.

Some participants may resist these discussions covertly by being silent or by outwardly appearing to support a multicultural agenda while inwardly hardening their opposition. Others may be more open about their disagreements, often blaming victims of discrimination for their disadvantaged state (e.g., "people are just lazy; they could be successful if they worked hard") (Devine et al., 2000).

Strategies for working with resistant people include promoting relationships between them and low-prejudice peers (fellow students, teachers, or parents) with whom they identify; fostering interpersonal empathy for individuals in groups that are targets of their prejudice; and pointing out how discrimination contradicts values that they *do* espouse, such as a belief in equal opportunity (Devine et al., 2000).

If a group is large, then it makes sense to break up into smaller groups. In some cases participants may choose to be divided by race, ethnicity, sex, class, abilities/disabilities, or sexual preference. Although these divisions may seem regressive, they do provide space and safety for people to struggle through difficult memories and defenses. After a staff meeting in which I attempted to facilitate a discussion about the pervasiveness of racism in our day-to-day interactions, one of my African American colleagues told me how painful it was for her to sit and listen to her White colleagues "discover" the racism that has defined her whole life. She suggested that the White staff meet separately to continue these discussions. Ideally, the grouping should be flexible, because, as people go through the different phases of thinking about their identities and biases, their needs change. For example, at one point an individual might want to be part of a group made up of only Asian Americans to explore her identity issues in that context; but later she might want to be part of a heterogeneous group to learn about common issues and collaborative possibilities.

*Topics and Questions for Identifying and Challenging Assumptions.* This section includes several topics and questions that follow a sequence from relatively safe disclosures to more risky confrontations. They can be used for journal-writing assignments or for stimulating group discussions. Many antiracism and diversity workshops and college courses follow a similar sequence (see Derman-Sparks & Phillips, 1997). They also complement the questions that I pose in the "Reflections" sections in Chapters 4–8. The following suggestions are written with a heterogeneous group of parents and teachers in mind, but they can be adapted for more homogeneous groups. The main point is that people meet over a period of time in order to support each other through the slow process of uncovering and challenging their assumptions.

At the first level, participants can get to know each other by talking about how they identify themselves. One way to get the conversation started is to have participants bring pictures or objects that have meaning for their lives and to use them to share information about how their backgrounds (race, social class, gender, and/or culture) have shaped their lives and values.

Another exercise is to see what images people associate with the label "American." Pang and Park (2002) asked their students to record what came to mind when they heard the following: "An American walks by. The American smiles. You smile back at the American and the American walks on" (p. 8). Interestingly, the majority of students, regardless of their gender, racial or cultural backgrounds, reported that the image of a White man spontaneously came to their minds, a pattern that stimulated some interesting discussions.

Probing a little deeper, participants can talk about how their respective racial, cultural, social-class, gender, sexual orientation, and ability/disability groups are viewed and treated by the immediate community and the larger society. For example, in the media, are they over- or underrepresented? positively or negatively stereotyped? in subordinate or dominant roles? Participants can learn from others' perspectives on how different groups are regarded. For example, because a number of television shows have Black characters, many European Americans assume that African Americans are well represented on television. However, many African Americans are critical of the limited and stereotyped roles available to Black actors.

As people get to know and to trust each other, the conversations can focus on more difficult and potentially contentious issues of inequities and bias and how they affect our long-term prospects and our daily interactions. One way of easing into these more difficult areas is to talk about participants' earliest memories of differences among people.

- What specifically did I noticed? physical appearance? language? clothing? foods? disability?
- What did I think and feel about it at the time? Was I afraid? curious? attracted?
- Did I ask any adults about it? If not, why not? If I did, what was the response? What underlying messages about diversity did I learn from adults?

Discussions and journal entries along this line of inquiry often help us to see how we learned stereotypes and biases and how they still influence our responses to others. Recalling and sharing these experiences also provide concrete clues about how children in our classrooms might feel about unfamiliar people.

Often the most difficult conversations are those in which people analyze their current day-to-day experiences and see how they are still reacting according to deeply held stereotypes and assumptions. Group members might ask themselves:

- When was the most recent time that I felt afraid or uneasy about a person or group of people?
- Exactly what features of their appearance, dress, or behavior made me feel this way?
- Were my reactions reality-based, or was I reacting to group stereotypes? How and where did I learn those stereotypes?

To understand more fully how our own stereotypes and attitudes potentially affect others, we can talk about times when we ourselves have felt misjudged and/or excluded. Being ignored or marginalized, even temporarily, can evoke anger, frustration, and feelings of helplessness. We can use our own experiences to begin to see how being stigmatized profoundly affects personal relationships and the ability to function. Questions to think about are:

- When have I felt that I was the target of discrimination?
- What was the reason for it (e.g., race, gender, occupation, size, sexual orientation, ethnicity, age)?
- Who had the power? What was the source of that power?
- Did I feel disempowered? If so, why?
- How did I react? feel? What did I do? wish that I had done?
- What kind of support would have been helpful in this situation?

Obviously, momentary slights from a patronizing garage mechanic or occasional snide remarks about one's profession ("You teach little kids—kind of like babysitting, huh?") are not the same as growing up bombarded by negative images of one's group or being systematically excluded from "good" schools and neighborhoods. However, people who have not been targets of long-term discrimination can use these situations to get a glimpse of its impact.

One way to heighten awareness of our biases and limited views is to form small diverse groups to discuss films, books (including children's books), and articles in newspapers and magazines. By comparing responses, we can see some of our own blind spots. One person might see the one-dimensional women's roles; someone else might notice the lack of people with disabilities in any roles; another might point out that the Whites are portrayed as heroic rescuers of victimized and passive Latinos or that the hero of the film was valorized for "conquering" nature.

Uncovering and challenging our biases is a lifelong process, and no book, writing assignment, workshop, or conversation can provide the magic "cure." Yet if we are open to learning, we can use each conversation to learn something new and push ourselves to critically examine our assumptions. Andrea Ayvazian (1997), a longtime antiracist educator, says it well:

> None of us have reached the promised land where we are free of stereotypes and prejudices. . . . For me it has been more useful to pledge continually to move forward on this journey rather than to be crippled with shame or to be tied in knots with defensiveness or denial. . . . We are not required to be perfect in our efforts, but we do need to try new behaviors and be prepared to stumble and then to continue. (pp. 15, 17)

## HOW CHILDREN LEARN ABOUT THEIR WORLDS

Like adults, children's current lives, future prospects, and attitudes about the world are influenced by their environments. This part of this chapter will explore how children form their worldviews as they learn and develop in their social environments.

As children grow up they expand their knowledge and change how they process information, as the following example illustrates:

> My son Daniel, then 4 years old, had chosen a biography of Martin Luther King for his bedtime story (he has the same birthday as Dr. King and has from a very young age felt a strong attachment to stories and pictures of Dr. King). When we got to the part about the assassination, Daniel said in a voice full of bravado, "I'd get my sword and kill James Earl Ray!" I smiled, thinking how simple things can be when all the "bad guys" can be killed by indomitable 4-year-old "good guys."
>
> Another night about a year and a half later, we were reading the same story, and afterward we talked for a while about good laws and bad laws and how today Blacks and many other people in this country often are still treated unfairly and how we need to be strong like Martin Luther King to change things in our country that are unfair. It was a familiar conversation, and as usual Daniel repeatedly asked why people were still mean and why the police did not arrest them. We talked

about how people who are in charge often don't want to change the way things are. Later, as I was rubbing his back while he fell asleep, Daniel started to cry. I asked what was wrong and he said, "I am scared; I don't want to go to jail."

I was surprised at Daniel's reaction because we had had this conversation and similar ones many times, but this time it had touched his sense of vulnerability. At first I felt guilty—had I been pushing my agenda onto my child too forcefully? Was I being a heartless "politically correct" mom? Then I realized that Daniel had turned a cognitive corner; he was now able to imagine himself as an adult—to project himself into the future, so that the story of Martin Luther King was no longer about a distant hero but potentially about himself. He was listening to an old story, but developmentally he was hearing a new one. This incident also made me appreciate yet again how, in our discussions with children about some of the harsh realities of their world, we are always walking a tightrope balancing honesty with hope, reality with reassurance—with the fulcrum shifting as children develop more insights and connections.

All of our children are growing up in a world full of contradictions. We teach them about equality, but every day they see and experience inequality. We tell them that they should share, but then they are bombarded with messages on the media telling them they need more possessions. We urge them to work hard for a better future, but many are surrounded by poverty and despair. How do we support children to become confident idealists and activists, yet able to live in and negotiate our very imperfect world?

We also face the monumental challenges of trying to make complex issues meaningful to young children without oversimplifying or trivializing them and of raising issues and concerns without making children fearful and hopeless. To these ends, we need to consider how children are learning about the world around them.

## Child Development Theories and Research: A Critique

Most studies of how children learn have been done by researchers trained in traditional child development theories and methodologies. These theories and methods are derived from the work of early psychologists, most of whom were European or North American men (e.g., Erikson, Freud, Piaget, Hall, Skinner) and wrote from positions of racial, economic, and gender privilege. Developmental theorists and researchers have also tended to ignore the context of children's lives and have assumed that developmental goals, stages, and trajectories are universal—the same for all children in all situations. Because these "norms" are based on research done on European and European American middle-class families, children from other backgrounds have often been judged "deficient."

Over the past two decades, researchers have begun to challenge the universalistic assumptions underlying child development theories and interpretations of research outcomes. The 1980s and 1990s saw the publication of several books and research reviews (e.g., *Child Development Special Issue on Minority Children*, 1990; Gibbs, Huang, & Associates, 1989; McAdoo, 1993; Spencer, Brookins, & Allen, 1985) that interpreted minority children's development and behaviors within their own contexts instead of measuring them with the norms, paradigms, and methods based on studies of White children.

More recently, Garcia Coll and colleagues (1996) have urged researchers and educators to view children's development within the larger context of social stratification—including racism, prejudice, oppression, and segregation—and to be aware of local manifestations of discrimination such as quality of schools, access to health care, and resources available in neighborhoods. While they do not dispute the deleterious effects of political and economic disadvantage, they argue against pathologizing groups of people. They note that many communities, families, and individuals develop adaptive cultures, competencies, and strategies to overcome and resist the effects of discrimination. People working with or studying children need to expand their definitions of developmental competencies to include abilities such as functioning in more than one culture and coping with discrimination and segregation.

Developmental theories and educational practices also reflect the European American ideal of individualism and independence. Thus, we often judge children on their individual achievements, which stimulates competition among children. We also expect that children will become autonomous and self-sufficient adults who go off on their own and start their "own families" often hundreds of miles away from their original family and community. These goals, which we commonly regard as universal, are not shared by societies that value family and community loyalty and cooperative living above individual achievement. As a result, developmentally based educational policies may be in conflict with local values. Ritchie (2001) describes a time-honored early childhood practice in New Zealand called "fruit time" that reflects Maori community values and practices. All the children in a class gather together, choose a piece of fruit from a supply that children have brought from home, and eat it while listening to a story. However, new government policies that reflect more individualistic goals require that children each bring their own snack, which they eat themselves rather than sharing food during snack time.

One might argue that, with all these flaws and limitations, we should simply dismiss all child development research. However, this work has provided much valuable information about how children change as they mature. As Stott & Bowman (1996) argue:

> What makes theories worth reading and discussing is not the assumption that they mirror reality but that they serve as suggestions or estimations—they help us to arrange our minds. Theories are helpful in that they organize and give meaning to facts, and they guide further observation and research. (p. 170)

In short, rather than "throwing the baby out with the bath water," we can use developmental theories and research to help us to be more aware of the nuances in children's lives and thinking. However, we must read this information critically; apply it cautiously; and develop new theories, research methods, and educational practices that reflect broad perspectives and challenge us to see the world in new ways.

## Developmental Trends and Processes

Many principles of early childhood education (and by extension parent education) are based on the theories of Jean Piaget (e.g., Piaget, 1951; Piaget & Inhelder, 1968), who provided some wonderful insights into how children's thinking changes as they get older. However, child developmentalists and early childhood educators—certainly including myself—have traditionally focused on children's cognitive limitations at each stage. We assume that 4-year-olds across the board are "preoperational" and are able to think of only one attribute at a time and are unable to understand more complex concepts such as class inclusion.

Foregrounding children's cognitive limitations may provide an excuse to avoid difficult and complex issues. Silin (1995) challenges the attachment to developmental stages and the tendency to protect children's innocence and asks whether we are simply trying to distance children from the "disquieting material realities in which they live" (p. 104). I am not suggesting here that children do not change over time. I firmly believe that they do. However, rather than use developmental theories to define children's capabilities and limitations at particular ages, we can use them to observe and hear children more accurately, to better understand where they are coming from, and to anticipate where they are going as they try to make sense of the world around them.

We can also shift our focus away from identifying children's stages of development to looking more closely at *how* they develop their ideas. One useful framework is Piaget's (Piaget & Inhelder, 1968) concepts of assimilation and accommodation—the continuous cycle in which children's expectations about the world are formed, confirmed, challenged, and changed. For example, a child shifts from assuming that all four-legged creatures are dogs (assimilation); to experiencing uncertainty as he notices differences in names, sizes, shapes, and sounds; to developing more refined categories, such as horses and cats (accommodation). As children go through this process, they experience disequilibrium when new questions and ideas emerge and take shape. This phase offers many possibilities for cognitive growth. Daniel experienced disequilibrium when he realized that being a good guy did not mean simply killing the bad guys with a sword; it also meant that he himself might have to take risks and get hurt. A familiar story converged with his growing understanding of himself as a vulnerable person with a future and precipitated new insights and discomforts.

Vygotsky (1978), like Piaget, viewed children as actively constructing their own knowledge. However, unlike Piaget, who focused on children's interactions with the physical world, Vygotsky believed that children's learning is a social process that occurs in a particular space and time that reflects the beliefs, politics, and practices of the adults around them. He also reversed Piaget's assumption that development must precede learning and proposed that learning makes development possible (Silin, 1995). These differences are reflected in Vygotsky's concept of the *zone of proximal development*, which refers to the difference between a child's level of *independent* problem solving and his *potential* level of problem solving that is evident when an adult or more mature peer provides assistance or guidance (often referred to as "scaffolding"). I recall watching a young child and her mother weaving in a small town in Chiapas, Mexico. As the girl worked on her small hand-held loom, her mother glanced over frequently and occasionally pointed to the child's work and made a comment or demonstrated an action on her own loom. A few times the child nudged her mother and asked her a question, pointing to her work. Through demonstration and a few verbal instructions, the mother was "scaffolding" her daughter's efforts to refine her weaving skills.

Disequilibrium and the zone of proximal development work hand in hand. As children experience disequilibrium, they are approaching new insights and absorbing new information, and often, with the support of an adult or older child, they move to the next level of understanding. Although teachers and parents rarely think in terms of *disequilibrium* and the *zone of proximal development*, they often apply these principles in their day-to-day interactions with their children. When a child comes storming in from a fight with a friend declaring that she will *never* again play with that child, an adult may try to help her rethink that assumption. By discussing what happened or reading or telling related stories, he can help the child come to some new understandings about why fights start and how friends can get mad at each other and still be friends.

When Daniel was crying about being put in jail, I have to say that the words *disequilibrium* and *zone of proximal development* did not enter my head. I only thought about what information would be useful in getting him to see beyond the scary part of being a social activist. I talked to him about the fact that people work together to change things and that they help each other out and that every time Martin Luther King was in jail people all over the country made sure that the police let him out right away. We talked about all the people who might work with Daniel to stop the "mean people." As together we listed friends, teachers, family members, and neighbors, Daniel seemed comforted and reassured. We shifted to talking about things in our town and his school that are unfair and should be changed and how he and his family and friends might go about that. At this point what had been a story about a distant historical hero had become a discussion about local issues, about what he and his friends and family could do, which created some new areas of disequilibrium. I did wonder at the time whether or not to mention all the people who were in jail and did *not* have people all over the country trying to get them out. I decided not to—I felt at that moment that I needed to shift the balance toward the hope and reassurance end of the continuum. There would be many more conversations.

As we talk with children about complicated events and issues, we need to listen for what they understand and feel at the moment, where they are trying to go, and what they are ready to absorb. To this end I will briefly review a couple of relevant developmental trends in children's thinking that are commonly observed in societies that value logical and linear thinking. These patterns may not be evident in cultures where intuitive or metaphorical thought are developmental priorities.

*Moving from Concrete to Abstract Thinking.* Young children are shifting from seeing the world in concrete and static terms to being able to engage in abstract speculations and to recognize causal relationships and events outside of their immediate realm of experience. Several years ago, after a gay couple had been visiting us for a week, Andrés, then 4-years-old, talked about "I jump on Stan and Bill! They throw me in the air!" His main interest was in their playmate potential. Daniel, then age 7, however, asked questions about whether they were "married together" or had wives and whether or not they could have kids. Although he already knew a number of gay families and was aware that some children have two mommies or two daddies, a week of close proximity apparently made him more conscious of the couple aspect of gay relationships. An event that was interpreted by a 4-year-old as simply "More people here to play with" stimulated a whole new set of wonderings and questions about adult relationships by a 7-year-old.

As young children grapple with new information and unfamiliar experiences, they often draw some erroneous conclusions on their way to understanding more abstract concepts, such as the relationship between traditional and contemporary lifestyles or geographical relationships. One teacher introduced her kindergartners to the idea that people in or from different countries speak different languages by teaching them some songs and a few words in various languages. Later she overheard two children arguing about whether or not the children who lived in the next town spoke English. The children were beginning to make connections between locale and languages, but the specific nature of that relationship eluded them. The children also may have heard people in their own family or community speaking other languages and then fused the concepts of town and nationality. The activity was not a failure—the children were clearly thinking about language in new ways. Moreover, this argument gave the teacher a whole new set of ideas to work with. She asked the children about people in their lives who spoke different languages, organized a project in which the children interviewed children and teachers in other classes about which languages they spoke and where they were from, and invited bilingual people to come into the classroom to talk about how and where they learned their different languages. She and the children found many ways to continue the discussion of the relationship between language and place—a complicated issue for any of us, but one filled with fascination for young children who are just learning the power of language.

*Categorizing Information.* All of us tend to categorize information because it is a way to make our thinking more efficient. If we have a category for a "fork," then we know what to do with one when we see it and do not have to "rediscover" it each time. The downside of categories is that we often overgeneralize and make unwarranted assumptions. This tendency is clearly a problem when it occurs—as it often does—in our judgments about people. Where do useful generalizations stop and prejudices begin? Fifty years ago, Allport (1954) described prejudice as "overcategorization" in which people assume that all members of a particular group will behave, look, feel, and think the same way. Moreover, these assumptions are impervious to new information that contradicts them.

Young children tend to organize information in broad categories that are often rigid and dichotomous. They sometimes see extremes rather than gradations and, if they decide that two groups are different, resist seeing similarities. When I was interviewing children about their racial perceptions, attitudes, and understandings (Ramsey, 1987), one White preschooler (who lived in a predominantly White rural community) was looking at pictures of both African American and Chinese American children and described the latter as "a little Chinese" and the former as "a lot Chinese." She was able to make distinctions between people who "look like me" (Whites) and people who "do not look like me" but was unable to refine them, even when I directly pointed out different physical features. As they get older, children are better able to see that similarities and differences can coexist. Try asking preschoolers whether or not bad guys can ever be good guys—usually the answer is a resounding "no!" However, a second grader may be able to explain how a person can be both bad and good.

Children who are able to use multiple and flexible categories on non-social items (e.g., being able to shift between classifying a red triangle by shape and by color) seem to be better at remembering counterstereotyped information about different groups (Bigler, Jones, & Lobliner, 1997). Thus, when we are working with children on any classification tasks (e.g., colors, shapes, leaves, animals), we may want to help them see how objects can be categorized in a number of different ways.

All children have unique experiences and perspectives. To work effectively with them, we need to learn what specific children do and do not know, what puzzles them, and how they react to different people and situations. Each chapter in Part II of this book includes suggestions for observing and talking with children to learn how they think and feel about the issues specific to that chapter.

## Guidelines for Challenging Children's Assumptions and Expanding Their Perspectives

To counteract children's limited and/or biased views about the social and natural worlds, we need to provide them with experiences and information that will expand their views and encourage them to reconsider their assumptions. Suggestions and examples related to particular issues will be discussed in Chapters 4–8. Chapter 3 will focus on children's social and emotional development and related teaching practices. This section contains general guidelines for how to assess and modify physical settings and materials to support children's awareness and understanding of the world. The suggestions below are not prescriptive and can be adapted for different issues, groups, and communities.

*Physical Settings.* Where children live and go to school profoundly affects what they learn about the social and natural worlds. All settings have their assets and drawbacks, and teachers need to find ways to work around the limitations while taking advantage of the possibilities to create multicultural environments.

One of the first things to consider is the relationship between the physical setting and the social world:

- Do the children at the school represent the diversity of the community? If not, why not? Are transportation, admissions, or financial aid policies discouraging particular families from sending their children to the school? How might these be changed?
- How diverse is the staff? If it is not diverse, what employment criteria and practices might be instituted to attract staff from a wider range of backgrounds?
- Does the staffing hierarchy replicate typical dominance patterns? Are Whites, especially White males, in charge, with members of other groups as subordinates? What jobs, if any, are held by people with disabilities?
- What are nearby potential learning sites outside the school (e.g., stores, small factories, farms, homeless shelters, museums)? What can children learn from these resources. What ethnic and occupational groups are represented? Are there places where children can see a range of jobs (not just the usual glamorous firefighters and doctors)?
- How can staff members develop closer relationships with the community? Are there senior citizens who might want to volunteer? local business people or artists who could visit the classroom and/or sponsor field trips to their workplace? community activists who could share information and involve the school in local struggles?

The second area to question is how the physical setting relates with the natural world:

- Do children have easy access to the outdoors?
- In places where access to the outdoors is limited, how can the natural world be "brought in" with plants, seedbeds, aquaria, terraria, and small pets?
- How is the natural world portrayed in classroom photographs? Do they stimulate children's awareness and appreciation of the natural world? its many climates and landforms? the many ways in which people and animals adapt to different environments?

*Photographs.* Photographs potentially expand children's awareness by visually representing both familiar and unfamiliar people and settings. However, like any other materials, we need to critically analyze the messages that are conveyed.

First, why do I recommend photographs instead of drawings or paint-ings? Commercial drawings on school posters often depict static and stereo-typed images and do not add meaningful information. Paintings, especially those that convey social justice themes (e.g., the works of Diego Rivera and Ralph Fasanella), often convey powerful messages and can provoke good discussions. However, to recognize unfamiliar people as individuals, chil-dren need images of real people in the context of their daily lives. Generally, photographs capture human variety and the range and depth of feelings bet-ter than most commercial drawings and paintings.

Photographs of persons from many backgrounds provide opportunities for children to observe and compare facial expressions and individual char-acteristics in unfamiliar people. I saw an innovative use of photographs in a computerized Concentration game at the "People Puzzle" exhibit at the Cleveland Children's Museum. About 15 pairs of identical photographs of children's faces that represented a broad range of racial features were placed face down. As in the game of Concentration, players had to remember the location of different faces in order to match the identical pairs. As I per-formed this activity, I was chagrined at how many errors I made but noticed that my awareness of individual differences increased as I played. This game can easily be constructed with photographs mounted on sturdy cards.

Ideally, collections of photographs consist of individuals who represent many varieties of skin color, hair texture, facial features, dress, and adorn-ment. They should also include people with and without disabilities and in scenes that show a range of occupations, homes, and family constellations. The people should be shown in situations and expressing feelings that young children can recognize in order to convey the message that people look, dress, and live differently but have similar feelings and activities. Photo-graphs that challenge common stereotypes should also be available (e.g., Black male executives and doctors, White males sweeping streets, women doing construction work, and people with disabilities participating in sports events). To support children's learning about social justice movements, pho-tographs of protest marches and strikes and other acts of resistance should also be included—again, representing as wide an array of people as possible.

Photographs of the natural world and of people living in different types of landscapes expand children's ideas of people and how they live their lives. They also illustrate how all people and living things share common experiences and needs and are connected because we all live on the same planet.

Calendars, magazines, catalogues, and websites are all potential sources of photographs. Several educational companies also have packages of poster-size photographs that are designed for schools. When selecting photo-graphs for a school collection, several people, including, if possible, members of the groups that are being portrayed, should review them before they are displayed to ensure that they are reasonably authentic and representative images. Contemporary images of groups doing daily activities should be emphasized more than historical or ceremonial images, so that children see them as real people, not as exotic "others."

Teachers and parents can collaborate to build up a large collection of photographs and organize them by categories. Then, when teachers are developing curriculum themes or challenging particular stereotypes that their students express, they can use relevant photographs from the collection.

*Electronic Media.* I am including electronic media in this chapter because the information and images in the media influence children's view of the world. As they are growing up, children watch and absorb millions of visual and verbal messages about people and how they relate to each other and to the natural environment. They learn information that can both undermine and support multicultural views. Thus, we need to make conscious decisions about the role of electronic media in children's lives.

Teachers, preferably in consultation with parents, need to decide whether or not to allow media-based play (derived from television, movies, or electronic games) in their classrooms. Some people believe that it is better to let the children enact and process what they have seen on the media, especially if it is scary. Others feel that school is the one place where children can explore other aspects of the world and that media-based play should be excluded (for more detailed discussions of these debates, see Carlsson-Paige & Levin, 1990). Whether or not media-based play is allowed in the classroom, I do feel that teachers should not encourage children's preoccupation with television and movies by having media characters and/or pictures displayed or used in the classroom except to critically analyze them. The world is full of exciting information and experiences, and to reinforce images that already bombard children is a wasted opportunity. One exception would be using media images to make an initial connection with children who are very uncomfortable with or alienated from school.

When teachers notice that particular children are exclusively enacting television characters and storylines, they might talk with parents about ways to expand their children's interests and to counteract their dependence on television. Parents can help each other to reduce the amount of children's "screen time" by making playdates and cooperating to get children involved in other activities (e.g., sharing rides to parks and recreational activities). They can also agree to monitor and limit screen time when children are visiting to reduce the pressure to go to homes where more screen time is allowed.

Because television, movies, and video games reflect many biases, they can be useful tools for teaching children critical thinking skills. Teachers can talk to children about the programs and advertisements that they have seen and encourage them to identify stereotypes and misinformation (see suggestions in Carlsson-Paige & Levin, 1990). Children can also discuss the underlying messages of stories and figure out why certain shows are so appealing. When children discover that a show is biased or an advertisements is misleading, they might write letters to the networks and advertisers. Elementary school children enjoy making videos, and these experiences often show how decisions about what to include and how to film it (e.g., distance and angle) affect viewers' interpretation of the image (e.g., how advertisers make toys look bigger than they are).

Despite the many drawbacks, electronic media are not all negative. We can learn a lot from shows about different cultures, social injustices, environmental issues, and movements for social change. However, even the most careful documentaries reflect particular points of view, often ones that are compatible with the priorities of corporate sponsors. As we watch these programs with children, we need to talk about what is *not* shown (e.g., the effects of bringing in tourists and photographers on the animals and habitat being portrayed). Another problem is that documentaries have a hard time competing with violent cartoons for children's attention.

All of us who care for children need to put hard economic pressure on the communications industry to shift their programming from violent, racist, sexist, product-driven shows for children to substantive ones. These issues may be a way to galvanize teachers and parents to become activists and advocates for their children. They can work together to take back control of the airways (which are as much a part of the public domain as our highways) by supporting public television and local community-access channels. They can also pressure local stations to air grassroots programs, to investigate and report local problems and success stories, and to resist the dictates of the networks to air violent and biased shows. It is a daunting challenge, but a lot of teachers and parents are angry and frustrated about trying to raise children in a media-saturated environment. Their frustration can become a force for change.

*Toys and Materials.* Toys and materials should be consciously selected, not simply purchased because "all the other kids (or classrooms) have one." Teachers do not experience the same pressure to purchase advertised products as parents do. However, they may feel compelled to stock their classrooms with materials that are counterproductive to multicultural education (e.g., reading series or computer programs that contain stereotypes and/or teach rote skills instead of critical thinking) because they are supposed to accelerate children's learning. Teachers in some schools are required to use specific materials such as test-preparation packets and state-adopted reading series. In these cases, teachers can try to negotiate with their colleagues and principals to find ways to include other materials and to prevent the mandated curricula from defining the whole curriculum. They can also organize parents and fellow teachers to resist community and state regulations that they see as counterproductive to authentic education.

When selecting toys and materials, we want ones that potentially encourage children to expand their views, develop social and cognitive skills, question their assumptions, and explore and solve interesting problems. As we look around our classrooms or choose new toys and materials, we can ask the following questions:

- What groups are represented? not represented? Is the diversity of children in the class, community, and country represented?
- How are different people and places represented? Are the figures in the puzzles, the doll area, or blocks stereotyped? or do they represent realistic images?
- What values about the natural environment are conveyed in the images and materials in the classroom?
- How can material or pieces of equipment be used? Can they be used by more than one child or only by single children? Do they promote cooperative or competitive play? Are they open-ended activities (such as blocks) or do they have defined endpoints (such as a puzzle)?
- Are materials made out of natural or synthetic materials? made by hand or machine? How durable are they? Will they last for a long time, or will they soon be taking up space in the local landfill?
- What do we know about the manufacturers? What are their of environmental and employment practices?
- How many of a particular tool or toy do we need? Are we assuming that we need one for each child? or do we want to get a few for the whole group to share?
- Do we really need a new piece of equipment or toy? or can we help children adapt an old one for the same purpose? How might we use existing materials instead of purchasing new ones?
- In addition to manufactured materials, do we have a lot of natural ones (e.g., grasses for paint brushes, small logs for construction) that will challenge children's expectations that tools and materials are all made exactly to specifications (e.g., uniform paint brushes and unit blocks).
- How can we use these materials to enhance children's appreciation for natural forms and their understanding of physical properties (e.g., the challenge of building with uneven logs)?

*Books.* Children's literature is a valuable resource in our efforts to support children's ethnic identity, introduce them to unfamiliar people in a personalized and appealing fashion, challenge stereotypes, and raise social and environmental issues. Books can also "affirm models of resistance and social justice—'to know if something's wrong, they can try to do something about it' and 'to feel a sense that if they have the power to find the solutions'" (Sara, a Head Start teacher, quoted in Wilson, 2000, p. 71).

However, writing children's stories that fulfill these goals is not easy. Some books that attempt to portray a broad range of human experiences have been criticized for their stereotypical or romanticized portraits. In other cases, authors try so hard to make a political or social statement that the stories have a dogmatic tone and are not appealing to young children. Teachers, together with children and parents, can review and critique a number of books for stereotypes and misinformation and select ones that together authentically represent diverse experiences and perspectives and raise issues in ways that are appropriate for their particular children.

A number of publications (e.g., *Rethinking Schools* and *Multicultural Perspectives* [the journal of the National Association for Multicultural Education]) review new children's books. I find that reading the reviews not only gives me information about the books themselves but also sharpens my own critical awareness of images and issues in other books.

Some critics have raised the question of whether authors who are not members of a particular ethnic group can authentically write stories about the experiences of that group (Sims, 1982). It is a valid point. Some stories written by White authors subtly undermine other groups by portraying White protagonists rescuing less competent or victimized persons of color or valorizing the people of color for having "made it" in the White world. Often White authors and readers do not see these biases because they mesh with unconscious beliefs about White superiority and fantasies of White rescuers and role models.

In general, stories written by members of the groups portrayed are preferable. However, publishers often reject books by unknown authors or ones that they think will appeal only to a limited segment of the population. Teachers, parents, and children can write to publishers and urge them to publish authors from underrepresented groups.

Books authored by people other than those who are represented should be scrutinized carefully for subtle ways in which they may patronize the group or misrepresent its experiences and perspective. The acknowledgments and biographical information also provide information about whether or not the authors have worked with or at the very least consulted with members of the group that they are portraying.

All books, regardless of their content, reflect particular values, even though at first glance they may appear to be "culture-free." For example, although most of its protagonists are animals, *The Story of Babar* (De Brunhoff, 1984) extols the virtues of French colonialism and contains many disparaging images of African people and animals before they were "civilized." The plot of Silverstein's *The Giving Tree* (1964), ostensibly a story about a boy and a tree, reflects our culture's patriarchal and exploitative view of nature. Not only does the story reinforce the idea that people (or at least White males) have private property that they can use and destroy however they wish, but it also perpetuates the assumption that boys/men are the takers and exploiters and that nature, depicted as a woman, is the willing and passive provider.

Another consideration is the balance between realism and optimism. Books for young children usually have happy endings, and some have been criticized for trivializing the complexities and minimizing the pain that people experience. At the same time, we want children to grow up to be hopeful as well as knowledgeable and concerned. *Out of the Dump* (Franklin & McGirr, 1995), a book of poems and photographs by children who live in the dump in Guatemala City, is a good example of balancing despair and hope. It is an unflinching portrayal of the hardships these children face, yet it manages to convey a sense of courage, resilience, and even joy. The children create toys out of scavenged materials and play games in a desolate dump. Their experience is a good foil for talking to more affluent children about their "need" for every new toy and game. As the authors and photographers of the book, the children also provide an inspiring example of how children can learn skills and use them to fight back—in this case, to reveal to the world the plight of a group of poor families in Guatemala.

Nonfiction books are good resources for background information and images of people who are underrepresented in the media. Several books and series published in the 1990s about different countries and groups within the United States have fairly current information and in many cases good photographs to show children different natural environments, ways of life, dwellings, clothes, and foods in meaningful contexts. *Material World: A Global Family Portrait* (Menzel, 1994) is a fascinating series of photographs from all over the world. Each one portrays a family, their house, and their possessions. This collection illustrates both cultural similarities and differences and the huge disparities in material wealth across countries. The *Cultures of America* series (published in the 1990s by Marshall Cavendish) describes the lives and histories of different ethnic groups in the United States, such as Mexican Americans, French Americans, Korean Americans, and African Americans. They are good sources of background information for teachers and parents and have photographs that children can look at. The

*Our American Family* series (published by PowerKids Press) are short books, each about a particular ethnic group in the United States. Each volume has photographs and information about the group's history, family life, and traditions and is written by an author from that group. The books in the *Kids Explore* series (Westridge Young Writers Workshop, 1992, 1993) have a lot of information about different cultural groups in the United States and are written to appeal to young children. The book for each group is written by elementary school children and teachers, the majority of whom come from that particular group. The books in the *Journey Between Two Worlds* series (published in the late 1990s by Lerner Publications) describe particular families' immigration experiences. They include information about the home country and fairly detailed explanations about the political and/or economic reasons that led the families to emigrate. The stories give realistic but hopeful accounts of the hardships that families faced moving and adjusting to life in the United States. As with the *Cultures of America* series, young children will not be able to read these books by themselves, but teachers can use the photographs and information to tell the stories to children in age-appropriate ways.

Children's stories can also be used to explore social justice issues and dilemmas. However, many books that allude to injustices and hardships often fail to critique the systemic causes of these inequities. To challenge some of the overly benign interpretations of events, we need to look for books that have more critical analyses. One good source is the *Perspectives* series, published in the mid-1990s by Marshall Cavendish. They include a number of books, such as *A Multicultural Portrait of Colonial Life*, *A Multicultural Portrait of the Civil War*, *A Multicultural Portrait of Life in the Cities*, and *A Multicultural Portrait of People at Work*. These volumes show how racial advantages and disadvantages have been part of our history and continue to permeate our current society. The reading level is too advanced for young children, but teachers can use the pictures and modify the information so that it is appropriate to the age and interests of the children in their particular class.

Biographies of people engaged in struggles against injustice are also valuable resources. I am not advocating that we return to the "heroes and holidays" approach, which has rightly been criticized from many quarters, but rather that we use biographies to help children learn to hope and to persist by learning about the lives of people who have taken risks and have made a difference. Many children are especially interested in how people were able to overcome their fears and limitations to act courageously, whether it was refusing to change a seat, leading slaves to freedom, overcoming multiple disabilities, speaking out and facing ridicule, or going to a school or joining a team where no one wanted them. Hearing or reading these accounts can stimulate conversations about being strong and brave in ways that children can understand and can relate to their own lives. When my son Daniel was in kindergarten, he was afraid of the dark. He had me read a biography of Harriet Tubman over and over again as he marveled at how she went out into the woods *at night* and led people to freedom.

Biographical accounts also provide a compelling antidote to the violent images of power and strength that dominate television shows and the toy market. We can point out to children that superheroes have to use their magical powers and weapons to win, but Martin Luther King never used a gun or magic and changed this whole country using his brains and his words and his faith in people. We can ask them, "What do you think is harder? to jump into the Batmobile and to push buttons that provide lots of gadgets or to learn to read and speak when you cannot see or hear, as Helen Keller did?"

Collections of biographies should include not only well-known people but also people who have led relatively ordinary lives. The books in the *Kids Explore* series have biographies of people who are not famous but have overcome discrimination and poverty to become successful contributors to society and agents of social change. With the help of older children or adults, young children can also interview family and community members and create their own biographies, which can provide many close-to-home examples of people conquering hardships and resisting injustices.

An annotated list of suggested children's books is found in the Appendix. It is not an exhaustive bibliography but will give teachers a place to start.

This chapter has focused primarily on the cognitive goals of multicultural education—on identifying and challenging assumptions and broadening the perspectives of both adults and children. The next chapter will focus on social and emotional aspects because authentic multicultural education can *only* occur in the context of caring classrooms and communities.

# CHAPTER 3

# Creating Caring
# and Critical Communities

At the core of all multicultural endeavors is the creation of "communities of critically thinking, morally courageous, and politically engaged individuals, who work together and share power to reform society and who genuinely value diverse realities, voices, individuals, and cultures" (Gay, 1995, p. 181). This chapter will focus on how we can foster caring and collaborative connections among adults and children that lead to critical involvement with broader concerns.

According to Nel Noddings (1992), caring involves an "encounter between two human beings . . . an open, nonselective receptivity to the cared-for" (p. 15). In other words, to care for someone means to give them our full attention and to see and hear them with an open heart and mind.

We often assume that caring only occurs in private, intimate relationships that protect the innocence of children and provide a refuge from the world. Noddings (1992), however, argues that caring is a way to engage with the complexities and difficulties of our world. She articulates the following eight centers of care: "care for self, for intimate others, for associates and acquaintances, for distant others, for nonhuman animals, for plants and the physical environment, for the human-made world of objects and instruments, and for ideas" (p. xiii). Noddings criticizes most educational programs for caring only about ideas and argues that authentic education must address all the centers of care.

Valerie Pang (2001) echoes these views and argues that all aspects of multicultural education flow from caring relationships—among children, teachers, families, schools, and communities. Both Noddings and Pang make explicit connections between caring and social justice work. Noddings (1992, 2002) demonstrates how caring leads to a greater understanding of ourselves and others, a willingness to connect across racial and cultural boundaries, and a critical awareness of how our actions affect others. Pang (2001) asserts that "caring and social justice in a democracy are intimately connected. When we care, we act . . . social justice flow[s] directly from what we care about" (p. 63).

43

Audrey Thompson (1998) makes a similar point, from a Black feminist perspective. She points out that, for poor people and people of color, caring can never be confined to the personal realm. Because there is no escape from racism and poverty, loving and caring *must* be about confronting and transforming inequities. She asserts that caring in Black communities has always been a shared endeavor and has focused on giving children strategies to survive and challenge racism. In contrast to the White middle-class value of protecting children's innocence, Thompson points out that in the Black community honesty is more valued than innocence and that Black children *must* learn about racism in order to be prepared for the dangers they will face. Thompson also argues that caring includes reaching out across communities, to "demythologize race relations and make it possible to see ourselves and one another as we really are and to see ourselves together as we might be" (pp. 539–540).

In short, caring is a powerful emotion that energizes concern for ourselves and others and our willingness to confront and change inequities. Thus, it is an essential component of multicultural education.

The willingness to collaborate with others is also vital for creating multicultural communities. One of the challenges in this effort is the individualistic orientation of many people and most institutions in the United States. Our reverence for individual liberties and achievement has fueled great creativity, productivity, and innovation. However, it also leads to maximizing self-interest with little attention to others' needs and experiences. Competition, which is a natural outgrowth of individualism, fuels a desire to dominate rather than enjoy experiences and to ensure victory by sabotaging and undermining others (Johnson & Johnson, 2000). These values permeate our educational and economic enterprises. As individuals, we push ourselves to get the best grade or get the highest raise. At an institutional level, schools are judged by their test scores or athletic championships, and businesses expend huge amounts of money and energy to outperform their rivals.

In contrast, cooperative communities, in their most ideal form, are based on members' commitments to contribute to the success of the whole group; to take responsibility for doing one's fair share and for supporting others; to respect and learn from the diverse strengths of community members; to respond with compassion to others' needs; and to strive as individuals, not to win, but to have the intrinsic satisfaction of learning and growing (Johnson & Johnson, 2000). However, in many cases these ideals are elusive, and some tight-knit cooperative communities become hierarchical and repressive and, at worst, dictatorial and totalitarian.

The challenge is to form communities that are sufficiently flexible to support individual growth yet cohesive enough to work toward common goals. The following ecological principles accommodate these tensions and provide some direction for creating collaborative communities among adults and within classrooms (Bowers, 1995):

- *Interdependence*—honoring and supporting the web of relationships among children, families, teachers, administrators, and community people; facilitating energy and information flow throughout the system, not only from the top down
- *Sustainability*—supporting people and nature to thrive over the long haul and focusing on long-term rather than short-term effects of actions
- *Flexibility*—developing fluid dynamic systems that adapt to changing needs
- *Diversity*—supporting diverse experiences, backgrounds, and learning strategies
- *Partnership and co-evolution*—working together, understanding each others' needs, and mutually adapting as members' needs and interests change and evolve

## CREATING CARING AND CRITICAL COMMUNITIES AMONG ADULTS

Positive relationships among adults are crucial to creating caring communities and to developing shared commitments to work for social justice. In the following sections I discuss relationships among staff and between parents and teachers and between schools and communities.

### Staff Relationships

To create sustainable communities, staff members must feel secure and well compensated in their jobs and supported by peers and the administration. They need working conditions and schedules that allow them to enjoy and savor their work and to participate in professional development activities. If a teacher is working two other jobs in order to make ends meet, then she is not going to have the time and energy to meet with parents, to participate in community activities, or even to emotionally connect with all of the children. These considerations relate to ongoing concerns about the poor wages and benefits of many early childhood teachers (particularly those in the private sector). Some schools have taken a proactive stance to this problem by lobbying legislators to more fully fund child-care programs. However, these changes involve sweeping shifts in national spending priorities and, unfortunately, probably will happen slowly. Thus, in the short term, staff members need to set clear priorities and be creative in scheduling and allocating responsibilities to ensure that, as much as possible, people have the energy and time to enjoy their work with children and engage in professional development and community activities.

All staff members, including teachers, support staff, and administrators, need to feel that they are valued participants in the decision making of the school. As described in the ecological principles, we should encourage partnerships and co-evolution, rather than hierarchical decision making. The system needs to be flexible enough so that all members can grow and expand their knowledge and skills. When staff members feel devalued and frustrated, the whole school suffers. For example, in many public schools the undesirable task of monitoring the cafeteria falls to low-status workers, often referred to by the derogatory term *lunch ladies*. Some children, fully aware of the status differentials among the school staff, test the limits and act in ways that they would never dare to do with their classroom teachers. The cafeteria workers, who often have little training and may feel unsupported, then react punitively to children, and conflicts escalate and spill into the playground and classrooms. Sometimes racial, ethnic, and class differences enter in, creating particularly tense situations that can affect the whole school.

To create a caring community, staff members need to take responsibility for mutually supporting each other, recognizing and addressing diversity in all of its forms. By engaging in conversations like those described in Chapter 2, staff members can become more responsive to each others' values, needs, and interests.

In short, the emotional, social, and physical well-being of the school staff is key to creating a caring community for children and their families. If staff members feel empowered, supported, and respected, they will participate more fully in community decisions and activities and create caring settings for children. Sometimes administrators feel that they cannot take the time for staff retreats, full-day workshops, and pot-luck dinners. However, they may gain back that time and more if staff members feel connected and energized by these experiences.

## Family–School Relationships

To engage in meaningful multicultural practice, families and schools need to operate as interdependent, mutually respectful partners. However, establishing these relationships is challenging for many reasons.

First, many families are rarely in the schools and have little contact with any of the staff. Their children may arrive and depart on a bus, and many parents' work schedules and/or lack of transportation make it impossible for them to get to school when the teachers are available. Except for occasional phone calls, teachers and parents may rarely speak with each other. Moreover, if parents feel intimidated by schools, then they will find excuses to avoid contact. Staff members need to be creative in finding ways to make meetings appealing and accessible to as wide a range of families as possible (e.g., trying out different formats, schedules, locations). Also, teachers can use their phone contacts with parents not simply to exchange information but to more fully explore the parents' feelings about the school and their children's progress.

Another impediment to meaningful connections is when parents and teachers do not speak the same language. Every effort should be made to have staff, family members, or community people who can translate available at class meetings and conferences. However, using an intermediary makes conversations stilted, and nuances of meaning are often lost. If mono-lingual teachers find that they are working with many children from one particular language group, they may want to study that language so that they can begin to communicate with parents more directly. Administrators might also work with local adult education groups to organize English classes for parents that focus on vocabulary relevant to schools and children.

An additional obstacle to honest parent–teacher communication is that we often expect that families and schools have—or should have—common philosophies and practices. Yet many families in the United States find that the goals, values, and practices of school personnel are incongruent with, if not antithetical to, their child-rearing goals (as will be discussed in more depth in Chapter 6).

Often parents and teachers are constrained from openly acknowledging and discussing their differences because of status issues. Throughout our educational system, teachers are considered the experts (Silin, 1995). This dynamic is true even in early childhood education, which—with its history of parent cooperatives and parent boards—has traditionally been more re-ceptive to parent input than most public schools. The tacit assumption is that "when differences of opinion [between parents and teachers] arise [teachers] should listen, explain, compromise, but never give in" (Tobin, Wu, & Da-vidson, 1989, p. 210). Many parent education programs ignore the profound problems of inequities, racism, and poverty and put the burden on parents to "improve" their parenting practices by imitating those of the White mid-dle-class teachers and parents. Even very open and well-intentioned teachers often slip into the role of the expert, especially with parents who are dealing with poverty, divorce, homelessness, or other hardships.

These status differences are sometimes reversed in affluent communi-ties, where some parents treat their children's teachers as employees or "in-stitutionalized versions of . . . nannies" (Tobin et al., 1989, p. 209). Parents may exert their influence to limit school closures for staff training or bad weather or expect the teachers to give their children special attention and modify the program to fit their families' schedules and goals. Many teachers understandably resent these high-handed approaches and avoid communicating with the parents.

To create communities where roles are flexible and information is exchanged freely throughout the system rather than hierarchically, we need to develop new opportunities for teachers and parents to work and talk together. One inner-city elementary school increased parent involvement dramatically by implementing several strategies, including a new-parent breakfast and an outreach committee to get parents involved, a family center, a parent leadership team that was involved in the governance of the school, and the formation of reciprocal relationships between parents and teachers where ideas and feedback were shared and parents' ideas were given equal weight. Most important, the parents felt welcomed, honored, and connected with the teachers and administrators of the school (Mapp, 2002).

The schools in Reggio Emilia, Italy, are deservedly famous for their parent and community involvement. Cadwell (2003) describes how she has adapted this approach for a school in the United States. Her specific strategies include the following:

- Formation of a parent committee that meets regularly with the classroom teacher
- Discussions with parent groups about classroom projects
- Parent–child collaborative projects
- Parent volunteers, who share hobbies and skills with the children (not just drive on field trips)
- Teacher–parent planned celebrations
- Weekly newsletters describing the work in the classroom
- Daily classroom journals (featuring children's work and words and teachers' observations about that particular day)

The possibilities for involving parents are endless, and several are described in Chapter 9. As described in the following sections, parent–teacher conferences and class meetings can also be vehicles for developing collaborative and reciprocal partnerships.

One issue that immediately arises is time. To have more collaborative relationships between families and schools, we need time to talk, to plan, and to work together. As I mentioned earlier, many parents have difficulty getting to the school at all. And even those who can get there may struggle to fit in meetings. (As I write this, I see myself rushing out of the house to a meeting with part of my dinner wrapped in a napkin and the rest of it sitting in an unchewed lump in my stomach—wishing desperately that I did not have to go back out.) Yet think about all the things we *do* find time for: watching television, going to the mall, talking with friends on the telephone or on e-mail, attending self-help and exercise groups, to name only a few. If parents and teachers become a mutually supportive team, then meetings change from being burdensome obligations to opportunities to gain new insights about themselves and their children; to connect with other parents, teachers, and the community; and to generate activities and strategies for the classroom and home. Obviously, there are many logistical problems— transportation, child care, and incompatible work schedules. However, the bottom line is: If the meetings are supportive and meaningful, then people will find a way to participate. If not, then logistics and time will always be good excuses.

*Parent–Teacher Conferences.* Typically in parent–teacher conferences, teachers, acting in their role as experts, ask parents for background information about their children, then tell the parents how the children are doing in school, raise any concerns and problems, and sometimes offer advice to the parents. Usually teachers reveal little of their own backgrounds and feelings. These conferences, however, could be more reciprocal exchanges. What if we openly talked about our backgrounds and acknowledged our limitations? Parents often perceive teachers' biases anyway, so trying to mask them is probably futile. "I have found that if I want to learn how best to teach children who may be different from me, then I must seek the advice of adults—teachers and parents—who are from the same culture as my students" (Delpit, 1995, p. 102). If we are not trying to hide our uncertainties, we can more comfortably ask parents for advice on issues that are beyond our personal realm of experience: "One of the children in our class keeps insisting that Sara does not live with her real mother. How are you explaining Sara's adoption to other kids?" "What words do you and Lenny use to describe what happens when he has a seizure?" "How are you talking to Francis about his father's imprisonment? How do you feel about our talking about it in class if it comes up?" In cases where children are learning English as a second language, we can ask parents (through an interpreter if necessary) how we can complement the parents' efforts to teach English and/or maintain the child's home language.

When a child is not doing well in school, parents and teachers often blame each other (e.g., "If the parents did not let their kid watch so much TV . . . " or "If the teacher were more organized . . . "). Often both parties feel defensive and either withdraw or escalate the conflict. Parents and teachers need to openly acknowledge their differences and try to resolve them through compromises—or at least agree to disagree (Gonzalez-Mena, 1992). Optimally they can collaborate to find a good solution, but it may take time. Both need to be open about their concerns and willing to listen to the other person. For example, if an African American parent is worried about his child's discomfort in a predominantly White classroom, the teacher, instead of reacting defensively, can openly admit, "As a White person, I cannot know what it is like to be the only Black child in this classroom. Based on your experience, how can we make the class more comfortable for your child?"

Even if they thoroughly disagree with parents' views, teachers need to listen carefully and respectfully to parents' concerns and suggestions and keep in mind the contexts in which they are raising their children. By hearing how parents handle various situations, teachers can get ideas for coordinating their own efforts with those of the parents and, when necessary, help children adapt to two different sets of expectations.

In sum, I am not advocating drastic changes in parent–teacher conferences but rather a subtle, yet profound, shift from teachers as the experts reporting to parents, to teachers and parents openly sharing concerns and collaboratively exploring possible solutions.

*Class Meetings.* Class meetings for parents are usually held at the beginning of the year and maybe once or twice more during the year. Typically the teacher describes the program and gives a general overview of what the class has been doing and will be doing in the next few months. Often teachers feel pressured to impress parents with the quality of their program and spend hours fixing up their classrooms and setting out materials.

Class meetings can be adapted to support more collaborative relationships among parents and teachers. To make this shift, meetings need to be held more often, especially at the beginning of the year, and be oriented toward reflection and discussion instead of teacher presentations. In fact, some meetings might be led by parents or co-facilitated by teachers and parents.

In the first one or two class meetings, parents and teachers might get to know each other by talking about their own racial, cultural, class, and occupational backgrounds. To get the discussion going in a fun and non-threatening way, parents and teachers can pair up (obviously there will be more parent–parent than parent–teacher pairs) with someone they do not know and "interview" each other to identify one way in which they are similar and one way in which they are different. When they report their "findings" to the whole group, conversations about backgrounds and experiences often begin quite spontaneously. Starting the first few meetings with this activity helps everyone to make new contacts.

At the first meeting, parents can also "introduce" their children by describing them in terms of what kind of animal or plant they are most like.

These discussions are usually both amusing and informative. Parents as well as teachers gain a fuller view of each child that enables them to support the children's fledgling friendships and respond more knowledgeably to children's questions and comments. For example, if Josh's parent knows that a classmate, Selina, has cerebral palsy, he can help his son understand what that means if Josh comes home saying that "Selina is just a baby because she can't even walk yet."

At subsequent class meetings, parents and teachers might discuss their goals for the children and their ideas about how children learn. One way to start these conversations is to have parents and teachers describe their own experiences and visions (e.g., memories of what they liked best/worst in school, their best/worst parenting moment, their image of their child as an adult). These conversations may reveal a range of views about learning, behavioral expectations, and discipline. Although these differences may be unsettling, it is better to have them out in the open and discussed, not in terms of "bad" or "good," but rather as "we have different views of learning and ways of disciplining children; let's try to learn from each other and find some common ground or ways to compromise." Examples of children's work, videotapes, photographs of classroom activities, and records of children's questions and comments can provide material for parents and teachers to discuss how and what children are learning and how their expectations converge and diverge.

Another class meeting can be devoted to exploring children's previous experiences and thinking about how parents and teachers could build on that knowledge base and expand into new areas. Parents could describe memorable family visits and outings or trips they have taken with their children. As the conversation develops, teachers could ask some of the following questions as they seem relevant:

- How much contact have children had with people from different racial, cultural, and social-class groups? What has been their experience with people with disabilities?
- What have been the children's experiences with community services, such as police, welfare workers, and the schools? with more informal support systems of family members, neighbors, and co-workers?
- What workplaces are the children familiar with? Do they know people who have non-gender-stereotyped jobs (e.g., women construction workers)? Have they seen people from diverse cultural and racial groups and with different abilities and disabilities work together?
- What physical environments are the children familiar with? What experiences have they had in wilderness areas? in urban areas? How much do they know about ecological problems?

As they discuss and compare the children's experiences, parents and teachers may develop some curriculum ideas and plans for field trips and classroom visitors that would take advantage of resources and experiences of the families. They can also think of ways to compensate for the limitations in children's backgrounds. For example, a trip to a nearby city might be a priority for children living in the suburbs.

In short, instead of being an occasion for teachers to describe a predetermined program, class meetings can be opportunities for parents and teachers to become a cohesive teaching team—with everyone sharing their backgrounds and concerns, offering ideas, and becoming involved.

*Schoolwide Conversations About Multicultural Issues.* School staffs and parents may also organize discussion groups geared toward challenging their assumptions about social divisions and the natural world in a deeper way. To get people interested, a parent–teacher committee might sponsor a workshop on an aspect of multicultural practice that would be of particular interest to parents. Parents and teachers who are interested in pursuing these issues can form small ongoing support and discussion groups like those I described in Chapter 2. To avoid alienating parents and staff members who do not want to participate in a group, we need to ensure that no one feels pressured to join or excluded if they do not.

*Community Involvement and Taking Action.* The school or center can also sponsor discussions about issues that are affecting their families, school, and community. When individuals and groups start seeing how social and economic pressures are negatively influencing their lives and their children's futures, they are often eager to "do" something and may be interested in making action plans (for examples of how people develop their action plans, see Derman-Sparks & Phillips, 1997). Teachers and parents may decide to design new multicultural materials or activities. A group of parents and teachers might work together to critically review the children's books in the school library and raise money to buy new ones in order to broaden the collection, or they might build up a collection of photographs that counterbalance the limited and biased images children see on television. Families may join new organizations to break out of their racial or cultural isolation and/or begin to protest unfair town policies.

Meetings can provide a venue for sharing information, supporting school staff and families, and sowing the seeds for social action. For example, schoolwide discussions about children's passions for television, video games, and related products might address some issues described in Chapter 2. Moreover, they can provide opportunities for parents and teachers to explore ways of supporting each other to reduce the impact of media and consumerism on children and to develop strategies to pressure the networks to stop airing programs filled with commercials, violence, and stereotyped images.

Parents, teachers, and community people also can meet to discuss local, state, and national issues such as school funding, standardized tests, and welfare reform. They can share stories about how these issues are affecting families and communities. These discussions might lead to getting involved in local efforts to provide decent housing or parks in poor areas of the city or to force local companies to follow environmental or worker safety regulations. Individuals might choose to join national and international movements for causes that are the most meaningful to them (e.g., antiracism, disability rights, hunger projects, environmental protection). Obviously, no one can be involved on all fronts, but by meeting and talking together, parents and staff members can energize each other, stay connected, and explore ways of collaborating.

There are myriad possibilities for teachers and parents to support each other, to bring multicultural perspectives into the classroom, and to get involved in larger social justice issues. Teachers and parents can talk about their interests and choose projects that are most relevant and likely to engage young children. What is most crucial is that people are involved and active. Doing something—even something very small—can energize us and keep us going.

## CREATING CARING AND CRITICAL CLASSROOM COMMUNITIES

To develop connections with each other and with the social and natural world, children must learn to be caring and respectful. They need to make "room in [their] mind[s] for others" (Coles, 1996, p. 185)—a space for others' ideas, wishes, and perspectives—and develop a willingness to learn from people with experiences and backgrounds dissimilar to theirs. They need to be mindful of how their own actions affect others and be willing to sometimes set aside their own wishes in order to help others meet their goals and needs.

This emphasis on connecting with others does not mean, however, that children should be compliant and concerned with pleasing or conforming. To engage in social justice work, children also need to develop clear values, critical thinking skills, and confidence that they can be a positive force in the world. To this end, we need to create classrooms where children are caring *and* critical and are deeply engaged with each other and with the larger world.

Social development has traditionally been a high priority in early childhood programs. Unfortunately, recent mandates for skill-oriented testing for younger and younger children have forced teachers to spend more time on academic curricula, which can make it difficult to support children's developing friendships and social skills (e.g., more time in teacher-directed academic activities and less in child-oriented play). This shift, which contradicts everything we know about children's learning, is regrettable and hopefully will be short lived (as educational "reforms" usually are). Meanwhile, teachers need to be creative in developing strategies to teach the required skills in ways that encourage children to interact and collaborate (e.g., using cooperative games to teach math concepts).

Teachers and parents play crucial roles in children's social and emotional development. Close adult–child relationships provide the contexts for children to learn culturally appropriate ways to express and regulate emotions and to form relationships. To be effective in this role, adults need to be responsive to children's emotional states and willing and able to support children's efforts to learn social skills (e.g., modeling, coaching, explaining) (for specific teaching strategies, see Howes & Ritchie, 2002).

Early childhood social goals usually include empathizing with others, communicating effectively, initiating and maintaining social interactions and relationships with peers, playing cooperatively, and resolving conflicts. These interpersonal skills are relevant to multicultural education because they underlie children's capacities to connect with the larger social world, the natural environment, and social justice issues.

### Empathy

Caring, respect, and interdependence require the ability to empathize with how other individuals feel and to understand how they think. According to Hoffman (2000), children go through several phases in developing these skills during their early childhood years. I will summarize this development below. It is important to note, however, that the sequence and timing may not be true of all children and, in particular, may vary across social and cultural contexts.

Humans appear to be born with some innate ability to resonate with others' emotional states, as evidenced by the fact that newborns typically cry reactively when they hear other babies cry. As they get older, they develop a self-referenced empathy, an assumption that others feel the same way that they do. For example, toddlers frequently attempt to comfort friends with their own favorite dolls or blankets because they assume that the crying child will find them as comforting as they themselves do. However, they are beginning to see that other people have distinct perspectives and needs. Hoffman describes how David, a 2-year-old, first offered his crying friend his own teddy bear. When that did not work, David went and got his friend's teddy bear from the next room.

Preschoolers are learning how to read more subtle emotions and to understand that people may have their own information and ideas and may react differently to the same event. When they see a crying child, they may ask questions about what happened rather than assume that they know. They also begin to see how their own actions affect others (e.g., grabbing a toy makes the other child mad) and are able to resolve conflicts (often with some adult help). However, children this age still tend to interpret events in their own terms. For example, when they see a photograph of a father comforting a child, they may begin to talk about a recent incident when they themselves were sad rather than focus on the situation of the father and child in the picture.

As children enter and go through elementary school, they begin to realize that they themselves are the objects of others' ideas and feelings. This development enables children to be more considerate of others and better able to collaborate with other individuals and groups. However, this awareness can also make children self-conscious and worried about what their peers think of them. Some children respond by conforming to group norms (e.g., rigid ideas about appropriate dress) or by being antagonistic toward out-group members in order to ensure in-group peer approval. This trend obviously works against cross-group solidarity and illustrates how development is not a linear process but an ever-changing confluence of maturational, situational, and motivational factors.

We can foster children's developing awareness and interest in others by asking or pointing out how others may feel or think. When children are reading stories or looking at photographs, we can ask them how they would feel if they were engaged in that situation or doing that activity. For instance, if the class is watching construction workers carry heavy materials, teachers might ask: What do you suppose they are feeling in their arms? What does it mean when they wipe their brows? When learning about pollution, children can be encouraged to think about how plants and animals (including people) are experiencing the loss of clean air and water. Many children's stories have plots that encourage children to think about and empathize with others' feelings and to see how individuals and groups often have different perspectives and priorities. Dramatic play provides endless opportunities to experiment with taking multiple roles and perspectives.

In our highly technological society where machines do most of the menial work, children have few responsibilities for the well-being of others (e.g., we no longer need them to collect firewood to cook the family dinner). Thus, we have to make conscious efforts to teach children how to recognize and respond to others' needs. Teachers can encourage children to help each other get dressed to go outside, put on and take off smocks, move large tables, and hang up large easel paper to dry. Older children might visit preschool and kindergarten classrooms and help their younger peers to read and write stories, do woodworking, or make snacks. Instead of simply being chores, caring for classroom pets and plants can be opportunities to observe how plants and animals change day by day and to learn how to "read" and attend to others' needs. As one preschool girl said to me, "My plant looks really tired today. I'm gonna sing her to *sleep*."

We also need to encourage children to empathize with individuals and groups that they are not familiar with, to "reduce the gap between empathy toward kin and empathy toward strangers . . . to reduce the tendency . . . to make *negative* causal attributions to strangers . . . [and] to reduce the stereotyping, hostility, and down-right hatred toward [outgroups]" (Hoffman, 2000, p. 298, emphasis in original). Young children's capacity to emotionally resonate with others' feelings is a potential "handle" for teachers and parents to use in helping children to feel connected with unfamiliar people and to understand the effects of discrimination. Hoffman advocates that we foster children's empathy with a broader range of people by emphasizing emotional similarities among people. We can respect the diversity of cultures and group norms but recognize that underneath these differences everyone has similar feelings and reactions to life events such as death and birth. To make other groups' experiences more "real" to children and to trigger their empathy, we can read stories that personalize other groups' experiences and ask children to imagine how they would feel if they were in that situation. As children learn about and become emotionally aroused about unfair situations, we can work with parents and community activists to help them find effective ways to act on their feelings (e.g., raising money for a cause, writing letters to government officials).

## Communication

Effective communication requires paying close attention to what others are saying both verbally and nonverbally and genuinely trying to see and understand their perspectives, as well as making oneself understood. We can make children more aware of these skills by encouraging them to try alternative ways of communicating. For example, using nonverbal communication helps children to become more aware of facial expressions and gestures. By "mirroring" each others' gestures or facial expressions (either in partners or with the whole group), children become more attentive to others' gestures and expressions. Pantomiming feelings and events (e.g., first enjoying and then dropping an ice cream cone) gives children practice in expressing themselves nonverbally and interpreting what another person is conveying without words. Teachers might pantomime instructions or use only facial expressions and gestures to express reactions and see if children can understand.

In group discussions, young children often blurt out comments that have little to do with what else has been said. They need to practice listening carefully and speaking more clearly and precisely. In individual and small-group conversations, we can encourage children to slow down and hear others and perhaps repeat the question or statement that they are responding to before they speak. When children take turns instructing each other on how to do a particular activity or task, they quickly see whether or not they have mutually understood each other. One variation on this activity for kindergarten and primary children is to sit in pairs, back to back, and describe things to each other that the other one cannot see. For example, the first child draws a picture or builds a block structure; then the second one replicates it, based only on the first one's verbal instruction.

Children often assume that everyone speaks as they do and sometimes respond negatively when they hear other languages (e.g.,"that person talks funny"). By weaving sign language and words and songs from other languages into daily classroom life, teachers can help children broaden their ideas of how people communicate. This exposure meshes well with efforts to foster their empathic feelings towards a wide range of people.

## Peer Interactions and Relationships

As children experience the pleasures and challenges of playing with peers, they become more motivated to understand others' points of view, which in turn enables them to develop relationships and get along with a wider range of people. Friendships are critical learning opportunities for children and can support them in many ways.

The design of space and the selection of equipment and materials can influence the type and frequency of social interactions in classrooms (Kemple, 2004). For instance, in one study (Ramsey, 1986a), I found that single-entrance spaces such as lofts or small houses tended to be the scenes of more exclusionary behavior than were more open spaces. The single swings, which could accommodate only one child at a time, were frequently the scene of disputes and complaints about having to wait one's turn. The horizontal tire swing, on the other hand, was more fun with a group of children. The children riding it often invited passersby to join in, took responsibility for helping each other get on and off, and coordinated their motions in order to make the swing go fast. Interestingly, the tire swing was also the site for a number of conflicts, usually about who could join in and how fast or slow to spin the tire. However, these conflicts required more interpersonal awareness and complex negotiations than those that involved simply waiting for turns on the single swings.

The placement of furniture and equipment also influences the kinds of social interactions that occur. If the sand table, water table, and housekeeping furniture are placed against a wall, then children have less eye contact and direct interactions with each other. Moving them away from the wall facilitates more sociable and cooperative play. (*Note:* Be sure that any free-standing furniture is stable enough to prevent accidents and injuries.) In primary classrooms, tables and chairs should be movable so that children can work in a variety of groups, either at tables or on the floor.

Teachers can support children's attempts to initiate social interactions and develop friendships by setting up activities that children are interested in and then facilitating their play. Some children are not very skilled at starting social interactions, and adults can serve as a "bridge" between the children during these awkward moments (e.g., "Sally, can you show Mary and me what you are building? Mary, do you see how Sally is making her garage? Do you have some ideas how to help Sally make the door stand up?"). Adults can also "coach" children on how to initiate contacts. Several studies (Putallaz & Wasserman, 1990; Ramsey, 1996) have shown that children are more successful entering groups if they observe and then fit into the ongoing play than if they explicitly ask if they can play, demand materials, or try to dominate the play. (For more explicit suggestions for helping children initiate and maintain social interactions, see Kemple, 2004; Pellegrini, 1995; Ramsey, 1991a.)

Besides helping children initiate contacts, we can also support them to keep interactions going. When children seem to be running out of steam, we can sometimes enliven their interactions by introducing a new material (e.g., "I notice you boys are going to the store; here is a basket for carrying the groceries") or suggesting a new dimension of the plot (e.g., "I am so sorry to hear that the babies are sick; maybe you should take them to the doctor").

In addition to working with children to help them become more adept at interacting with their peers, we also need to help them be more receptive to a broad range of peers and not play exclusively with one or two best friends. Close long-term friendships provide rich contexts to learn about oneself and how to manage the ups and downs of peer relationships. However, playing with only one or two children is limiting and puts a lot of pressure on relationships that often fall apart, leaving both parties bereft. Thus, a balance of close friends and a wider range of good friends is optimal. Vivian Paley's book *You Can't Say You Can't Play* (1992) is a wonderful resource for talking with children about exclusionary behavior, why it happens, and its impact on other children. Many teachers have successfully implemented her ideas and have reported that having a "you can't say you can't play" rule has greatly improved the social dynamics of their class-rooms.

Children's friendships often reflect divisions by gender, race, social class, culture and language, and abilities (as will be discussed in more detail in Chapters 4–8). From a multicultural perspective, children need to learn how to play and work with peers who, at first, may seem different from them. We can help children to look beyond obvious dissimilarities and to discover potential shared interests. A good way to start encouraging cross-group contacts is to try to figure out why they are not occurring by observing children's grouping patterns and considering the following questions:

- How do children respond to overtures from peers who are different from them in some way—race, gender, culture, social class, language, abilities?
- What reasons do they give for rejecting certain peers?
- What factors appear to influence whether particular children are in-cluded or excluded (e.g., play styles, preference for certain activities, language)?
- Are there times and places when groups are more or less segregated? If so, what are they?
- What happens when activities are structured so that children are inter-acting with peers other than their customary playmates?

When teachers have a clearer sense of how and why children are sepa-rating themselves, then they can support children to cross borders and to expand their range of relationships. Teachers can change seating arrange-ments and create long- and short-term "teams" for various activities to en-courage children to get to know different classmates. Cooperative activities are especially effective in promoting cross-group friendships (as will be dis-cussed in the next section of this chapter). Photographs and story books that portray children playing with friends from different gender, cultural, and racial groups may legitimize cross-group relationships and be a reference point to counteract children's arguments that groups must be exclusive.

Teachers may also want to analyze how the physical environment (the location, size, accessibility, and attractiveness of the spaces) may be contrib-uting to divisions. If it is apparent that some groups—be they defined by race, culture, class, gender, or energy level—are always together in certain areas, then rearranging the physical space may help increase intergroup con-tact. In one classroom, teachers noticed that children tended to get into their favorite areas with their special friends and then not move for much of the day. After observing this pattern for a few days and talking with the chil-dren, the teachers realized that the boisterous play that often occurred in the open area in the middle of the classroom intimidated some of the quieter children and kept them from venturing out of the "safer" areas on the outside edges. After the teachers created an area for gross-motor play at one end of the classroom and moved some of the other areas into the center of the space, the children began to play with a wider range of peers and activities.

In primary classrooms, children can work in cooperative groups comprised of children from different backgrounds for a lot of activities, such as doing research projects, painting murals, putting on skits, or organizing classroom events. In elementary schools, a lot of exclusionary behavior occurs in the cafeteria and during recess, when children are in large groups and are less closely supervised. Assigning lunch groups composed of a variety of children and structuring the first part of recess with cooperative games may curtail this in-group/out-group dynamic.

When teachers notice exclusionary play, they can help children to articulate and challenge their feelings and assumptions. One teacher (described in De Gaetano, Williams, & Volk, 1998) noticed that his kindergartners, who were building a large town in blocks, had constructed a large wall down the middle of the town, with White children working on one side and children of color on the other side. He asked them why they had built the wall and supported them in explaining their reasons. With a number of activities and stories, he challenged their assumptions about similarities and differences and who could and did live and work together. After a while, the children dismantled much of the wall, although it never completely disappeared.

## Cooperative Activities

Cooperative activities provide a good counterbalance to our society's obsession with individual achievement and competitiveness. These activities promote children's sense of *inter*dependence, their awareness of others, and their flexibility. Moreover, they foster friendships among children of diverse groups (Johnson & Johnson, 2000; Slavin, 1995) and different abilities (Kemple, 2004; Kozleski & Jackson, 1993).

Because most of us have been so immersed in competitive activities and individualistic goals all of our lives, we may find ourselves unintentionally undermining efforts to encourage cooperation. One interesting exercise is to keep a tape recorder running in the classroom and at the end of the day listen to see how many instructions, reprimands, and praises reflect on individual orientation (e.g., "Don't bother the other children at the table; let everyone do their own work" "Wow! Look at that tall tower you made all by yourself!") or a more collective orientation (e.g., "You three children are really helping each other on your collage projects" "Willie, would you and Sarah please help each other move that table?"). Often teachers are surprised at how many times they reinforce individualistic behaviors and attitudes even though they may consciously be trying to encourage children to cooperate.

Young children may not see others' cognitive perspectives very well, but they can learn how to coordinate their actions with each other. Cooperative games, such as those described by Hill (2001), Kirchner (2000), and Orlick (1978, 1982), are appropriate for young children because they involve physical rather than intellectual coordination among two or more children. For example, in Turtle several children lie on the ground under a large blanket or mat; they have to move in a coordinated fashion so that the "shell" (blanket) stays on everyone. Children can also play Blob, which is like Tag except that people *join* "It" when they are tagged, so that eventually everyone is part of a large group moving as one.

Besides these physical games, older children can also collaborate on puppet shows, plays, and group art projects and stories, which require a more conscious and sustained coordinated effort. Competitive board and card games can sometimes be adapted to be more of a cooperative effort (e.g., having teams play or challenging the children to have everyone finish at the same time).

Many classroom routines can be done cooperatively, such as setting and clearing the snack tables, putting away toys, and putting on outdoor clothes. In many classrooms, a "special helper" sets up the snack, waters the plants, and does other classroom chores. This routine could be adapted to have two special helpers who then have to figure out how to do these tasks cooperatively. This pairing is also a way to get two children to know each other better.

Children need to have support to learn how to work and play together cooperatively (Kemple, 2004). We cannot simply put them into groups and hope for the best. Especially at the beginning, children need explicit instructions about how to do the task at hand and how to function as a group. Once groups are meeting, adults should be available to help them function equitably and to prevent the groups from forming hierarchies that replicate those in the outside world. Children may also need help resolving conflicts and making decisions. In particular, teachers need to watch for groups that appear to be doing the project cooperatively but in reality are being dominated by one or two members who are subtly excluding the others.

## Conflict Resolution

Children's conflicts are an inevitable part of classroom life. Although we often regard them as annoying interruptions, children potentially learn a lot about interdependence, flexibility, and diversity when they are embroiled in a dispute. Resolving conflicts requires that children know how to recognize different perspectives, balance their own wishes with those of others, manage anger and aggression, assess effects of their actions on others, be both assertive and respectful at the same time, and know when and how to compromise. These skills are germane to multicultural teaching because a "truly multicultural curriculum is contentious, raises more questions than answers, invites debate, and engages students actively" (Sleeter, 1993, p. 31). To teach children how to engage productively in conflict, we can use their day-to-day disputes to foster these skills (for more specific guidelines and examples, see DeVries & Zan, 1994; Kemple, 2004; Ramsey, 1991a).

Some teachers try to eliminate conflicts altogether by avoiding situations that potentially induce them. I remember one experienced teacher advising several neophyte staff members to provide each child with an equal share of the play-dough, clay, paper, paints, or whatever material was to be used, in order to prevent conflicts over the distribution of materials. She was unwittingly limiting children's opportunities to resolve conflicts and to engage in deliberations about fair distribution. Moreover, the children were learning that they could count on resources being distributed fairly, which obviously does not represent the real world. Instead, teachers can put the materials out and encourage children to figure out how to fairly distribute them.

When a conflict has blossomed, it is tempting to try to settle it as expediently as possible by giving both parties equivalent objects so that "each of you can have one." While that strategy often does stop the conflict, it also reinforces the value of having absolute control (i.e., private ownership) over an object. Instead, we can help children focus on others' feelings and needs and work out joint solutions that (at least minimally) satisfy all parties. For example, if two children are fighting over a truck, they can talk about why they want it and figure out a way to either take turns or, even better, to play with it together (e.g., loading it up with blocks and making it part of a construction game).

When an injury to a person or a piece of equipment or material has already occurred, children can focus on making some kind of restitution, which is a positive alternative to retribution (Schaffer & Sinicrope, 1983). By focusing on ways to aid and compensate the victim (e.g., helping rebuild the block tower that was knocked down or getting a cold compress to put on a bruise), the effects of the aggressive act become a shared problem instead of the object of vociferous blaming. Furthermore, the aggressor, who may be feeling some remorse, is able to reestablish a positive or at least neutral relationship with the injured child. If the target of the aggressive act is not receptive to help or if direct contact between the two parties is potentially too combustible at that point, the aggressor might perform an indirect but related restitutive act. For example, if a child has torn another's painting, she could put fresh paper on the easel so that the materials are available if the aggrieved child wants to paint another picture at a later point.

Conflicts can be used to help children reflect on larger social issues and possible solutions; these discussions, in turn, may help children see their conflicts from a broader perspective. For example, if one child is insisting on taking over the block area, a teacher might initiate a broader discussion about how it affects people when one person (or group) takes over and does not respect the rights of others: "Remember how many of you were mad that the field where we used to visit and play in got turned into a parking lot? We all thought that it was unfair that one person could ruin something for lots of other people just to make money. That's a little like what is happening here."

## Critical Thinking and Social Action

Besides creating cohesive classrooms, we need to help children see themselves as activists for social change. This goal poses some interesting dilemmas. We have to be sure that we have firm limits and clear authority so that children feel safe and are receiving enough guidance to function responsibly in groups. At the same time, we want to encourage children to raise questions and challenge adults when they feel that something is not fair or is not working for the group. We also need to be aware that, in some families and communities, teaching children to criticize and challenge rules and authorities may contradict traditional ways of learning and respect for adults. Teachers need to be sensitive to these cultural nuances and work with the parents to find ways to encourage children to see and respond to inequities but in ways that do not undermine their families' values.

*Rules and Procedures.* One way to support the development of both critical thinking and activism is to involve children in the process of deciding on classroom procedures and rules. Obviously the latitude that we give the children varies by age. For preschool children, we usually have to set restrictions that involve safety, since the children are unable to predict consequences of potentially dangerous situations. Older children can be involved with more regulatory decisions. Children at all ages have ideas about helpful and hurtful interpersonal behavior and usually eagerly contribute ideas about how to make the classroom "safe" for everyone (e.g., no hitting or no scaring kids). In the process of deciding on procedures and rules, children experience the interdependence of all members of the class and the need to be flexible. They learn to articulate their own needs; listen to the opinions of others; and think about the purpose, fairness, and enforcement of the rules. Moreover, children experience the effects of diverse perspectives. For example, children who are eager to curtail the rights of others realize that, when applied to them, repressive rules have their disadvantages. As children debate the merits of different routines and rules, they experience on a small scale what it takes for a society to function. They also begin to gain the insights and skills needed to organize democratic communities.

Decision making about classroom procedures is often a cumbersome process with young children, who have difficulty weighing various options and making decisions. When given the time and guidance, however, they often arrive at fair and wise solutions. DeVries and Zan (1994) describe and illustrate the process of making rules and deciding on consequences. However, instead of always voting, as suggested by DeVries and Zan, I recommend first trying to make decisions using consensus. With "majority rule" the emphasis often shifts children away from finding a common solution to pressuring each other to vote in a certain way. Also, when one side has "won," the "losers" may resist or undermine the decision. In the consensus process, the group works with the different opinions and all participants "move" a bit (show some flexibility in their position) and collaboratively reach an acceptable decision that is a compromise or, in some cases, a totally new and better plan that everyone can support. Decisions cannot be made in a single session, because participants need to get some distance from the pressures of different opinions and reflect about the various options. For this reason, consensus is a slow process. If a quick decision is necessary, or if after several sessions the children do not seem to be getting anywhere close to consensus, then voting would be appropriate.

One teacher described how his first-grade class used the consensus process over the course of several weeks to decide on a procedure about interrupting the teacher when he was helping another child. In the end, the children arrived at a plan that offered several alternatives, according to the urgency of need. The teacher also agreed to the students' request that he be available for questions at certain periods. Through their deliberations, the children came to see the problem from several points of view and to recognize a number of contingencies that made an absolute rule about not interrupting the teacher unfair and unenforceable.

To participate in critical analyses and social change, children need to learn how to think about complex situations and issues. We need to resist our usual emphasis on speed and efficiency and help children learn to live with confusion and frustration and to persist in working toward new ways of thinking and doing things. We can encourage them to define and pursue interesting projects by providing space and materials to allow them to try out their ideas. Reggio Emilia teaching practices (Cadwell, 1997, 2003) and the project approach (Helm & Beneke, 2003) offer many ideas for sustaining children's interest in long term projects.

*Routines.* Classroom routines can be adapted to be more meaningful and to foster interpersonal connections and critical thinking. For example, instead of just "doing" the calendar every day, we can discuss it less often but in more depth—perhaps when it is a new month or new season. These discussions could be opportunities for all class members to review the year so far and to think about the passage of time in terms of friendships and classroom projects. Children and teachers can talk about what they remember and see how people recall different details of the same experience. To see how they have an impact on their world, children and teachers could also reflect on problems that together they were able to resolve and identify current issues that they want address. Likewise, mealtimes can be occasions to talk about families, different traditions related to food, and comparisons of food likes and dislikes. They also offer opportunities to bring up issues like hunger, poverty, and pollution. We should not give children boring lectures about all the problems in the world but rather inject relevant information and questions and see how children respond (e.g., "You know when everyone was talking about how starving they were just before lunch, it made me think about an article I read about children in _____ who have only one meal a day. I wonder how that would feel . . . ").

*Conversations.* As children are trying to understand the many injustices, contradictions, and just plain absurdities of their world, they have many concerns and questions that they need to share and mull over. Thus, conversations are a critical part of multicultural teaching. Classrooms should be organized to enable teachers and children to have meaningful conversations—even if it means letting some other things go. Cadwell (1997) describes the thoughtful conversations that the teachers in the Reggio Emilia schools have with their children *and* the challenges of implementing this practice in classrooms in the United States. Teachers may find it difficult to have long conversations with individual children because other children are often clamoring for their attention. However, one child's questions can often be turned into a group discussion ("Silvio was asking me why, if the grown-ups want kids to learn to read, they are now closing our town library on Saturdays. It's a good question. Do any of you have ideas about what is happening?" or "Beth is sad because the boys won't let her play the chase game. What could we do about this situation?").

In these conversations, we do not need to explain all the complexities of an event but rather to puzzle along with the children and to try to help them deepen their own thinking and questions. When Daniel was 5 years old, he indignantly asked me, "Since Columbus was mean and cruel to the Indians, why do we have Columbus Day? Why don't we have Indian Day instead?" When questions like that come up, we can invite other children to share their views and affirm their feelings (e.g., "It makes me mad, too, that we celebrate Columbus Day, when many Native Americans are still suffering from losing their land and way of life"). We should not give children long lectures about Native American rights. However, we can encourage them to pursue their ideas and help them find answers to their questions (e.g., "How could we find out how American Indians feel about Columbus Day?"). Likewise, we can help them think of some possible actions to make a positive change (e.g., "What could we do to make the situation better?" "Whom might we talk to? write to?").

Many events, big and small, can give rise to conversations, and teachers should be prepared to "seize the moment" to encourage children to ask their questions and rethink their ideas and assumptions. Strikes or layoffs, reductions in municipal services, a stereotyped book, or exclusionary play during recess are examples of the many occasions when children may be open to challenging the status quo and engaging in social change.

We need to make space for conversations, hear children's concerns, and try to connect with them in a meaningful way. We will make mistakes—I can think of dozens of times when my response missed, and all I got was a blank stare or "I don't want to talk about this anymore." But other times we hit the mark and can have wonderful, enlightening discussions with children. In many ways, children are natural critical thinkers—they often ask questions that adults would rather avoid or have forgotten how to ask. When Daniel (then age 5) and I visited New York City and he saw a lot of homeless people for the first time, he asked, "Why don't people like us who have houses invite the homeless people to live with them?" Why not indeed? I did not have a good answer.

# PART II

# Contexts of Learning

This part of the book explores in more depth differences, divisions, and inequities related to race, class, culture (including orientation to the natural environment), gender (including sexual orientation), and abilities and disabilities.

Each chapter begins with questions to encourage readers to reflect about their experiences, identities, and attitudes related to the topic of the chapter. The questions are written in the first person but can be adapted for group discussions.

The second part of each chapter reviews research on how that particular social dimension affects children's life circumstances. Given the gaps in our information and the bias of much research, these reviews cannot be used to predict how specific children growing up in specific circumstances will fare. We can, however, use this information to question our assumptions and to respond more sensitively to the families and communities connected to our schools.

The third part of each chapter reviews what we know about young children's emerging ideas and feelings related to the topic of the chapter. Given the many influences on development, we cannot be certain what children at particular ages know, feel, or can learn. However, awareness of trends and patterns may help us to hear the nuances of children's concerns and questions and to develop meaningful ways to raise these issues.

The fourth section of each chapter includes specific suggestions for observing and talking with children to find out more clearly what they know, think, and feel about the dimension under discussion. The final section consists of composite examples drawn from a number of sites of how teachers have used this information to expand children's worldviews and to counteract their biases. Because children and families have different backgrounds and experiences, no curriculum can be applied across the board. I include examples not to prescribe activities but rather to encourage readers to develop ideas and practices most appropriate for their particular children. You may disagree with some of the strategies and/or feel that they would not work for your group. Use these moments to explore the source of your discomfort and to create strategies that better fit your particular situation.

Dividing these topics into separate chapters has the advantage of allowing readers to focus on each dimension in more depth and not be overwhelmed by too much information at one time. However, the disadvantage is that this organization implies that race, class, culture, gender, and abilities/disabilities are static categories that operate independently. *Nothing could be further from the truth.* Throughout the following chapters, I will point out how these dimensions are constantly changing and interacting. We need to think of them not as distinct categories but as permeable and shifting borders that individuals cross many times and in many directions.

Before turning to the next five chapters, ask yourself "Who am I?" and write down the answers as quickly as possible. This list will give you a quick overview of which attributes are salient in your identity and which ones you tend to ignore or take for granted. Keep your list in front of you as you record your responses to the questions and reflections at the beginning of each chapter.

I hope that as you read these chapters, you will work on developing "reflective and clarified" identities (Banks, 1997, p. 138) and gain new insights into how your unique history and worldview influence your identity, your attitudes toward others, and your work with children.

# CHAPTER 4

# The Context of Race

## REFLECTIONS ON RACE

On your list of attributes, did you mention race? In my experience, Asian, Latino, and African Americans are more likely to mention race than European Americans because Whiteness is the invisible norm of our society. To pursue these questions a bit further, we can ask ourselves some of the following questions:

- What is my racial background? Do I have a biracial or multiracial identity? Were my parents from different racial groups? Was I raised by adoptive or foster parents whose race was different from my own?
- What are my early memories of my racial identity? How has it changed?
- How do I feel about my racial group? Am I proud? ambivalent? Do I sometimes wish (or have I wished) that I belonged to another group?
- What are common attitudes toward my racial group(s)? How are we portrayed in the media? How are we stereotyped?
- Where does my racial group(s) fit in the power hierarchy of my community? country?
- How do I feel about people from other racial groups? Do I have close friends and neighbors in other racial groups, or is my social network racially homogeneous?
- What assumptions about particular racial groups do I have? How would I react if I found out that our new principal was Puerto Rican? the new gym teacher was Chinese American? a European American child in my class was homeless?
- How do I feel when the subject of race comes up in a conversation or conflict? Am I anxious? Do I try to avoid it? If so, why?

## GROWING UP IN A RACIALLY DIVIDED SOCIETY

As discussed in Chapter 1, "race" has no biological base but is a socially constructed concept, located in economic, political, and historical power relationships. Moreover, with the increase of biracial and multiracial children, racial categorizations have become even more blurred and ambiguous. In fact, using them at all is problematic (Ramirez, 1996), and perhaps some day they will no longer exist. However, despite these ambiguities, people in this country and many others are still formally and informally classified by "race" and often judged by stereotypes of genetically determined physical and mental characteristics that are associated with their particular group. Thus, race is "real" for those who are targets and perpetrators of racism in its many overt and covert forms.

### Racial Privilege and Disadvantage

People have come to the continent we now call North America under a variety of circumstances. The history of each group is complex and fraught with hardships and losses (see Takaki, 1993). However, some groups have attained higher levels of success and acceptance into the dominant society than others. Those who have been particular targets for discrimination include Native Americans and Mexicans, who were conquered; African Americans, who were enslaved; and Asian Americans, who faced stringent immigration and segregation rules. The lines of advantage and disadvantage are such that people who look most different from the Anglo-Saxon settlers have been the most marginalized. This system of racial advantage, in which one group has unearned privileges and power over other groups by virtue of its physical characteristics (Tatum, 1992), has prevailed in this country since the arrival of the earliest European settlers. One compelling example is that during World War II, when the United States was at war with both Japan and Germany, many Japanese Americans were put into concentration camps but very few German Americans were.

To this day Asian, African, and Latino Americans continue to suffer discrimination in all areas of their lives: housing, employment, and education (Cose, 1993; Feagin & Sikes, 1994; Gibbs, Huang, and Associates, 1989). Many families face a constant and debilitating confrontation with racism and prejudice that has been described as *mundane extreme environmental stress* (Peters, 2002). For example, when a Puerto Rican American family takes a trip to the mall, they are more likely to be rudely treated, ignored, and/or suspected of shoplifting than a European American family. Needless to say, these conditions profoundly affect all aspects of family life. West (1993) describes the psychological costs of discrimination with his devastating picture of the "nihilism of black Americans": "the lived experience of coping with a life of horrifying meaninglessness, hopelessness, and . . . lovelessness . . . a numbing detachment from others and a self-destructive disposition toward the world" (p. 14).

However, many communities, families, and individuals facing oppressive circumstances create structures and cultures that have enabled them to resist, survive, and even flourish (Garcia Coll et al., 1996). Extended families, fictive kinships (groups of nonrelated people who function as an extended family), churches, social and service organizations, and neighborhood groups have all served and continue to serve as buffers between individuals and the devastating effects of poverty and oppression.

In contrast, people who are identified as White are racially privileged in every aspect of their lives. Whiteness is the "invisible norm" that sets the standards for everyone else's experience (Levine, 1994; McLaren, 1994; Sleeter, 1994). Whites often have a hard time "seeing" the privileges that they enjoy on a day-to-day basis (McIntosh, 1995). Much as we take for granted the air that we breathe, those of us who are White are not conscious of the privilege that underlies our daily encounters with the world. However, many people who live outside of the circle of power and privilege see it clearly. One of my earliest lessons in racial privilege occurred many years ago in a casual conversation about clothes with my African American housemate. Having grown up in a White middle-class family that valued utility over fashion, I was—I have to say—subtly bragging about my thriftiness and ability to resist the pressures of clothing fads. My housemate turned my self-congratulation on its head when she said, in an exasperated voice, "*You can look like a slob and still go into stores and offices. I can't!*" I was shocked to realize that this "virtue" reflected not simply the positive value of frugality but also my privilege as a member of the White middle class. Still later, I came to understand more clearly how clothing symbolizes resistance as well as respectability for people struggling against oppression (hooks, 1990). I have not changed my clothes-buying habits, but I am cautious about judging others' "extravagance."

Racial privilege enables Whites to be pretend to be "color-blind." While Whites' assertions that "all children are just alike" are often well intentioned efforts at overcoming barriers, they in fact exacerbate interracial tensions.

> What passes for polite race discourse in education, therefore, is usually either racial obliviousness or the bestowal of honorary Whiteness on all students. . . . Politely pretending not to notice students' color makes no sense unless being of different colors is somehow shameful. Colorblindness, in other words is parasitic upon racism: it is only in a racist society that pretending not to notice color could be construed as a particularly virtuous act. (A. Thompson, 1998, p. 524)

Obviously, those of us who benefit from racial privilege cannot know what it is like to live without it, but we can become more aware of the small, concrete ways in which we experience privilege throughout the day.

Often, as I walk down the street, I try to imagine how familiar places would appear if I were not White. Would the same smiles come my way? Would I feel as much "at home"? Would that police car make me feel afraid instead of safe? How would it feel to encounter only 3 people who look like me instead of the 40 or so that I *do* encounter? Watching television, I ask myself similar questions. How would it feel to have my life and my image reflected only in stories about crime and sports? What if all the anchors and reporters were Black and were talking about White crime? What if I saw only Asian American faces on television? Going into stores, I wonder if I would be getting this courteous service if I were a Latina instead of a White woman? Would they let me take all seven garments into the dressing room? Would they so readily accept my check or credit card?

## Racial Identity Development

Despite the ambiguities and contradictions inherent in the concept of race, all of us are treated differently according to our race. As a result, we all, consciously or not, develop racial identities and attitudes. In the following sections, I will discuss three patterns of racial identity development. Like other aspects of development, it is complex and convoluted,

> a process in which contradiction, opposition, incongruity, gaps, tensions are constantly present.... There is no endpoint ... for the cultural dynamics are always changing, the contexts in which identities are claimed and in which meaning is made, are continually being erased and remade. (Scholl, 2002, p. 6)

As with theories of child development, we can use these models to help us anticipate and understand nuances and changes, but we cannot assume that the sequence is inevitable or that the process is the same for everyone.

Because identity formation differs across Whites, people of color, and bi- and multiracial individuals, I will discuss them separately. However, many individuals identify both as a White and as a person of color, so these divisions are more permeable and complicated than is implied by discussing them separately. For example, Adler (2001) found that Asian American parents identified themselves as people of color on some items and as Whites on others. (For more detailed accounts of how people move through these phases, see Derman-Sparks & Phillips, 1997; Tatum, 1997.)

*Racial Identities of White People.* Janet Helms (1990) formulated the following model of White identity development, primarily based on her work with adults. During the first stage, called *contact*, people understand racism only as overt individual acts, such as cross burnings. They are naive about their own role in maintaining a more pervasive system of racial privilege. Often these individuals have very limited contact with people of color and believe the stereotypes they have seen in the popular press. Many Whites live out their lives at this stage.

At some point a White person may have an experience, such as developing a close working relationship with a person of color or taking a course or reading a book that challenges the old comfortable assumptions. This experience sets off the second stage, *disintegration*. During this stage, people often feel uncomfortable and guilty about their privilege. They begin to become aware of the racism that prevails in the media, recognize it in interactions with their friends and families, and may try to confront other Whites.

Often the pervasiveness of racism (especially when people begin to identify its subtle manifestations) and the resistance of fellow Whites tempt individuals to *reintegrate* and return to their familiar assumptions, sometimes with a vengeance ("Yeah, I went through that bleeding heart liberal stage of thinking that the system was to blame, but now I know better; some people just won't help themselves and want to live off of *my* taxes!"). Given the prevalence of these messages in the media and popular culture, it is easy to find excuses to retreat from the harsher truths of racism, which is not an option for people of color (McIntosh, 1995). One particularly strong pull toward this retreat is White bonding (Sleeter, 1994), often expressed in snide comments about people of color that enhance a sense of solidarity among Whites (e.g., "With all these families and their problems moving here from the city [a common code word for poor people of color], *our* kids aren't getting the attention they need!"). Many Whites, even if they disagree, may remain silent in order to avoid antagonizing their peers. If they do directly confront racist statements or jokes, they may find themselves belittled and/or ostracized by their friends and family. These tensions may pull them back to their old assumptions and racial isolation.

However, individuals might have additional experiences that push them to continue their journey toward a deeper understanding of racism, and they may enter the *pseudo-independent* stage. At this point, they might begin to question more deeply their assumptions about White superiority *but* very possibly still act in ways that perpetuate the system. Some White people at this stage try to deny their racism by attempting to affiliate with Blacks or other marginalized groups, who understandably may be suspicious of the Whites' motives and inconsistencies and avoid contact. At this point, learning about other Whites who have struggled with their own racism and have participated in antiracist movements can help White individuals see ways to overcome guilt and shame and to participate in challenging the social and economic inequities of our society (Tatum, 1992, 1994; see also Aptheker, 1993; Brown, 2002; Virginia Durr's biography in Colby & Damon, 1992;

Howard, 1999; Kivel, 2002; McIntyre, 1997; Stalvey, 1989). People engaged in this process are at the *immersion/emersion* stage of racial identity development.

The final stage articulated by Helms is that of *autonomy*, when a person has a clear and positive sense of herself as White and actively participates in antiracist movements as a way of expressing her White identity. However, this stage is not an endpoint but rather a readiness to see and hear new information and be prepared to question and challenge even dearly held ideals and practices. Uncovering and unlearning racism is like peeling layers off of an endless onion. Each time we think that we have gotten rid of one set of assumptions, we hit another set and have to start working on those.

*Racial Identities of People of Color.* People from marginalized groups go through similar stages in their racial identity development, but they start at a different vantage point. Whereas most Whites need to unlearn a false sense of universality and superiority, many people from other groups need to overcome false assumptions of inferiority. William Cross (1991) has identified five stages in achieving Nigrescence, the point at which African Americans have a clear and positive identity and a commitment to working to improve the conditions for all Blacks. Although this theory is based on research with Black adults, similar stages have been identified in studies of other groups of color.

The first stage is called *preencounter*, in which individuals accept the dominance of European Americans. Some may acknowledge that racism exists but feel that they are exceptions and that they have been able to transcend it and are accepted by Whites. Alternatively, they may deny that they are a member of a marginalized group. One of my students, a Korean adopted and raised by European American parents, told me that until she got to college and became friends with other Korean Americans, she thought of herself as White. Many individuals at this stage internalize the negative stereotypes and the blaming-the-victim ideology of the dominant group, which can lead to a sense of hopelessness and victimization.

At the next stage, called *encounter*, individuals may experience racist events or come into contact with peers or teachers who have more critical views of society and cast the harsh light of reality on former illusions of being accepted by Whites. With this disillusionment—often accompanied by anger and bitterness—individuals then enter the *immersion/emersion* stage, in which they immerse themselves in their own group, often avoiding contact with Whites and rejecting all symbols of White dominance, including White definitions of success such as doing well in school. College students' desires for ethnically separate dorms, meeting places, and dining rooms reflect this stage of racial identity development. During this time individuals often immerse themselves in the literature, music, art, politics, and history of their group, which contributes to the formation of a positive racial identity.

With this kind of experience and support, pro-Black, or pro-Asian, or pro-Latino attitudes then shift from being anti-White to being more expansive and less defensive as individuals emerge into the stage of *internalization*, in which they develop a positive, healthy, and stable racial identity. At this point they both maintain their close connections with their own racial community *and* seek equal and reciprocal relationships with Whites and other groups. Unlike their preencounter relationships, individuals no longer deny their race in order to be accepted by Whites; rather they engage in mutually respectful relationships.

The final stage, according to Cross's paradigm, is *internalization/commitment*. Now the strength of a person's racial identity is translated into a commitment to challenge the status quo and to work to address the inequities of our society. As with White identity development, the process is more complex than this linear stage theory suggests. Often people who have achieved a stable racial identity find that some years later, they still have vestiges of their preencounter selves and may again go through an immersion/emersion stage as they lay these assumptions to rest.

*Identities of Biracial and Multiracial People.* Many people identify with more than one racial group. As the world becomes smaller and groups become more interdependent, the numbers of people who identify as bi- or multiracial are increasing. Also, children in adoptive, blended, and foster families often have parents who are from different racial and ethnic backgrounds, which raises the question of "Who am I?" in new and complex ways. My own children, Daniel and Andrés, have gone through several stages of identifying as White, Latino, and both, as they develop their understanding of the social world and who they are as individuals and members of groups.

In some communities bi- and multiracial children and adults face the challenges of negative attitudes toward interracial marriage and transracial adoption or a mutual antagonism between their identity groups. In many cases children feel pressured by peers, schools, and community members to choose one aspect of their heritage and to deny the other(s) (Wardle, 1996). Sometimes, children are not accepted by any of their heritage groups. The two books edited by Maria Root, *Racially Mixed People in America* (1992) and *The Multiracial Experience: Racial Borders as the New Frontier* (1996), contain many accounts of how people have experienced and negotiated these tensions and pressures. In the first book, a chapter authored by Kich (1992) outlines three stages of identity development of biracial youth and adults that are somewhat parallel to the two theories just described. Unlike Cross's and Helms's theories, he ties his stages to developmental changes in children. However, adults may also pass through these stages. As discussed with the other theories, these stages are not as linear and the endpoint not as clear and definitive as the following discussion implies.

First, biracial individuals become aware of *differentness and dissonance* and often confront questions about who they are. In some cases they find that their differentness is devalued and feel caught between groups. The next stage, *struggle for acceptance*, often occurs during adolescence and is characterized by conflicts in loyalties—between parents and friends, between communities, and between different groups of friends. During this time people may feel that they need to choose one part of their identity and to reject the other, but they feel diminished by "passing" as something they are not. Difficult as this stage is, it is also a time when people can learn how to understand multiple points of view and how to successfully negotiate between groups. Often they engage in a lot of self-exploration and learn about the lives of other interracial people in the United States and other parts of the world—much as in Cross's *immersion* stage. The needs of individuals at this stage may conflict with those of individuals who are in Cross's immersion/emersion stage, who may insist that loyalties to more than one group are impossible.

*Self-acceptance and assertion of an interracial identity*, the third and final stage, often occurs in late adolescence or early adulthood. At this point people have developed a stable self-acceptance of themselves as bi- or multiracial and no longer feel threatened by questions about their background. Aspects of their identities may become more or less salient as relationships with their communities change as they grow up (e.g., a biracial child who grew up in a White community may choose to live in a Black community as an adult) (Daniel, 1996), but they basically accept their multifaceted backgrounds. At this stage, bi- and multiracial people may become involved in activities that address discrimination against multiracial people (e.g., policies that force families to identify themselves as only one race).

All of these theories of racial identity development are parallel in several ways. People confront their illusions; deal with the anger, disillusionment, and disequilibrium that result; and then use information about their own group and the larger society to develop more secure and realistic identities and a commitment to change the conditions that made this development so hard in the first place. At some points in the process, individuals from different groups (including multiracial people) may need to work separately. This temporary separation often gives rise to fears of resegregation but can provide the space for people to grow.

Racial identity formation sounds very neat and well defined in theory, but in reality it is complex and convoluted. Not everyone passes through all these stages in the prescribed order, and many may recycle through the same stage(s) several times. Even during a given time period, a person's racial identity may shift across situations (e.g., a supportive and honest interracial dialogue may give rise to positive feelings about one's own racial identity, but a threatening and/or diminishing interracial encounter may propel a person back to an earlier stage).

These theories also offer hope—hope that everyone can at least try to transcend the damage that they have suffered from racism and to challenge their racist environments. While we can never eliminate all the wounds of racism from our hearts and minds and lives, we can struggle to overcome its most deleterious effects.

## CHILDREN'S RESPONSES TO RACE

A number of researchers have studied how children view race in a range of different populations and with a wide variety of methods. These studies have not been done to support the validity of race as a concept but in recognition of the fact that racial distinctions—with all their inconsistencies and contradictions—define people's lives and inevitably become part of children's earliest social categories.

Most research in this country has compared European and African American children's responses to same- and cross-race people, often depicted by dolls, drawings, or photographs. Only recently have researchers begun to include a broader range of participants and stimulus materials. Thus, our knowledge about children's reactions to racial differences is still incomplete and fragmented. However, the trends that have emerged may help teachers to observe and ask questions and respond to children's questions and concerns more insightfully.

Children's responses to racial differences involve a complicated set of cognitive, affective, and behavioral dimensions (Katz, 1976, 1982; Sigelman & Singleton, 1986), and this review will be organized around these dimensions. However, as will become apparent, they continuously interact and mutually influence each other.

### Do Young Children Notice Race?

This is one of the first questions that teachers ask when the issue of race comes up. Often it is asked as a statement of denial: "Do young children *really* notice race? Kids just see other kids; they don't see color!" Contrary to this color-blind myth, young children *do* notice race. Infants have been observed to consistently react to racial differences by 6 months of age (Katz & Kofkin, 1997). By the age of 3 or 4, most children have a rudimentary concept of race and can easily identify, match, and label people by racial group (Holmes, 1995; Katz, 1976; Ramsey, 1991b; Ramsey & Myers, 1990; Van Ausdale & Feagin, 2001). During their elementary school years, children elaborate their concepts of race as they begin to associate social information with the physical attributes that they see (Katz, 1976). As this shift occurs, they rely less on color cues and begin to grasp the social connotations of racial distinctions (Alejandro-Wright, 1985).

The timing, clarity, and salience of racial awareness appears to be related to children's contacts with people from different racial groups (Katz, 1976; Ramsey, 1991b; Ramsey & Myers, 1990). In our interviews, one European American 3-year-old who lived in a predominately White community looked at a picture of a smiling Black child and said, "His teeth are different." Then he looked again and said with some hesitation, "No-o-o. [pause] His *skin* is different." However, European American children of the same age who lived in more racially integrated neighborhoods readily categorized the same photographed child as "Black."

Because young children have a hard time coordinating multiple attributes, they may appear color-blind in one situation but intensely aware of race in another, as illustrated in the following conversation I had with one of my White interviewees.

> Four-year-old David was looking at photographs of African American children. "I'm gonna kick all those Black people out of the workplace!" He clenched his fists as he spoke. "They can't be there," he exclaimed. "They're bad! I'll punch and kick them if they go there!" Later in the interview, David was selecting friends from photographs of classmates. Two of his designated playmates were African American. When I casually observed that "some friends are White and some are Black," he emphatically disagreed. "Oh no! Michelle is Brown!"

## What Do Children Know and Think About Race?

Children's understanding of racial differences changes as they get older, as illustrated in their questions about race, which shift from questions about physical attributes to ones about the social significance of racial distinctions (Derman-Sparks, Higa, & Sparks, 1980). Their explanations of racial differences reflect their changing understanding of the physical environment (A. Clark, Hocevar, & Dembo, 1980; Ramsey, 1986b). Children shift from attributing racial differences to supernatural causes and arbitrary physical reasons to understanding that racial characteristics are inherited from one's biological family.

A number of studies have suggested that children probably do not understand that race is an irrevocable characteristic until after they have acquired gender permanence (usually between ages 4 and 6) (Katz, 1976, 1982; Ramsey, 1987; for a review, see Ocampo, Bernal, & Knight, 1993). Gradations in skin color may make racial distinctions more confusing (as indeed they are) than the more clearly defined genital distinction between boys and girls. Young children often confuse skin-color difference with color transformations that they either observe or experience, such as sun tanning, painting, and dyeing, in which colors usually change from lighter to darker. In my interviews with children (Ramsey, 1982), virtually all of the 4- and 5-year-olds believed that everyone was inherently White and that Black people had been painted, sunburned, or dirtied. Only one child, an African American, had another theory: "If those White kids had left their skin on, they would be nice and Black and shiny like me!"

However, some children may know more than these findings suggest. After conducting a series of studies in which preschoolers accurately predicted the race of older children and adults based on their parentage and their characteristics as babies and young children, Hirschfield (1995) concluded that preschoolers *do* understand that race is an inherited and unchangeable characteristic. Moreover, according to Hirschfield, they have a relatively sophisticated view of race that does not rest simply on physical characteristics but also includes the elaborated views of race found in the popular culture. These findings clearly diverge from earlier ones and suggest that children today may have a more accurate understanding of racial differences than we previously thought. Alternatively, their level of understanding may be influenced by their circumstances (e.g., racial composition of the group; available information about racial differences; discussions about race) and by the particular questions that researchers ask.

## Do Children Identify Themselves by Race?

Children's racial identity development varies across groups and across historical periods. In many early studies (e.g., K. B. Clark & Clark, 1947; Morland, 1962; Radke & Trager, 1950), European American children *never* expressed a wish to be Black, but African American children frequently appeared either to wish or to believe that they were White. Goodman, who wrote at about the same time (1952), offered a poignant example of an African American child in a predominantly White nursery school who assured her friends, "This morning I scrubbed and scrubbed and it [my skin] came almost white" (p. 56). This attitude was not unique to African American children. In his autobiography, Mexican American author Richard Rodriguez (1981) described his efforts as a child to "shave off" his dark skin with his father's razor.

Studies that have been done after the 1960s suggest that the positive images of African Americans, now more evident in schools and in the media and consciously promoted in families and communities, may be reducing this dissonance. In more recent studies African American children usually express a Black reference group orientation (e.g., Cross, 1985; Farrell & Olson, 1982). Some Black children appear to have a stronger White preference in preschool but then in elementary school develop a stronger own-race identity than their White peers (Aboud & Amato, 2001; Aboud & Doyle, 1993; Burnett & Sisson, 1995). In my research (Ramsey, 1983), African American children readily identified themselves as Black or Brown, but some adamantly pointed out that they were not as dark as some of their peers. As one African American child said, "I like Brown people, but not real, real Black people." This bias may reflect the preference for lighter skin tones that prevails in many African American communities (Averhart & Bigler, 1999; C. P. Porter, 1991), which in turn reflects the racism of the larger society.

Cross (1985, 1987, 1991) suggests that these patterns of White identification and preference may be an attempt to resolve the contradiction between feeling personally valued yet disparaged because of group membership. As evidence of this, Corenblum and Annis (1993) found that White children's personal self-esteem was positively related to attitudes about their own group, whereas the reverse was true for a comparable group of Canadian Indian children. Spencer and Markstrom-Adams (1990) point out that children who have been targets of discrimination have to negotiate the conflict between loyalty to their own group and the negative images that prevail in the larger society. In the face of these pressures, some children focus on the values of European Americans and deny their racial heritage, which results in identity confusion.

### How Do Children Feel About Racial Differences?

Children's emotional reactions to racial differences may be affected by cognitive limitations, namely, a tendency to exaggerate the intergroup differences and minimize individual ones (Aboud & Amato, 2001; Holmes, 1995; Katz, 1976, 1982; Ramsey, 1987; Tajfel, 1973). Adults often sheepishly admit that they have trouble distinguishing individuals from cross-racial groups. Young children, who tend to focus on one characteristic at a time, may be particularly distracted by racial differences. Katz (1973) found that children more readily distinguished skin-color variations among individuals of their own racial group than among those of others. One time a woman whom I identified as an Algonquian visited our classroom of 3-year-olds. She had long braids and wore some beaded jewelry, but the children did not realize that Algonquians were "Indians." The children happily heard her stories and sang with her until she told them that she was an "Indian," whereupon several children shrieked with fright and refused to stay in the group. Here an immediate association of pleasurable experience was overwhelmed by the children's preconceived notions of "Indians."

Children absorb prevailing attitudes about race as they grow up. By the preschool years, children begin to express stereotypes of groups (Ramsey, 1987, 1991b; Ramsey & Williams, 2003; Tatum, 1997; Van Ausdale & Feagin, 2001). Some children may be more likely than others to develop and maintain stereotypes. Bigler and Liben (1993) found that White children (ages 4 to 9) who had more rigid classification systems in general formed stronger stereotyped images of African Americans and Whites. Moreover, they also had more trouble remembering stories that were inconsistent with these stereotypes than did their White peers who had more flexible classification systems. In a later study, children who learned to make multiple and flexible categorizations about both social and nonsocial items improved their recall for counterstereotyped information (Bigler, Jones, & Lobliner, 1997).

As children become more aware of different groups, their feelings change. Doyle and Aboud (1993) found that as children went from preschool through the early elementary years, they became more racially prejudiced. During this time the children increasingly focused on intergroup differences and had difficulty identifying individuals in other groups. However, in middle childhood (after the age of 7) prejudice declined as children's cognitive skills increased. Children also shifted from emphasizing intergroup differences to seeing similarities between groups. They were also more able to distinguish individuals in different groups and to see others' points of view (Aboud & Amato, 2001; Aboud & Doyle, 1995). However, not all children become less prejudiced as they get older. Whether children become more or less own-race biased may depend in large part on their racial environment, the values that they are learning, and whether or not their assumptions and stereotypes are challenged.

Some evaluative comments do not explicitly refer to race but reflect prevailing attitudes about color values. In one of my studies (Ramsey, 1983), both African American and European American children frequently made disparaging remarks about the colors black and brown when referring to African Americans. Some researchers (e.g., Williams & Morland, 1976) argue that this aversion stems from an innate fear and dislike of the darkness. It could be argued, however, that these feelings may be influenced by the prevalent negative connotations of darkness, such as in *blackball, blacklist,* and *black lie* in contrast to *pure white, whitewash*, and *white lie*. Most environments and materials designed for children are brightly colored; dark colors are avoided or used to depict frightening figures. Some marker and paint sets and books about colors do not even include the colors black or brown. In their fledgling efforts at art, children are apt to hear praise for their "pretty blue picture that looks like the sky," whereas the brown color that usually results from mixing several colors is frequently regarded as a "mess" by adult appraisers. These adult reactions probably are not deliberately racist but rather reflect many years of associating light colors with positive values and dark ones with negative ones. However, some children *are* connecting race with color preferences.

## How Does Race Affect Children's Friendship Choices?

Children's friendships in racially balanced preschool and elementary classrooms generally show a stronger same-gender bias than same-race preference (e.g., Asher, Singleton, & Taylor, 1982; Ramsey & Myers, 1990). Since gender is usually a more reliable predictor of activity preferences, it is not surprising that children prefer same-sex peers. However, when children in one study (Asher et al., 1982) were asked to nominate their "best friends," they usually chose same-race (as well as same-gender) children, so race may still be exerting some influence. Likewise, in a more recent study Aboud, Mendelson, and Purdy (2003) found that elementary school children reported that they enjoyed their cross-race friends but felt more comfortable talking about private issues with same-race friends.

Across three decades of research, White children have consistently shown stronger same-race preferences than their African American classmates do (Fox & Jordan, 1973; Newman, Liss, & Sherman, 1983; Ramsey & Myers, 1990; Rosenfield & Stephan, 1981; Stabler, Zeig, & Johnson, 1982), and this difference appears to increase with age (Aboud & Amato, 2001). Conversely, Black children are more accepting of cross-race peers (Hallinan & Teixeira, 1987; Ramsey & Myers, 1990). This pattern is not surprising because White children's in-group preferences are generally supported by the prevailing power codes and social attitudes.

Only a few researchers have studied children's actual cross-racial behavior, and the findings about younger children are mixed. J. D. Porter (1971), Singleton and Asher (1977), and Urberg and Kaplan (1989) observed few signs of cross-race avoidance or antagonism in young children's choice of play partners. Holmes (1995) also found little evidence of cross-race avoidance in the multiracial kindergartens that she observed. However, she did notice that when children were fantasizing about potential romantic relationships, they always referred to same-race partners. In other studies (Finkelstein & Haskins, 1983; Fishbein & Imai, 1993; Ramsey & Myers, 1990), cross-race aversion was more apparent; preschool and kindergarten children, especially White children, played more with their own-race peers. Sometimes cross-race rejection is more explicit. Van Ausdale and Feagin (2001) observed several instances of White preschoolers using explicit racial terms and beliefs to exclude and demean their classmates of color (e.g., a White child refused to let her African American classmate hold a white doll because "I don't want an African taking care of her. I want an American. You're not an American, anybody can see that" [p. 86]).

During the elementary years, racial cleavage often increases as children absorb more of the prevailing social attitudes, and the awareness of "us" versus "them" becomes more established (Aboud, Mendelson, & Purdy, 2003; Katz, 1976). This trend continues, and accounts of interracial contacts in middle schools and high schools show how vehemently and explicitly peers discourage cross-race contact (Patchen, 1982; Schofield, 1989; Ulichny, 1994). However, Howes and Wu (1990) found that in a very diverse setting, the third graders had more cross-ethnic contacts than the kindergartners did, suggesting that the trend toward racial cleavage in the early grades is not inevitable. With sustained cross-group contact, some children become friends with individuals in another group, although they may still have negative attitudes toward the group as a whole (Schofield, 1989). Research on racially integrated cooperative learning teams suggests that children who participate in these groups have significantly more cross-ethnic friendships (Johnson & Johnson, 2000; Rosenfield & Stephan, 1981; Slavin, 1995) but only if the cooperative activities are structured to ensure that all members contribute in positive ways and that their roles do not simply recreate the patterns of domination that occur in the larger society (Hertz-Lazarowitz & Miller, 1992).

Despite the great number of studies that have been done, many questions remain unanswered. However, we can generally assume that children are not color-blind and that, by the age of 3 and possibly even younger, they are aware of differences in skin color, hair, and facial features and can label and categorize people by race. Moreover, they may have a harder time recognizing individuals from races different from their own. Early on, children begin to absorb stereotypes about particular groups that may affect their racial identity development and their cross-racial feelings and relationships. Children's racial concepts are often characterized by overgeneralizations, erroneous associations, and some confusion about the source and permanence of racial differences. Those who have rigid categorization schemes rely more on stereotypes to interpret information about other groups. Children commonly express a dislike of dark colors, and some extend this aversion to darker skin tones. Many children prefer same-race people, especially when they see unfamiliar people or name their "best friends." White children in particular are at risk for developing racial bias.

## HOW TO LEARN WHAT CHILDREN KNOW, THINK, AND FEEL ABOUT RACE

Children often do not directly say what they feel about racial differences. However, we can observe how they interact with peers from different racial groups—not only who plays with whom but also the emotional quality of same-race and cross-race interactions and the dominance hierarchy in the classroom. In their study, Van Ausdale and Feagin (2001) heard preschoolers express many racial ideas and stereotypes among themselves. The children, however, were adept at hiding these conversations from their teachers, similar to surreptitious bathroom talk and gun play. Thus, teachers should try to observe as unobtrusively as possible in order to hear children's racial references in conversations among themselves. In classrooms with little racial diversity, they need to rely on children's responses to stories, pictures, dolls, and puppets that portray different groups of people.

To more directly elicit children's ideas (in both monoracial and multiracial settings), teachers might try some of the following activities:

1. Show children photographs of people who represent a range of racial groups, and ask them to describe all the things that they notice about a person in the photograph or to tell stories about different people. Their comments may reveal how much they notice race and whether or not they are making racially related assumptions.

2. To get a sense of children's assumptions about intergroup relationships, ask them to group photographs, dolls, or puppets "who might be friends with each other." You can also show them different groupings of photographs, dolls, or puppets, some that are racially homogeneous and others that are racially balanced, and ask them questions like, "Do you think that these kids play together a lot or not so much?"

3. Do activities with children that focus on bodies (e.g., self-portraits or faces or full bodies) or that highlight different-colored skin, eyes, and hair (e.g., matching skin color to paints, making a list of who has what color eyes and hair), and see how children respond. In particular, do they make any disparaging comments about particular attributes of themselves or other people?

## ACTIVITIES TO CHALLENGE RACIAL BIAS

There are myriad ways to address racial issues in early childhood class-rooms. As with any anti-bias work, engaging experiences that lead children to see and question assumptions are more effective than lectures about racism. Here are one strategy and one example of what teachers can do.

As I mentioned earlier in this chapter, children (both White and Black) often explain their antipathy toward darker skin as a dislike of the colors black or brown. We cannot erase the pervasive attitudes regarding color that children are exposed to from birth, but we can try to challenge them by using dark colors in decorating classrooms and encouraging the children to explore and appreciate browns and blacks. Before reading any further in this section, make a list of the colors used in your classroom. Think of the toys, the walls, the furniture, the partitions, and so forth. Now think about your art supplies and what colors of paint and paper are usually left over at the end of the year. Unless your situation is unusual, most of the colors used in the decor of your classroom are light and bright, and the unused colors are the browns and the blacks.

Children may initially complain about the black water in the water table or the five different shades of brown at the paint easel, but we can encourage them to express their negative reactions and then to challenge them to re-think their assumptions. For instance, if the children assume that the brown play-dough will smell "like poopy," as one child assured me, we can encourage them to smell it and see that it smells just like any other play-dough. One preschool teacher and her class mixed colors of paint for several weeks. As the culminating event, the children put all the colors together and came up with many rich shades of brown. In contrast to the negative associations that are often made, here the color brown was seen as the most exciting color because it included all the others.

Tatiana, a Mexican American teacher in a racially diverse Head Start, overheard Sara and Alison, two White girls, say that Amanda, a Black class-mate, could not play at the water table because she would get the water dirty. Tatiana was very concerned, and she and her colleagues Beth (White) and Clarissa (African American) developed multiple responses that reflect several of the goals mentioned in Chapter 1.

At the first level and at the moment, Tatiana helped the three girls resolve their conflict. She encouraged Amanda to express her frustration and anger at being rejected; Sara and Alison acknowledged that they had been wrong and apologized (albeit a bit reluctantly).

For the next few days, all the teachers listened closely to conversations of all the children to see if other children were making negative racial comments. Although it did not seem to be a general pattern, the teachers realized that racism is contagious and introduced some class activities to counteract any incipient racial bias. For example, they organized water play with soap bubbles and doll-washing activities to give children a chance to explore and express their questions about skin color and what does and does not come off in water.

The teachers, who usually changed the books and photographs in the classroom every month, rotated in books and photographs that portrayed African American children and families to support Amanda and other African American children in the classroom and to counteract the negative views that Sara and Alison had expressed. They listened carefully to comments that children made, particularly those of the White children, when they looked at the photographs and books. Children's questions and misinformation often became topics for group discussions. The teachers also put out and read books about the physiological basis for skin-color differences, which led to self-portraits done in skin-toned paints. These projects helped the children see skin-color gradations in a more realistic and less polarized way (e.g., no one was "white" and no one was "black").

Later in the year, the ongoing conversations about race led to discussions about how people from different groups were portrayed in the media. Seeing the potential for social activism, the teachers helped the children make posters about common TV stereotypes. These were hung in the hall of the school to encourage parents, teachers, and community people to write and complain to producers.

Because the teachers felt that the original comments reflected deeper racial antipathy than mere misunderstanding of the properties of skin color, they talked with Sara and Allison about what darker skin meant to them. They heard many comments that sounded as though they were quotes from adults. Beth spoke to their parents about the children's attitudes. The parents were initially very defensive, but Beth, working hard to keep the lines of communications open, continued the conversations whenever she had a chance during the rest of the year, often talking about her own struggles with recognizing and unlearning racist attitudes. She also created situations to bring those parents into nonthreatening collaborative relationships with parents of color (e.g., a committee to plan the end-of-the-year party). Obviously the parents did not immediately or drastically change their views but they seemed to become more open to connecting with other groups of people.

# CHAPTER 5

# The Economic Context: Social Class and Consumerism

## REFLECTIONS ON SOCIAL CLASS

Embedded in much of the discussion about racial power and privilege is the question of social class. In your responses to the question "Who am I?" did you list your social class? Often adults who are from middle- or upper-income groups do not mention their class background when answering the question "Who am I?" whereas those from working-class or poor families often *do*. As with race, the salience of class increases the further one is from the "norm"—in this case, middle- or upper-class affluence.

To clarify your relative level of affluence and your assumptions about different social-class groups and possible causes and remedies of unequal income distribution, ask yourself the following questions:

- When I worry about money, am I afraid that I won't be able to pay the rent or feed my children? Or am I concerned that I might have to forgo taking a vacation or purchasing a new car?
- Do I have a savings account? money for retirement? Or do I have to spend all of my available funds on day-to-day necessities?
- What do I assume about the race, gender, education, and character of people in different jobs? What images come to my mind when I hear that someone is a sanitation worker? a doctor? an assembly-line worker? an executive? a chambermaid? a manager?
- When I think about people in different jobs, which ones do I assume are more like me? Who might or might not be part of my social network?
- What are my assumptions about why some people are affluent and others are poor? Do I think it is fair? inevitable?
- Whom or what do I blame for disparities in wealth and opportunity? poor people? wealthy people? the system?
- What do I think needs to be changed? What reforms do I actively support?

- What would I be willing to give up to ensure that everyone in the world had adequate shelter, food, and education?

People who enjoy at least some financial security are often unaware of the role it plays in their lives. A number of years ago I worked for a federally funded day-care center in a low-income neighborhood. At first I was impatient with families and fellow teachers who always seemed to have "a crisis a minute." After a while, however, I realized how much my crisis-free life depended on my relative affluence. If my car broke down, I could get it repaired right away and did not spend weeks relying on friends for rides. When I needed to go to a doctor, I made an appointment, went, and was back in an hour or so; I did not have to waste a day waiting in a hospital emergency room to get the same service. Many requests from schools reflect this same blind spot. Money for field trips, requests for supplies, help with typing and photocopying a newsletter—all require money and/or some equipment that may seem trivial to middle-class parents but may be a burden to poor or working-class parents.

Ironically, many people express their discontent with economic inequalities, but very few actually *support* egalitarian reforms (Furnham & Stacey, 1991). Most people justify the unequal distribution of wealth because they themselves need economic resources to survive and do not want to give them up; they fear that major economic changes might mean the loss of their familiar way of life. Even individuals who are currently economically disadvantaged are committed to the current system because they expect to be upwardly mobile in the future. Finally, very few people have any vision of how things could be different.

## SOCIOECONOMIC DIVISIONS IN THE UNITED STATES

Despite our egalitarian principles, the United States has been moving *away from*, not toward, a more equitable distribution of wealth, especially during the last two and a half decades (Huston, 1991; McLoyd, 1998a; T. Thompson & Hupp, 1992). "The magnitude of economic disparities in the United States has taken on crisis proportions" (Lott, 2002, p. 100). Between 1979 and 1997 the average after-tax income of the poorest 20% of the population declined from $10,900 to $10,800, while the income of the top 1% rose from $263,700 to $677,900 (Lott, 2002). During the 1980s the numbers of children growing up in very poor (deprived) households and in very affluent (luxurious) households increased, whereas the number of children growing up in "frugal" (i.e., working-class) or "comfortable" (i.e., middle-class) households declined. One out of every six American children (16.7%) under the age of 6 are living below the national poverty level (Children's Defense Fund, 2003).

Most analysts attribute this trend to the reduced numbers of well-paid semiskilled and low-skilled jobs, cutbacks in federal programs that supported poor families before the 1980s, welfare "reform" that further eliminated these supports in the 1990s, deregulation and tax cuts that favor the wealthy and penalize poor and working-class families, and the changes in family configuration that have resulted in higher numbers of female-headed households. These economic shifts have had a devastating effect on families who are living in poverty and highlight the need to examine and challenge the inequitable distribution of wealth in this country.

These inequities intersect with race, gender, and age. Disproportionately more families of color, female-headed households, children, and elderly people fall below the poverty line (31.5% of African American children, 28.6% of Hispanic children, 11.6% of Asian and Pacific Islander children, 9.4% of non-Hispanic White children [Children's Defense Fund, 2003]). In contrast, White two-parent families and White single males are more likely to be among the affluent. As discussed in Chapter 4, racial discrimination in education, employment, and housing accounts for much of these disparities. Also, because of their long-term privileged status, European Americans are more likely than members of other groups to have inherited wealth and financial capital (e.g., investments and home ownership) that provide more financial stability and a buffer against the effects of unemployment.

Socioeconomic status is "an encompassing structure . . . it relates to virtually every aspect of human psychological development and across a considerable period of time" (Gottfried, Gottfried, Bathurst, Guerin, & Parramore, 2003, p. 204). As teachers, we need to be aware of the economic circumstances of the families in our schools and centers and to orient our teaching to helping children overcome the effects of economic inequities. Some children have to cope with material deprivation caused by poverty, and others need to let go of overblown materialistic expectations induced by affluence and consumerism. I will focus first on the pervasive effects of poverty.

## GROWING UP POOR

When thinking about the effects of poverty, we need to distinguish transitory poverty (a short-term decline in living standard due to divorce or job loss) from persistent poverty (an ongoing state of poverty with no prospects of change). Although both present hardships to families, the latter is most damaging, because children in those families may grow up with no hope or confidence that there is a place for them in the mainstream (Huston, 1991). Children from these families—across all racial groups—have more pervasive academic and peer problems than those from families who suffer intermittent economic hardships (Bolger, Patterson, Thompson, & Kupersmidt, 1995). Stability of income is another factor; families who face economic uncertainty and fluctuating incomes also experience high levels of stress (Yeung, Linver, & Brooks-Gunn, 2002).

Being poor in and of itself does not necessarily impair development (T. Thompson, 1992). Many families face the daunting challenges of poverty with fortitude and resolve and protect their children from its most deleterious effects. However, common consequences of growing up in poverty—malnutrition; inadequate health care; exposure to violence, toxins, and diseases; unsafe living conditions; neighborhood disorder; frequent moves; and poor educational facilities—do pose enormous risks for children (Brooks-Gunn, Duncan, & Maritato, 1997; Jackson, Brooks-Gunn, Huang, & Glassman, 2000; Kohen, Brooks-Gunn, Levanthal, & Hertzman, 2002; McLoyd, 1998b). Economic stress sometimes causes parental depression and family tensions that can spill over into conflicts with children (Conger, Ge, Elder, Lorenz, & Simons, 1994) and in turn make children more vulnerable to depression, low self-confidence, poor peer relationships, and conduct disorders (McLoyd & Wilson, 1992; Yeung et al., 2002).

Recent welfare "reforms" have aggravated these problems. New regulations forcing women with young children to work have resulted in many poor infants, toddlers, and preschoolers spending their early childhood years in substandard and even dangerous child-care centers and day-care homes. Given the well-established link between quality of early childhood care and school success, these arrangements may undermine children's educational prospects and erase any benefits of having a "working" parent (Polakow, 2000). These hardships are exacerbated when a family has a child with special needs. Because of all the environmental risks, a disproportionately high number of poor families have children with special needs. Not only is it more difficult to find child-care placements for children with special-needs, but their parents have to juggle numerous visits to doctors and specialists around their work schedules (Rosman, Yoshikawa, & Knitzer, 2002).

Violence is "as American as apple pie," and all communities have their share of it, but it is especially pervasive in poor areas (McLoyd & Ceballo, 1998) and has a devastating effect on children, families, and neighborhoods. In their study on the effects of violence on children, Garbarino, Dubrow, Kostelny, and Pardo (1992) found that, compared to their peers in low-violence communities, children in high-violence communities were more likely to suffer from learned helplessness, grief and loss reactions, school problems, delayed moral development, and feelings of hopelessness and futurelessness. They also tended to identify with aggressive people and/or objects. However, children whose families were able to provide a secure base that buffered them from the effects of violence were less likely to develop these symptoms.

Another common outcome of poverty is homelessness. Without a home, parents face huge obstacles supporting their children's development and education (Stronge, 1992). Homelessness is associated with severe physical problems (e.g., poor nutrition, lack of immunizations, high lead levels in the blood), socioemotional stressors (e.g., depressed parents, abuse, and neglect), and poor educational outcomes (e.g., inconsistent attendance, grade retention, poor performance on tests) (Molnar, Rath, & Klein, 1990). Children often face bureaucratic and logistic barriers to attending school (e.g., lack of permanent addresses and transportation to school) and frequent disruptions in their schooling due to moves. Once they get to school, they are often stigmatized by peers and teachers. When they get "home" to the shelter or the cramped quarters of a temporary placement, they do not have a space free of distractions to complete homework assignments or to get adequate rest. Tim, a child living in a shelter, described his school experience: "She [his teacher] hates everything I do—she made red checks on all my worksheets and anyhow I can't do homework and stuff in the shelter—there's always noise and stuff going on" (quoted in Polakow, 1993, p. 145). The observer in Tim's classroom also noted that when children ate lunch or worked in pairs, Tim was always alone and that the teacher made no attempt to help him find a partner or become part of a group. Tim fell asleep several times in the afternoon and each time was "jerked back to attention by Mrs. Devon's voice calling his name" (p. 145).

Unfortunately, educational and political systems, as well as schools and teachers, often exacerbate rather than mitigate the effects of poverty. First, the devastating inequalities between the public schools in affluent communities and those in poor communities ensure that children from different economic groups do not obtain equal educations (Kozol, 1991). Polakow (1993) points out that "programs organized for children of poverty are designed to provide the minimum amount of the least expensive instruction allowed under federal and state guidelines" (p. 149).

Second, despite the heterogeneity of children in all social-class groups, teachers and administrators often classify children by their socioeconomic backgrounds and base their expectations of the children accordingly (Bigelow, 1995; Gollnick & Chinn, 1998; McLoyd, 1998a; Rist, 1970). In an analysis of teacher attitudes and practices in low- and high-income schools, Harvey (1980) found that teachers of low-income children were concerned about their students but not optimistic about their futures. They discouraged active behavior, used directive teaching techniques, and stressed basic skills. In contrast, teachers in the middle-class schools encouraged active and independent learning, emphasized science and art as well as basic skills, and were more positive and optimistic about their students.

The high rates of school failure among children who are poor is especially ironic and frustrating because Stipek and Ryan (1997) found that, across all racial groups, economically disadvantaged preschool and kindergarten children entered school equally optimistic of school success and as motivated to do well in school as their middle-class peers were. However, they were already behind the middle-class children in academic skills and so, despite their high expectations, they came in with an academic disadvantage, which, along with the other pressures described in this section, eventually eroded their optimism and motivation.

What these statistics and studies fail to show are the daily—and often heroic—struggles of poor people to provide a decent life and education for their children against incredible odds. In a series of interviews (Cook & Fine, 1995), low-income African American mothers talked about how they are caught in a terrible bind. Their children need enormous support, monitoring, and advice in order to negotiate the unrelenting hardships of growing up poor—situations that would terrify and paralyze most middle-class families. Yet the jobs that they can find are usually low paying, have long inflexible hours, and often require several hours of commuting. So these mothers are less available than their middle-class counterparts for supervising and supporting their children. Cook and Fine challenge parents and teachers who are protected by racial and economic privilege:

> Imagine . . . a context in which you can no longer lie to your child [about being safe] because she hears shots out the window; where public institutions, your only hope, evince a strong ambivalence, sometimes antipathy, toward you and your kin; where the most enduring public institutions are the prison and the juvenile justice system, and the most reliable economic system involves underground drug trafficking. Imagine further that despite your best attempts to get your children to believe in "what could be," your children see little hope for themselves. . . . What kind of child rearing practices would you invent? (p. 137)

Against this backdrop of every imaginable frustration and indignity, these women bravely fight on. One described her attempts to influence the schools. "I have been to [the Board of Education]. I called, I got letters, both the student's rights, parent's rights and everything, . . . because I do believe in the telephone, you know. And I works on it" (p. 129). Several parents had also formed parent clubs to support each other and to maintain parent involvement in the schools.

Despite the grim statistics and daily hardships, many children growing up in poor families do succeed in school and in life (Gramezy, 1992). Werner (1989) identified three protective factors. First, the children themselves made a difference. If they were active and sociable, they were able to get more support and opportunities. Second, emotional support from their family was a crucial factor. Finally, external support systems such as church and community groups often provided the emotional and material support needed to succeed at school. Yeung and colleagues (2002) found that when children and parents engaged in cognitively stimulating activities and maternal stress levels were low, children performed better on academic tasks and had fewer behavioral problems than their peers from similar economic backgrounds.

The quality of schools also makes a difference. Gramezy (1992) found that schools associated with lower levels of delinquency were characterized by high expectations, effective management, clear reward systems, firm disciplinary control, and high-quality after-school programs.

The protective factors identified in a number of studies give some direction for how practitioners can effectively work with families and schools to provide optimal environments for children growing up in poverty. We also need to identify and build on developmental competencies that children growing up in disadvantaged circumstances develop, such as their abilities to function in different value systems and to deal with racism and social stratification (Garcia Coll et al., 1996). Furthermore, neighborhoods should be judged not only by what resources they *lack* but also by ways in which they *support* families and children, such as providing a sense of ethnic belonging or a buffer against prejudice in the larger community (Garcia Coll et al., 1996).

Most important, we need to avoid pitying and/or blaming families for their economic distress. Instead, our focus should be on the economic and social structures that contribute to the unequal distribution of resources and the widespread resistance to changing them. Rather than considering how children are "at risk," we need to ask, "Is privilege at risk?" (Swadener, 2000, p. 126) or perhaps *"How can we put* privilege at risk?" Teachers, children, families, and community people can engage in discussions about how our national and local economic, political, and educational systems support the ever-diverging worlds of poverty and privilege (e.g., business practices that put downward pressure on working-class wages while exponentially increasing executives' salaries; reliance on property taxes to fund schools). At the local level, we also have to scrutinize school policies, teachers' assumptions, and classroom practices to see whether and how they are exacerbating the educational challenges that poor children face.

Families, teachers, and community people need to work together to create schools where poor children can learn and thrive—not with watered-down curricula that prepare them for menial jobs or with replicas of "successful" middle-class schools. Instead, we must develop challenging and rigorous educational experiences that provide tools for children to critically understand their circumstances and create ways to overcome and change them (e.g., learning math skills by analyzing the extent and causes of the unequal distribution of wealth; studying history from the perspective of social and economic protest and change). All of us—children, families, teachers, and community people—have to learn about the causes and costs of increasing economic polarization and collaborate in political actions to reverse this trend.

## CHILDREN'S AWARENESS AND FEELINGS ABOUT SOCIAL CLASS DIFFERENCES

Young children are not likely to notice indices of social class such as education and occupational prestige, but they do notice more concrete clues such as differences in clothing, homes, and possessions. Moreover, they daily experience the effects of economic privilege or disadvantage by watching how their parents interact with employers, retail personnel, agencies, and institutions. In subtle ways, their images and expectations are being formed. When interviewing a number of elementary school children from different economic groups, DeLone (1979) found that children with comparable IQ scores but different social-class backgrounds had disparate perceptions of the world of work and the relationship of school to their futures. For example, a middle-class child said that she worked hard in school in order to get into a good college. Her lower-income counterpart said that he worked hard in school in order to get out.

As children learn about the sources of economic disparity, they also absorb the prevailing attitude that being rich is better than being poor (Leahy, 1983). Cottle (1974) quotes a child as saying, "Rich folks like you are lawyers and poor folks like me go into the army" (p. 136). Even preschoolers tend to assume that rich people are happier and more likeable than poor people (Naimark, 1983; Ramsey, 1991c).

Leahy (1983), who conducted a major research project (720 subjects, aged 6 through adolescence) on children's views of social class, found that children's understanding of social class goes through three stages. Early elementary school children are likely to both describe and explain poverty and wealth in observable concrete terms, such as number of possessions and type of residence. When they are around 10 years of age, children begin to refer to psychological traits, such as motivation, in their explanations of why people are in different circumstances. Finally, adolescents are capable of seeing the role of social and economic structures in the unequal distribution of wealth. During childhood and adolescence, children increasingly make the connection between having a job and getting money and learn more about the status and financial benefits associated with specific occupations (Furnham & Stacey, 1991).

Young children are beginning to develop a sense of fairness and to notice inequities, which may affect their responses to disparities in wealth. Damon (1980) found that children in the United States typically passed through several levels of positive-justice reasoning that reflect a growing awareness of others' perspectives. They go from expecting that they should get whatever they want, to insisting that everyone receive exactly the same amount of resources, to understanding that equity does not necessarily mean absolute equality and that distribution of resources may be adjusted according to need and merit.

When I asked preschoolers if it was fair that some people had more money than others, only a few of them tried to answer, but those who did said that it was not fair, and some suggested that the rich should share with poor people (Ramsey, 1991c). Leahy (1983) and Furby (1979) found that elementary school children also advocated equalizing the wealth between rich and poor. However, older children and adolescents are more likely to justify inequalities by claiming that poor people get what they deserve (e.g., "They didn't work hard enough") (Leahy, 1990). Taken together, these findings illustrate how children in our society, even as they are developing their ideas about fairness, are caught in one of the underlying contradictions of our society: the ideal of equality versus the economic competitiveness and individualism that inevitably result in inequality (Chafel, 1997).

Virtually no studies have been done on the effects of social class on children's friendships. However, teachers often comment about how children divide themselves by social class. In one rural White community, kindergarten teachers expressed concern at how quickly their children separated themselves by income group. Not only did the children come from different neighborhoods, but many families already knew each other from their preschools, which were economically segregated—with the low-income children attending Head Start and a federally funded day-care program and the middle-class children going to tuition-based preschool programs. One pilot study of peer interactions in a racially and economically diverse third grade (Kang & Ramsey, 1993) showed that children divided themselves more by gender and social class than by race. In their conversations, children talked about possessions, interests, and activities that often reflected different levels of affluence (e.g., computer programs, dancing lessons, skiing, social events in certain neighborhoods) that potentially inhibited cross-class contacts.

In summary, young children have a limited understanding of social-class differences. However, in preschool and early elementary school, they are developing ideas and attitudes about rich and poor people and their own economic futures. One disturbing developmental trend is that young children often assert that unequal distribution is unfair and that rich people should share their wealth with poor people, but older children are more apt to accept it and to blame people for their poverty. As teachers, we need to counteract the blaming-the-victim ideology that prevails in our society and help children recognize the economic inequities that define the lives of all people—rich and poor.

One impediment to engaging children in critiquing the economic system is the fact that they are so attached to it—in particular, to the hyperconsumption that has become a way of life for many people in our society. Thus, we need to consider how this pressure affects us and our work with children.

## REFLECTIONS ON CONSUMERISM

All of us engage in the market economy, but the relative importance of consuming varies across cultures, families, and individuals. To address these issues with children, we first need to understand how we relate to acquiring and owning goods and how that affects our relationships with others. Here are some questions to ask yourself:

- How often do I engage in nonmonetary activities, such as watching a sunset or enjoying the company of friends versus activities that involve spending money, such as shopping, going to the movies, or taking expensive trips? Which type of activity do I tend to value more?
- How much time do I spend shopping at stores? online? How much time do I spend looking at advertisements? catalogues? home-shopping networks?
- How do I feel when I see someone with a new purchase (e.g., clothes, car, sports equipment)? Do I immediately want to get one, too?
- How do other people's material wealth and ability to keep up with the latest fashion affect my opinion of them?
- What proportion of my income do I spend on food, shelter, and transportation? on charities and social justice work? on nonessentials?
- When something breaks, do I fix it or go out and get a new one?
- What factors do I consider when I am contemplating a purchase? Do

> I consider whether the new item is worth the raw materials and the space that the old one will take up in some landfill?
> - What are my motives for shopping? Do I shop when I need a specific item? for fun? to feel better about myself?

An interesting historical perspective is that in earlier times (and still today in some remote areas), towns and villages had "market days," one day each week or month for everyone to do their shopping and bartering (Bowers, 2001). As we think about our purchasing patterns, we can ask ourselves how our lives would be different and how we would feel if we were suddenly transported to that time rather than living in a society where we have access to 24/7 shopping.

## LIVING IN A CONSUMERIST SOCIETY

Over the years, I have watched in dismay as more and more open land near where I live is covered by malls. At the same time, the population in the area is not growing, which means that I and my neighbors are buying more and more. This hyperconsumption is not unique to my town—it is a national trend. The fact that many of us have far more than we need is evident in the commercial storage units that are sprouting up all over the country. What does this material abundance mean? Are we happier? According to a number of studies, the answer is *no*. Once people have sufficient food, shelter, and clothing, increased material wealth tends to bring not happiness but rather a "hankering for more; envy of people with the most perceived successes; and intense emotional isolation spawned by resolute pursuit of personal ambitions" (Luthar & Becker, 2002, p. 1593). Moreover, pursuit of material wealth tends to squeeze out alternative sources of satisfaction, such as creating works of art or spending time with family and friends. It has also "progressively eliminated every alternative that in previous times used to give meaning and purpose to individual lives" (Csikszentmihalyi, 1999, p. 823). Societies once respected members for their physical skills, wisdom, humor, or artistry; now these abilities are admired only if they have market value (e.g., athletes who command huge salaries, painters whose works carry high prices).

Competitive consumerism also aggravates economic disparities. Even if people have sufficient food and shelter, the lavish lifestyles of others often make them "feel poor," which affects their psychological functioning (Csikszentmihalyi, 1999; McLoyd & Ceballo, 1998) and can lead to shame and, in some cases, violence (Vorrasi & Gabarino, 2000).

Consumerism, class, race, and gender interact in some particularly damaging ways. As mentioned before, a disproportionately high percentage of people of color and female-headed households are in the low-income groups. However, the one place where all people in our society are welcome to participate is the marketplace—assuming that they have the money or available credit. For people excluded from other avenues of success and satisfaction, "with a limited capacity to ward off self-contempt and self-hatred" (West, 1993, p. 17), purchasing power is their only power and may become an exaggerated source of self-esteem and sense of well-being. Also, people who are targets of discrimination are judged more harshly on the basis of their appearance and possessions and feel pressured to dress in the latest styles and to buy the latest cars and equipment. Merchandisers, fully aware of these dynamics, often mount intensive advertising campaigns in poor communities (Nightingale, 1993). Parents get drawn in because dressing up their children is one way of compensating for all the things that they cannot do for them. Thus, people who can afford it the least often end up spending considerable amounts of money on expensive clothes, cars, stereo equipment, and other luxury items. The competition and financial pressures can, in turn, create interpersonal tensions and undermine the sense of community and potential for political action. The seductive images of consumerism "contribute to the predominance of the market-inspired way of life over all others and thereby edge out nonmarket values—love, care, service to others— handed down by previous generations" (West, 1993, p. 17). "It is the intrusion of white 'consumer capitalism' into black life that has been responsible for the erosion of community and political solidarity" (Haymes, 1995, p. 31).

## CHILDREN'S UNDERSTANDING OF CONSUMERISM

Money is one visible symbol of our economy, and most children growing up in the United States (and other money-based economies) are very interested in money at a young age. Preschool children in these economies often go through a series of phases as they develop an increasingly accurate understanding of the value of specific coins and bills (Berti & Bombi, 1981). As children enter elementary school, their understanding of money begins to reflect logical thinking and an early understanding of mathematical relationships (Edwards, 1986; Furth, 1980).

However, when and how children learn about money depends in part on the cultural and economic environment. Young children who are handling money independently at 4 or 5 years of age (e.g., selling candy and crafts on the street or running errands for their parents) probably learn about the specific values of currency and the concepts of costs and prices sooner than children who rarely handle money on their own. In communities where people primarily barter goods and services, children may not learn about money until much later.

Although most children in our society are avid consumers and therefore think a lot about money and things that they want to buy, children under the age of 11 or 12 are usually not very aware of the larger economic system. Harrah and Friedman (1990) asked children about money, salaries, prices, and taxes. They found that 8-year-olds had only a fragmentary and rudimentary understanding of the economic system and that only the 14-year-olds had a grasp of the overall system of the economy and how all the pieces fit together. Thus, when we want to teach children about resisting consumerism, we need to work on fairly concrete levels.

There is little formal research about the effects of growing up in a consumerist society where children are bombarded by messages that they need more and more (Burnett & Sisson, 1995). However, several research studies have shown that affluent children tend to be less happy and more at risk for drug and alcohol abuse than their less affluent peers (Csikszentmihalyi, 1999; Csikszentmihalyi & Schneider, 2000; Luthar & Becker, 2002), suggesting that consuming does not bring contentment to children but rather stimulates new desires. Teachers and parents often regale each other for hours about how their children have been obsessed by particular advertisements or products. We have all been horrified by news reports or the sight of children fighting and on occasion killing each other for high-status clothes. In my children's elementary school, trading cards were banned because children were bullying each other in attempts to make advantageous trades.

Teachers sometimes unintentionally encourage children's consumerism. Discussions around the Christmas holidays often revolve around anticipated toys—a time when children from lower-income families (not to mention those who do not celebrate Christmas) may feel left out. In some classrooms, children bring in toys for "sharing," which can aggravate possession-oriented competition. One parent told me about how her kindergartner worried for days about what to bring in for sharing; if his toy was not the glitzy attention-grabber of the day, he came home bitterly disappointed.

As they grow up in a consumerist society, children are learning to relate to physical objects, especially toys and in some cases clothes, in terms of *getting* and *having* instead of *using* and *enjoying* (Kline, 1993). Many of the toys promoted on children's television programs are specific to that program; when the fad dies, the toys lose their appeal. Furthermore, children's play with these toys revolves around the identities that have been created for the characters on television—not around the children's own ideas and feelings. Much of their play involves pre-scripted violence and stereotyped roles (e.g., action figures, Barbie dolls). In contrast, children create elaborate and ever-changing play with favorite old teddy bears or well-used blocks. Several years ago I kept track of the different roles played by our sons' two favorite teddy bears over the period of an hour. In this short period of time, the bears were spectators, misbehaving and crying babies, karate kickers, bicycle riders, water skiers, naughty dogs, and a pirate's parrots. Meanwhile, the much-begged-for action figures remained untouched.

Children are also learning to identify themselves solely as consumers and owners (Kline, 1993). Their sense of efficacy rests not on contributing to the family or community welfare or creating games but on getting the resources to purchase new toys and clothes. Children either pressure their parents to give them money or, in some cases, get drawn into illegal activities in order to acquire highly desirable goods.

Children are also learning to judge each other—and themselves—by the desirability and quantity of toys owned. "It's mine!" and "I had it first!" have echoed in schoolyards in the United States for generations. However, nowadays the competition and exclusion based on toys are fierce. With rapidly changing toy fads, it is no longer a matter of children bringing their kites or dolls or baseball mitts when they go to play. You cannot arrive with any old doll if the other children are all playing with their American Girl dolls. Pokémon figures won't do if everyone else has shifted to Digimon. These pressures often set off competitive comparisons among children as well as demands to parents to buy yet one more toy.

We need to be asking ourselves: What are the long-term effects of this passion for consuming on children's self-images and their social relationships? Some children may tire of this pressure and unhook themselves from it as they get older. Others, however, may grow up to be adults who always have to prop themselves up with the latest gadget, outfit, car, or piece of sports equipment. Of particular relevance to multicultural education, what does hyperconsumerism mean in a world of limited resources and unequal distribution of wealth? How can children think about racial and social justice, equality, and community when their sense of well-being is tied to getting more toys or clothes than another child? "In fact, to the extent that most of one's psychic energy becomes invested in material goals, it is typical for sensitivity in other [nonmaterial] rewards to atrophy" (Csikszentmihalyi, 1999, p. 823).

## HOW TO LEARN WHAT CHILDREN KNOW, THINK, AND FEEL ABOUT SOCIAL CLASS AND CONSUMERISM

Children are not likely to talk explicitly about social class since they probably have only a vague awareness of what it means. So teachers need to observe and ask more direct questions to see what income-related concepts and attitudes children are developing. The role consumerism plays in children's lives, however, may be more obvious as they engage in conversations about possessions they have and wish they could have. To learn how social class and consumerism are influencing children's ideas and relationships, teachers can use the following strategies:

1. To get an idea of how social class might be affecting peer relationships, teachers can observe grouping patterns and playmate choices to see if there are social-class divisions. If so, what factors seem to be contributing to them (e.g., topics of interest, after-school activities, neighborhood gatherings, friendships among parents)?

2. To learn what knowledge and beliefs children are developing about social class, teachers can show children photographs of people who have different kinds of jobs and represent different levels of affluence (be sure to have a good distribution of different racial groups across income groups to avoid reinforcing stereotypes), then ask the children to describe what they notice and/or tell a story about a person in the photograph to see what (if any) characteristics they associate with particular jobs and income levels.

3. If children talk about *rich* and *poor* (the most common terms for young children), teachers can ask them why some people have more money than others to find out if they are beginning to absorb a blaming-the-victim ideology. They can also listen to hear whether children are expressing negative assumptions about poor people and/or positive ones about rich people.

4. To learn what children assume about the impact of affluence on intergroup relationships, teachers can ask them to arrange the photographs into groups of people "who might be friends with each other" and ask them why they made the choices that they did.

5. To get a sense of the role consumerism plays in children's lives, teachers can listen to children's conversations to see how much of their time is spent describing and comparing clothes or toys that they have or want to have. How concerned are particular individuals with their possessions? For those who are very concerned, what role are possessions playing in their sense of self?

6. As teachers watch children socialize, they can observe how possessions affect children's social interactions. How much do they talk about them? Are children included or excluded on the basis of possessions?

## ACTIVITIES TO CHALLENGE ASSUMPTIONS
## ABOUT SOCIAL CLASS AND CONSUMERISM

As teachers learn about their students' ideas and attitudes about social class and consuming, they will see ways of helping children expand their knowledge and challenge their assumptions, as the following illustrations suggest.

Doreen, a European American who taught in an affluent and primarily White community, was tired of hearing her third graders complain about their lunches and seeing them throw away large amounts of food after every meal. One day she distributed special snacks. However, only 10% of the children got the ice cream and cake; another 40% each received two crackers and juice; and the remaining 50% got water and half a cracker. As the majority of the children vociferously complained about the lack of fairness, Doreen showed them graphs of food consumption around the world so they could see how their snack distribution had matched those figures. Later, after all the children had had the ice cream and cake, Doreen encouraged the children in the different snack groups to express how they had felt during the exercise. As they spoke, children began to talk about how it was unfair that some people were hungry and generated ideas for ways they might help (e.g., collecting food, working at homeless shelters), which Doreen passed on to the parents. Over time, this activity sparked an extended exploration about the political and economic causes of hunger and led the children to make posters and write letters to editors and government officials about ways to reduce world hunger.

Sandra, an African American, and Silvia, an Argentinian American, taught in a child-care center in a diverse low- and low-middle-income urban neighborhood. They decided to use their preschoolers' fascination with "going to the store" to talk about economic inequities and consumerism. The teachers set up a store in the pretend area, where each item cost one bill of play money. Then they gave each child a bag with different numbers of bills. As the children came and "shopped," some were delighted and others dismayed at how many or how few items they could "buy." At the end of the activity, the teachers had the children stand in a circle next to their "purchases." As the children saw the discrepancies and expressed their outrage at the lack of fairness, the teachers talked about how these discrepancies affected everyone in the country, including their own families. Several children chimed in with how their parents worried about money and often did not have enough. The teachers worked with the children in small groups to plan ways to make the game—and, in a few cases, the larger world—more fair.

Another day, the teachers put new empty containers into the "store," some of which had labels of highly advertised products and others no brand labels at all. They also included plastic replicas of vegetables and fruits. They then gave children equal amounts of money but assigned different values to the products—the advertised ones cost two bills, whereas the brand-free ones and the fruits and vegetables each cost one. They watched as children were first drawn to enticing brand logos and then struggled with deciding how to spend their money. Afterwards the teachers had the children talk about why certain products were more appealing than others. This discussion led to children looking at advertisements in magazines, talking about ones they had seen on television, and discussing how they make children want that product even if it is more expensive and not good for them.

Jan, a European American first-grade teacher in a small racially and economically mixed town, was concerned about the socioeconomic split in her class that also followed ethnic lines (relatively affluent European American children and low-income Latino and African American children). Jan realized that playing soccer was one activity that many of the middle-class children did every weekend. However, since it cost $45 to join the soccer league and required parents to transport their children to the playing fields, none of the children from low-income families were participating. She contacted the soccer association and (with much persuasion and the help of several current soccer parents) convinced them to waive the fee for children who could not afford to pay. She then asked parents of children who were already participating if they would help provide transportation. Several of them agreed, although some expressed concerns about driving into certain neighborhoods. In a few cases, Jan accompanied them on their first trip. This plan not only helped the parents overcome their fears; it also meant that the parents of both groups got to know each other as they made plans for transporting children and rode to games together. It also led to a number of postgame play dates.

Later, Jan and a few other teachers from her school met with the town recreational services to look at other activities that required money, equipment, and transportation (e.g., Little League, after-school ski program). They worked out a plan to provide equipment exchanges and sliding fees to reduce the economic barriers, which made some difference, although White middle-class children remained the primary participants.

# CHAPTER 6

# The Context of Culture

## REFLECTIONS ON CULTURAL INFLUENCES

Culture is a multifaceted and amorphous concept, yet it profoundly affects how we perceive the world and relate to people, objects, and nature. To help readers identify the many complexities and influences of their cultural backgrounds, this section consists of several discussions followed by series of questions, each addressing a specific aspect of culture.

Because we typically associate culture with different countries and bygone traditions, many people, especially those whose families have lived in the United States for several generations, assume that they have no culture—that they are "just plain American" as one of my students told me. Yet everything we do reflects cultural traditions—from singing a good-night lullaby to a child to ordering in a restaurant or stopping at a red light (Bowers, 2001). These conventions are not biologically encoded in our brains; they are rituals and rules that have evolved within our cultural context. However, because we take them for granted, we often do not see them as "cultural."

We also usually associate culture with specific customs or artifacts. However, cultures function on two levels. The *explicit* culture includes cultural expressions and symbols, such as clothes, food, tools, holidays, rituals, crafts, artifacts, and music. The *implicit* culture embodies the values, meanings, and philosophies that underlie the overt symbols (Garcia, 1990). For example, many ancient pyramids in Mexico are dedicated to the rain gods, explicitly symbolizing the concerns of people living in an arid climate. In a more contemporary example, shopping malls in the United States are concrete expressions of our culture's competitive consumption. Likewise, graduation ceremonies reflect our national interest in formal schooling.

Take a few minutes to think about the cultural influences in your life, at both the explicit and implicit levels, and ask yourself:

- On my list of identifying attributes, did I mention language? religion? country of origin?
- When I think of my family and my childhood, what foods, rituals,

holidays, artifacts come to mind? What culture(s) do they represent? What underlying values do they reflect?

- How do people in my family and community relate to each other? Do they value community over individual success or vice versa?
- How do they define success? What are their aspirations? fears? How are these reflected in their child-rearing practices?

Many people see cultures as clearly defined and frozen in time, with static rituals, values, and artifacts being passed down through generations. In fact, cultures are not pure or fixed entities with clear boundaries. They continuously change, merge, and diverge in "restless uneasy processes in which the fusion of elements is often . . . dislocating, jarring, and discomforting" (Scholl, 2002, p. 6). Across generations, the relationships within and among cultural groups evolve. Many individuals, especially in the United States and in other highly mobile societies, belong to a number of cultural groups (e.g., family of origin, school, recreational groups, workplace). They shift among them many times during their lifetimes and even in the course of a day, sometimes with ease and at other times with discomfort and conflict.

Within cultures, traditions connect us with the past, and we rely on them to guide our behaviors. At the same time, "their sheer existence disposes those who possess them to change them" (Shils, 1981, p. 213). With new experiences, insights, and knowledge, people adapt traditions to evolving realities. For example, the tradition of schooling has changed over the course of the last two centuries to adapt to everchanging social and economic needs.

To consider how your cultural contexts and traditions have evolved, ask yourself the following questions:

- How do my values and practices differ from those of my own parents and/or teachers? What traditions and priorities have I given up, maintained, changed, or reclaimed?
- How is my current life influenced by intergenerational knowledge passed down in my family or community?
- What new values and traditions have I incorporated into my life? Where did they come from?
- Are there conflicts between and among early and contemporary influences on my life? If so, how do they affect me and my relationships with others?

Cultures also intersect with racial, gender, and social-class backgrounds. In some cases, race and culture overlap, but not always. We need to be sure that we do not assume that people who may look alike to outsiders (e.g., African Americans and Haitian Americans; European Americans and recent Russian immigrants) share the same culture. Gender groups and disability groups also develop distinctive cultures, as do occupational groups, which, in turn, reflect social-class differences.

## REFLECTIONS RELATING TO THE NATURAL ENVIRONMENT

Besides determining how we relate to the social world, cultures also influence how we relate to the natural world and experience the rhythms of the day, the year, and the life span. Because this relationship is core to the goal of creating equitable and sustainable societies, we will explore it in some depth.

To examine how you and your community/culture relate to nature, you can ask yourself:

- How attuned am I to the natural rhythms of the day and year?
- Do I and other members of my community try to live harmoniously with nature and view ourselves as part of the ecosystem (e.g., use renewable energy sources, buy food from local farmers)? or do we try to control or overcome natural forces (e.g., build houses on floodplains, construct dams, and grow crops that are not indigenous to the area)?
- How conscious are we of the amount of oil, gas, water, food, and other natural resources that we consume in a day? in a year? Do we know where these resources come from and how much they cost in terms of environmental impact?
- Do we think about how much we contribute to sewage systems, landfills, or air pollution in a day? a year?
- How does my community relate to land use? How much of it is being "developed"? What efforts are being made to conserve local ecosystems?
- How connected do I feel to the place where I live—the climate, landforms, vegetation, and animal life?
- What do I know about the history of human habitation where I live—especially traditional wisdom about how to live sustainably in this area?

As we think more deeply about our relationship with the natural world, we begin to identify cultural beliefs that may not have been obvious before. I have always loved the outdoors and have enthusiastically supported environmental causes. However, after reading works by American Indian writers,

I have come to see how my "appreciation" for nature is still built on the European tradition that nature exists to be used and enjoyed by people like myself. The following quotation from Paula Gunn Allen's book *Sacred Hoop: Recovering the Feminine in American Indian Traditions* (1992) is one of many that has made me stop in my mental tracks and recognize the profound difference between my *homocentric* perspective, which places people in the center, and the *biocentric* view that we are all part of the same ecosystem—plants, animals, water, landforms, and humans—and that no one species has the right to dominate or destroy the habitats of others.

> The notion that nature is somewhere over there while humanity is over here or that a great hierarchical ladder of being exists on which ground and trees occupy a very low rung, animals a slightly higher one, and man (never woman)—especially "civilized" man—a very high one indeed is antithetical to tribal thought. The American Indian sees all creatures as relatives . . . as offspring of the Great Mystery, as cocreators, as children of our mother, as necessary parts of an ordered, balanced, and living whole. (p. 59)

Many of us are caught between our desires to create an ecologically sustainable and equitable world and the pressures of our day-to-day lives. For example, as a "soccer mom" I spend many hours driving a minivan from town to town taking children to soccer games, which directly contradicts my desire to use as few natural resources as possible.

We may also feel conflicted between ecological principles and the Western scientific assumption that "progress" means increasing our control of natural forces and using ever more complicated technology to fulfill our basic needs (e.g., the cultivation and preparation of food) and to create new ones (e.g., our dependence on a wide variety of electronic entertainment) (Bowers, 2001). I am not suggesting that we condemn and/or rid ourselves of all scientific theories and inventions, but we do need to take a hard look at the downsides of the constant push to mechanize and globalize. For example, thousands of people throughout the world—especially in poor areas— are suffering from environmental degradation and have lost their livelihoods, cultures, and communities because multinational corporations have taken over the land, the means of production, and the markets.

In this country, environmental issues often exacerbate tensions between social-class groups. A proposal to build a factory on farmland may pit middle-class environmentalists who want to preserve open space against unemployed workers who would benefit from an influx of manufacturing jobs. In many rural towns, environmentalists and loggers fight about protecting versus harvesting old-growth forests. These conflicts often create tensions in communities and can affect classroom dynamics. Pressures to maximize

short-term profits push companies to constantly cut costs and reduce ex-
penses (e.g., build new factories rather than to rehabilitate old ones; clear-
cut rather than selectively cut forests; mass-produce new items rather than
repair old ones). As children and teachers analyze how these issues affect
their communities, they may think critically about the system as a whole
and see how these pressures hurt both the environment and the workers (e.g.,
in 5 years the new factory may close when a still cheaper alternative becomes available; clear-cutting forests means fewer long-term logging jobs).
As grassroots concerns about the environment have grown, some environmental groups and corporations have started collaborating to develop more
sustainable practices that are also cost-effective (e.g., shifting to biodegrad-
able packaging).

Cultural and economic contexts and views of the natural world also
influence our spatial, temporal, and quantitative relationships. In the United
States and most other industrialized market-based economies, time, space,
and value are precisely defined and are measured by standard units such as
hours, feet, and dollars. In other societies, they are measured in a more
relative and continuous fashion and within the context of the natural cycle
of the day or year and immediate human needs.

In some cultures time is linear and in others it is more cyclical (Allen,
1992). Most people in the United States see time as linear, and many feel
as though they are constantly racing against it. With our watches, daily plan-
ners, palm pilots, and cell phones, we try to control our time and never
"waste a minute." Children are also learning these values as they see thousands of easy and immediate solutions in televised stories and advertisements of particular products. They are learning to value speed and quantity
over deliberation and quality and to consume rather than savor experiences
(e.g., wolfing down fast food from a drive-up window as they are on their
way to the next activity).

The passage of time has a different meaning, however, when we are no
longer racing against it. You might think about your experiences with time.
Do you tend to think of time as something that is used up and lost, or do
you focus more on the rhythm of days and the recurrence of events such as
sunsets and ceremonies? Do you focus on the present, or are you always
thinking about the next thing you have to do?

Two familiar children's stories illustrate contrasting views of time. In
*Mike Mulligan and His Steam Shovel* (Burton, 1939), the protagonists, who
are a White man and a machine, are in a race against time to finish making
a cellar within a designated number of hours. If they succeed, they will be
rewarded. In the Navajo story of *Annie and the Old One* (Miles, 1971), the
completion of the blanket means that Annie's grandmother will die. When
the granddaughter tries to postpone that time, the grandmother admonishes

her for trying to interfere with the natural rhythms of life and death. These two stories also convey different messages about the relationship between people and nature: The construction of a new building, which is celebrated in *Mike Mulligan*, destroys the plants and animal habitats on the building site; weaving a blanket, on the other hand, involves using natural materials but does not damage the environment.

We all grew up in particular cultural contexts, but often we do not "see" our cultures because we take them for granted and assume that everyone lives—or should live—the way we do. As we become more conscious about the values and priorities that guide our decisions, we can see other cultural contexts in a more authentic and respectful way. This broader perspective also enables us to envision possibilities beyond the mainstream U.S. cultural preoccupation with the exploitation of natural resources and individual and material success.

## CULTURAL INFLUENCES ON CHILDREN'S DEVELOPMENT

How we want our children to grow up is defined by cultural values and mores that influence every detail of sleeping, feeding, playing, and schooling routines. The following questions highlight a few of the daily decisions that parents and teachers make that reflect culturally defined child-rearing goals.

- Should toddlers feed themselves or should they be fed? Should they be carried or encouraged to walk alone?
- At what age should children be toilet-trained?
- When should children start doing chores? When is a child old enough to care for younger siblings?
- How should children act around adults? Do we want them to be respectfully quiet or to seek attention and praise?
- Do we think that children learn best by watching the adults in the community or by being explicitly "taught" by professional teachers?

Cultural differences influence child-rearing goals, strategies, and outcomes such as level of independence (e.g., Gonzalez-Ramos, Zayas, & Cohen, 1998), discipline practices (e.g., Kobayashi-Winata & Power, 1989), play patterns (e.g., Farver, Kim, & Lee, 1995; Farver & Shin, 1997; Roopnarine, Lasker, Sacks, & Stores, 1998; Whiting & Edwards, 1988; Whiting & Whiting, 1975); sleeping patterns (Lebra, 1994), family responsibilities (Whiting & Edwards, 1988), and emotional development (Farver, Wells-Nystrom, Frosch, Wimbarti, & Hoppe-Graff, 1997).

Thus, teachers working with children from different ethnic groups need to learn about the cultural roots of the children in their classrooms and understand how they may affect the course of development (De Gaetano, Williams, & Volk, 1998). At the same time, we need to recognize that cultures are changing and that individuals within groups vary a great deal and not make assumptions about them based on cultural affiliation.

## CULTURAL AND LINGUISTIC DISCONTINUITY

Many children and their families feel culturally alienated from schools at some point in their lives. They may have recently immigrated to this country or perhaps have moved to a new region, or from the country to the city or vice versa. They may have lived in the community all of their lives but still find that their cultural values do not mesh with those of the schools. Whatever its cause, cultural discontinuity can be the source of considerable stress for children and their families *and* for teachers who realize that their classrooms are not "working" for at least some of their children. The following discussion will focus primarily on the experiences of recent immigrants, but many of the dilemmas described are relevant to families who feel culturally disconnected from schools for other reasons.

Children of recent immigrants suffer from the dislocation and confusion that inevitably accompany leaving the familiar and coping with a whole new language and school structure. Igoa (1995) eloquently describes the initial confusion, exhaustion, and fear that immigrant children feel and the different stages that children go through as they become more comfortable with their new surroundings. As one child said, "When I first went to school in the U.S., I wanted to cry. . . . It was very confusing. I did not understand. . . . I did not know anyone" (p. 44).

Learning a new language is an enormous challenge for children and adults alike and can delay children's academic progress and integration into the social world. Since the early 1970s bilingual education programs have been available to ease these transitions for many children by helping them maintain both of their languages and cultures and by making schools more hospitable for parents. Many of these programs have been very successful, and in some cases parents and teachers collaborated to create two-way bilingual/bicultural programs (e.g., Vasquez, Pease-Alvarez, & Shannon, 1994). Unfortunately, in the 1990s bilingual education was the target of a great deal of political opposition (see Crawford, 1999; Minami & Ovando, 1995; Moran & Hakuta, 1995). As a result, in many states bilingual programs have been curtailed and, in some cases, virtually eliminated and so are no longer available to many families. Thus, the burden now falls more heavily on regular classroom teachers and parents to ease children's entries into new language environments.

If only one or two children speak a particular language, they may be isolated from their peers, especially at the beginning of the year. One time I was visiting a first-grade classroom and noticed that when the children went out to recess, all the children found someone to play with at recess except for Andrew, a new arrival from Cambodia. I casually pointed out to a girl with whom I had been talking that maybe she could play with Andrew. She replied in a very matter-of-fact voice, "He doesn't speak English." Then, before I could say anything, she hurried to add, "Anyway, he's really shy; I don't think he wants to play with anyone." Children, reacting to the awkwardness of not having a shared language, may simply avoid each other unless teachers help them make connections.

Immigrant parents often have difficulty providing their children with support because they themselves are going through the same transition and are exhausted and confused. Vasquez and colleagues (1994) describe how family members and friends (including children) spend long hours pooling their knowledge and helping each other fill out forms for taxes and immigration and negotiate contracts such as leases.

Another stress that accompanies cultural and linguistic discontinuity is that children usually learn the new language and customs more rapidly than their parents do because they are in school all day. As a result, they frequently serve as translators, negotiators, and teachers for their parents. This role reversal enables children to learn to be responsible and to further develop their English-language skills, but it can also undermine respect for parental authority. In some cases children begin to refuse to speak their home language. This communication gap also means that parents have difficulty teaching their children their values, beliefs, and wisdom, and families become less intimate (Wong-Filmore, 1991). Moreover, because language and culture are inextricably bound (Nieto, 2004), the loss of language also diminishes children's knowledge of their culture.

Parents and grandparents often feel threatened and displaced as children shift their allegiances from the family and community of origin to the popular culture of their peers and the expectations of school. Vasquez and colleagues (1994) describe how Mexican American parents feel undermined when teachers—speaking from their own cultural perspectives—tell children that individual achievement and rights are more important than family loyalty. A child who stays home from school in order to accompany his mother to the doctor or is absent for two weeks to go to a family funeral in Mexico may be criticized by the teacher and feel caught between two different sets of expectations (Valdés, 1996).

When values, learning goals, and social expectations differ between home and school, children, parents, and teachers often miscommunicate and fail to develop good working relationships, which further adds to the stress. Tharp (1989) describes four dimensions of cultural differences that account for some children's discomfort and underachievement in classrooms:

1. Social organization (e.g., emphasis on individual accomplishments versus peer cooperation)
2. Conventions and courtesies of speech (e.g., the length of time one waits for a response, rhythms of speech and responses)
3. Patterns of cognitive functioning, in particular the difference between verbal/analytic and visual/holistic thinking
4. Motivation (e.g., responses to rewards versus affection)

As a result of these differences, children's behaviors at school are often misinterpreted, and their skills are underestimated by teachers and peers who do not understand a child's culture. Children who are taught to quietly respect adults are likely to be seen as withdrawn when compared with their outspoken, attention-seeking peers. In contrast, children accustomed to more spontaneous conversations may feel frustrated waiting for teachers to call on them. Children growing up in more collective cultures may be uncomfortable with the emphasis on individual achievement that dominates most U.S. classrooms and may be judged as unmotivated.

Variations in language use and construction also potentially disrupt communication. In one observation a first-grade African American girl was talking during circle time and, in her narrative, was moving from topic to topic in a chaining style. Her European American teacher, who was accustomed to hearing children develop a single theme, mistimed her responses and kept asking irrelevant questions that interrupted the child's thinking (Michaels, cited in Phillips, 1994).

Different views of what information is important and how it should be conveyed are another source of discomfort for children. Delpit (1995) describes how Native Alaskan children accustomed to learning from observing their parents and grandparents engaged in daily tasks had difficulty learning isolated skills and abstract concepts.

Cultural differences in children's emotional expressions also may interfere with teachers' abilities to see and meet children's needs. One example of this miscommunication occurred in my classroom many years ago but remains a vivid memory and will probably haunt me for the rest of my life. An Iranian child, who had been trained not to cry or complain if he was hurt, fell from the climber. We rushed over to see if he was hurt, but he got up and brushed himself off and did not cry or seek any comfort, so we assumed that he was all right. To our horror the next day, his father, who was much more attuned to his son's subtle signs of pain, told us that he had broken his arm.

Beyond simply adjusting to and surviving in an unfamiliar culture, how children develop their identities and orientations to both (or more) cultures has long-term ramifications. Darder (1991) describes four possible outcomes for children growing up biculturally, including those in groups that have been historically marginalized (e.g., Puerto Ricans, African Americans, Native Americans) as well as new immigrants:

1. *Alienation.* Children identify only with the dominant culture and do not acknowledge their ties to their home culture.
2. *Dualism.* Children separate their lives, behaving and thinking one way at home and another way at school.
3. *Separatism.* Children live totally in their home culture and avoid or reject the dominant culture.
4. *Negotiation.* In this most positive outcome, children live in both worlds and affirm both identities but maintain a critical stance and use experiences in one culture to understand and critique the other one.

A wonderful and inspiring example of this fourth possibility is Gloria Anzaldúa's book *Borderlands/La Frontera* (1987), in which she linguistically and psychologically moves back and forth between the United States and Mexico and reflects on the possibilities and drawbacks of both cultures.

All these accounts of children's difficulties coping with cultural discontinuities sound pretty discouraging, but the good news is that when parents, community people, and teachers work together, they *can* create effective programs for children who otherwise may feel alienated and unsuccessful in school. In the well-known Kamehameha Early Education Project (KEEP), teachers adapted their practices so that they were more compatible with the Native Hawaiian culture (Tharp & Gallimore, 1988). Children who had been doing poorly had much more successful school experiences after these changes were made. Tharp (1989) argues that educators should develop practices to increase the cultural compatibility between home and school but at the same time support children as they develop new skills so that all children (including members of the dominant group) can function a wider range of modalities. A cross-age tutoring program in a Mexican American community described by Vasquez and colleagues (1994), in which older children helped their younger peers learn how to read and write, was compatible with the sibling caretaking that was common in the families. At the same time, both groups, the tutors and their students, improved their literacy skills and developed more confidence in them.

Both parents and teachers need to be aware of how cultural discontinuity affects children and collaborate to help children negotiate between home and school cultures. Through conversations with parents and home visits, teachers can begin to review their practices and consider how to make their classrooms more accommodating and empowering to a wider range of children and families (Delgado-Gaitan & Trueba, 1991; Phelan & Davidson, 1993).

Teachers also need to see and work with the strengths of families and ethnic communities (Valdés, 1996). Much of the literature presents a "pathologized" view of immigrant families and other marginalized groups as disorganized and overwhelmed by the challenges of adjusting to the mainstream society. In fact, many families have extended kinship and friendship networks that provide social and financial support. Social and religious organizations give communities identities and provide families with a sense of security and continuity. These organizations are potential resources for families, and teachers should be aware of them and support families' participation in them. Parents, for their part, need to help teachers and administrators understand the specific issues and mores of their communities and, when necessary, to correct their misperceptions. Together parents and teachers can help children learn to negotiate between two (or more) cultures and benefit from these multiple perspectives.

## CHILDREN'S UNDERSTANDING OF CULTURE

Despite the profound influence of culture on all aspects of learning and development, the concept of culture itself is abstract, and most children are not consciously aware of their own or others' cultures. If they have traveled or if they live in a community that includes people from other cultures, they may notice some differences, but they probably do not see them as "cultural." During our first year in Mexico, I tried several times to get Andrés (then 4 years old) to talk about the differences between our lives in the United States and in Mexico. He invariably answered, "I miss my red tricycle." Although his life had greatly changed—food, language, and social context—he did not have a schema that encompassed these differences. Even Daniel, at age 7, described concrete differences, often more related to climate than to culture (e.g., "It's warmer," "There are more flowers and prettier houses," "People wear hats more"). At the beginning, he frequently talked about people speaking Spanish, but as the year wore on and he became more fluent, he rarely mentioned it. As illustrated by the account in

Chapter 2 of the kindergarten children arguing about whether or not English was spoken in a particular town, most children have only a vague idea of how geography relates to national, cultural, and language differences (Lambert & Klineberg, 1967; Piaget & Weil, 1951).

At the same time, culture shapes children's expectations of the world at an early age (Longstreet, 1978). A teacher of 2-year-olds heard a great outburst in the housekeeping corner one day. When she arrived at the scene, she discovered an Israeli girl (whose parents kept a kosher home) pushing a play milk bottle from the table that was set for "dinner." Her playmate, who was not Jewish, kept putting the milk bottle back on the table. Although neither child had a concept of kosher laws, each one had internalized particular expectations about serving milk with dinner.

Furthermore, when confronted with the practical demands of cultural differences, children adapt. For example, bilingual preschoolers switch between languages depending on the language being used by their current playmates and in the particular fantasy roles they are enacting (Orellana, 1994). Unfortunately, they also sometimes divide themselves along these lines. In a study of Canadian classrooms containing both French- and English-speaking children, Doyle (1982) found a striking amount of segregation between the two ethnolinguistic groups. Because many children were competent in both languages, Doyle concluded that the segregation was not simply a matter of linguistic fluency. She attributed these patterns to the following cycle: Children play more actively with same-culture partners and develop common repertoires, which means that their play is more engaging; children then seek out same-culture playmates more often, precluding opportunities to create the same shared experiences with children from the other group.

Preschoolers also notice and remember concrete cultural differences, especially when they emerge in a familiar realm such as food and clothing. In my interviews (Ramsey, 1987), 3- and 4-year-old African American and European American children often labeled pictures of Asian American children as "Chinese" and then talked about Chinese food and shoes and "those stick things" (chopsticks). Because children have trouble coordinating multiple pieces of information, they sometimes over generalize cultural attributes and may use a single aspect to define a whole group. One of the 4-year-old rural White children that I interviewed declared "All Chinese people eat in restaurants," which probably reflected the fact that her contact with Chinese American people (and any Asian Americans, for that matter) had been limited to eating in a few local Chinese restaurants. When I asked her if Chinese people ate all their meals in restaurants, her reply was a confident "Yep!" I pushed a little further, trying to create some disequilibrium, and queried, "What about breakfast, when kids are getting ready to go to school?" "They still eat in restaurants," was her reply. "Even babies?" I asked, still trying to shake her assumption. "Yep! Even babies," she replied without a quiver of hesitation.

As children approach middle childhood, they begin to acquire a sense of cultural relativity—the ability to see familiar conventions as unique to one's particular culture rather than as universal. However, this capacity does not necessarily make them more receptive to cultural differences. Carter and Patterson (1982) found that kindergartners were more tolerant of unfamiliar social conventions than were 8- and 9-year-old children. Apparently, while children are developing the capacity to see other cultural perspectives, some are also acquiring an in-group bias against unfamiliar cultures. Teachers can take advantage of young children's flexibility and convey in concrete ways the notion that "there are many ways of doing things" in order to predispose them to resist peer and media pressures that assume that "our way is the best—or only—way."

One kindergarten teacher used her children's intolerance to encourage them to develop more awareness of their own cultures and a sense of cultural relativity. Several children in the class were calling a boy from India "gar-bage head," because they noticed the smell of the coconut oil on his hair. In response, the teacher planned a series of activities in which she and the children compared the scent of coconut oil with a variety of shampoos, cream rinses, hairs sprays, and setting lotions. After many discussions about all the different things that people put on their hair, the children recognized that everyone's hair has a particular smell and realized that coconut oil was simply one of an array of hair products.

Culture influences the language, behavior, interactional styles, and so-cial expectations of young children, even though they generally do not un-derstand it at a conceptual level. However, they do notice and increasingly reject people who do speak or act in unfamiliar ways. We need to counteract this tendency by helping children maintain an open and flexible view of the world.

## HOW TO LEARN WHAT CHILDREN KNOW, THINK, AND FEEL ABOUT CULTURE

Finding out what children know, think, and feel about cultural differences is difficult because they may not be consciously aware of them. We also have to fight our own tendencies to give minigeography lessons or quick "touristy" descriptions of different cultures. Instead, we need to keep the focus on children's own feelings, ideas, and questions related to the similari-ties and differences that they notice. As we learn more about their reactions, we can provide them with information that is relevant to their particular interests. Here are some ways to elicit children's ideas about cultural differences.

1. Show photographs of people engaging in familiar activities (e.g., cooking, eating, going to school) in ways that are unfamiliar to the children and note how they react to these differences. Do they immediately reject the people as being "silly" or "yucky," or do they appear curious and interested in knowing more? What questions and explanations do they have?
2. Provide children with opportunities to play with clothing, tools, and other materials that represent diverse cultural groups and see how they react. Are they curious and eager to use them? Or are they dismissive or derisive?
3. Observe children's responses to their classmates who speak different languages. In particular, notice how children with a first language other than English feel about speaking that language. Do they deny that they speak Thai or Japanese, or are they willing to teach other children some words from their home language?
4. If all the children in the class are English speakers, then recordings with songs and stories in different languages can be used to stimulate discussion about the fact that people speak in many ways. Listen to children's reactions. Do they assume that people who speak a different language cannot talk (a common misperception)? Or are they interested and eager to learn new words?
5. Observe children's reactions to peers or visitors who are from different cultures. How do they react to unfamiliar behaviors, clothing, and languages? What questions do they ask? What assumptions do they make?
6. If children bring lunches from home, how do children react to unfamiliar foods? When parents do cooking projects, how willing are children to try new foods?
7. Ask children and their parents to describe some of their routines to help them identify their family traditions (e.g., Friday night pizza, special Sunday morning breakfasts, and other rituals that at first glance may not seem very "cultural").

## CHILDREN'S UNDERSTANDING OF THE NATURAL ENVIRONMENT

How children understand and feel about nature is influenced by their cultural context. Unfortunately, we have very little information about how children develop concepts about nature and virtually no information about how this development varies across cultures. Thus, the following discussion is drawn from informal observations and the few studies that have been done in the United States. The patterns that have been identified may be very different in children raised in more biocentric cultures.

Children's perceptions and understanding of the natural environment appear to change as they get older. Preschoolers often approach the natural world with a sense of wonder and excitement. They eagerly watch and ask questions about natural phenomena (e.g., sprouts popping out of seeds, water freezing, brown grass turning green in the rainy season). At this age, children are also likely to relate to the environment in a personalized way. Taking care of plants and pets or observing seasonal changes in a particular tree are the most meaningful types of activities. Kindergartners and first graders are able to observe natural phenomena more systematically and broadly. They may be interested in studying small ecosystems or learning about distant phenomena such as volcanoes, asteroids, and dinosaurs. Children in second, third, and fourth grades can analyze larger ecosystems and participate in cooperative research projects. As children develop their abilities to see multiple perspectives, they potentially shift from using exclusively homocentric reasoning (e.g., "Pollution is bad because it could kill people" "If you litter, people will get mad") to using biocentric reasoning (e.g., "We shouldn't destroy what nature made" "Fish need the same respect as people") (Kahn & Friedman, 1995).

Children's cultural contexts influence how they perceive and react to their natural environment. Most children in the United States readily absorb the values of conquering nature and are learning that nature is something you tame and exploit. Toddlers and preschoolers often "build roads" or "dig to find treasures" when they are playing in the sandbox. In our school we tried putting small cardboard trees in the sandbox to see if children would shift to other themes. A few children started playing "in the forest," but most "chopped down the trees" on their way to making new constructions. Children from families and groups that believe in the sacredness of the earth may feel uneasy and alienated by the "conquering earth" assumptions that prevail in the mainstream culture. Likewise, it may be difficult for children who admire backhoes and construction sites to understand those misgivings. As children learn about different cultural responses to the environment, they can experience physical properties and environmental phenomena in new ways and possibly rethink their assumptions.

Children's perceptions and feelings about natural settings also seem to be related to where they live. Wals (1994) found that suburban children saw nature as a *threatened* place that was rapidly disappearing because of new construction, reflecting a concern with protecting the wilderness. However, in this same study, urban children, whose sole contact with the natural environment had been visiting city parks, saw nature as a *threatening* place where "murderers and rapists use the trees to block what they're doing" (p. 190). In another study (Simmons, 1994), urban elementary school children chose photographs of places they would like to visit. They clearly preferred school playgrounds or small green areas in the city over more remote wilderness areas. When asked about visiting wilderness areas, the children said that they were afraid of natural hazards (e.g., drowning, falling, getting lost), threats from people in isolated areas, and lack of physical comforts such as no shelter from sun or rain. As these responses indicate, children's concepts and feelings about the natural world reflect their personal experiences. In planning curriculum, we need to start with those and build from there.

One approach is to reduce children's aversions by making natural elements more familiar. In a recent study, Pina (2002) tried this strategy with children's reactions to animals. After identifying which animals children disliked, Pina and her fellow teachers implemented a month-long curriculum in which children observed, handled, drew, read about, and enacted spiders and worms—two of the animals the children strongly disliked. During the curriculum, the teachers not only provided activities and information but also observed children's reactions to the animals and helped them express and rethink their aversions. At the end of the curriculum and 2 months later, the children's views of spiders and worms were much more positive than they had been before the curriculum.

A number of studies report on successful and unsuccessful environmental programs and provide some guidelines for parents and teachers. Not surprisingly, they have shown that children learn the most when they actually spend time outdoors seeing and experiencing firsthand natural ecologies, solving practical problems, and enjoying nature as well as learning information (Dressner & Gill, 1994; Milton, Cleveland, & Bennett-Gates, 1995; Simmons, 1994). Writers also argue that for young children teachers should avoid organized nature walks and/or factual lectures, and instead encourage children to enjoy and feel competent in their natural environment (e.g., scrambling up rocks, climbing trees) (Wilson, 1993, 1995). Sobel (1996) argues that deeply connecting to their local natural surroundings is the best way to interest children in the well-being of the environment. He points out the irony that children are spending more time indoors and away from their immediate natural surroundings and yet learning about distant animals and environments from the electronic media. He advocates that children spend a lot of time in nearby and familiar natural places—whether they are small parks or vast woodlands—so that these places become well-loved "homes" that the children want to protect. From this deep connection, Sobel argues, comes the commitment to care for the environment.

Programs that emphasize local environmental problems that are highly relevant to families have more impact on children and their families than more abstract information (Sutherland & Ham, 1992). We also need to be careful not to over-emphasize frightening information about the destruction of rain forests and the extinction of animals that may make children feel helpless and scared (Sobel, 1996).

## HOW TO LEARN WHAT CHILDREN KNOW, THINK, AND FEEL ABOUT THE NATURAL ENVIRONMENT

We can learn how children think about the environment by observing what fantasies they enact in their play and what they say and do when they are in natural settings or see pictures of them. Here are a few possible questions.

1. What themes arise when children play in the sandbox or with blocks? Are they intent on building roads and making towers? Or do they sometimes talk about protecting the land? What do they do when plastic animals and plants are in these areas?
2. How do children react to pictures of different natural settings? the same setting at different seasons and at different times of the day? What are their questions and comments? How attuned are they to different environments or the rhythms of days and seasons?
3. How do children respond to photographs of litter and air and water pollution? clear-cut forests? stories about animals and people whose habitats are threatened?
4. Take children to different natural sites (e.g., city parks, wooded areas near the school, small corners in the schoolyard). Listen to their questions and comments to see what ideas they are developing about the natural world. Observe their reactions to plants and animals. Do they whack at plants with sticks? stomp on ant hills? Or do they seem respectful and curious about the natural world?
5. Take children to a construction site or show them pictures of one and see how they react. Are they mostly interested in the machines and progress of the building, or do they also notice the number of trees that were cut down and think about the animals that have lost their habitats?

## ACTIVITIES TO CHALLENGE ASSUMPTIONS AND BROADEN PERSPECTIVES ABOUT CULTURES AND THE NATURAL WORLD

Because celebrating holidays has been a misunderstood and controversial aspect of multicultural education, I am starting this section with a more general discussion about the possibilities and drawbacks of holiday celebrations in a multicultural curriculum. Then I will describe a specific example of how teachers have developed curricula that incorporate cultural and environmental issues.

Holidays provide opportunities to explore cultural differences and similarities and the rhythms of the natural world. These occasions generate a lot of interest, and children are usually very motivated to participate in the many related activities (e.g., cooking, games, music, art projects). However, by focusing on holidays, we risk portraying groups in a superficial, exotic, or touristy way (e.g., how accurately does a traditional New England Christmas celebration represent the many groups, traditions, and regions of the United States—or even the people who currently live in New England?). As discussed earlier in this chapter, holidays and rituals are overt manifestations of deeply held values and should be portrayed in the contexts of those values and the contemporary daily life of the groups that observe them.

For these reasons, specific holiday celebrations should focus primarily on cultures that are represented in the school and immediate community. Families and community members can share their past and present experiences with particular celebrations so that the children hear about them from real people, not from secondary sources. These occasions also provide opportunities for children to connect with each others' families and community people and to engage in intergenerational learning. Children and their families can also share rituals that are not necessarily official "holidays" but are their families' ways of observing seasonal changes (e.g., a picnic to celebrate the first day of spring, going fishing on the first day of the fishing season). For children who are socially isolated because they are new to this country or community and/or not proficient in English, sharing their holiday traditions may help to incorporate them into the classroom and give them more status and visibility among their peers.

Activities should be designed to be meaningful to young children. Instead of a long description of the history and traditions associated with the holiday, teachers and parents can read or tell stories about how children celebrate it. Foods, dances, and clothing are also high-interest possibilities. However, we need to be sure that we are not conveying stereotypes or violating sacred ceremonies. In our school, we stopped having the children do sand paintings after a Native American visitor told us that they were part of sacred rituals and were not appropriate activities for non-Indians and children.

We can use holidays to explore the continua of cultural similarities and differences in meaningful ways. People all over the world share similar experiences, concerns, and aspirations as they go through the year (e.g., celebrating the harvest, the new year, the longest/shortest day). At the same time, climate and custom have led to different expressions of these common experiences. For instance, by looking at images of Christmas celebrations in northern Europe, Africa, South America, or Australia, children see how seasons and landscapes differ across hemispheres and how that affects people's lives in every detail, including their celebrations.

Children's awareness of the natural cycles underlying many holiday celebration can be heightened by having them observe the seasonal changes in a particular plant or the different angles of the sun and lengths of shadows. The Reggio Emilia schools have developed wonderful curricula on natural rhythms and celebrations that are an excellent resource for this work (e.g., Cadwell, 1997).

Celebrations—whether they are connected to a particular holiday or not—are expressions of the collective classroom or school culture and are opportunities to build community. Harvest, winter solstice, and spring festivals or school anniversaries are times when children, teachers, family members, and community people gather and honor the season and the work that children, teachers, and families have all done together. On these occasions children also have to think about others' interests and needs as they plan and prepare food, performances, and art shows for their guests' enjoyment.

Finally, weather changes and holidays are times that highlight the inequities in our society and people who suffer most from them. When the weather turns hotter or colder, we can talk with children about the hardships of people with inadequate shelter or clothing. Class groups can write letters to the local government or the newspaper about homelessness and the need to provide enough shelters. Holiday observances can also include participating in local food drives and/or community dinners.

*Celebrate!: An Anti-Bias Guide to Enjoying Holidays* (Bisson, 1997) is an excellent resource for thinking about the complexities of holiday celebrations. The author talks about how to deal with holiday-related issues such as religion and choices about which holidays should be celebrated. She also illustrates how to avoid the exotic, touristy aspects of holidays and to help children understand their underlying meanings and view them in the context of an anti-bias framework.

Phila, who had moved from Cambodia to United States when he was a young child, and Kendra, who had grown up in a White poor rural community, taught kindergarten together in an economically and ethnically diverse public school in a small city. From the very beginning of the year, they were both struck with how much the children talked about new toys, often bragging about which ones they already had and which ones they were going to get. Despite the fact that the children came from a number of different cultures, all their toy preferences closely followed the latest media events and advertising blitzes. Phila and Kendra recognized that these media-inspired passions did serve to create a base for connections among children who, in some cases, did not have a shared language and culture. However, they were concerned that the children's obsessions with expensive toy fads were, in some cases, undermining families' efforts to teach children about their home cultures and aggravating financial pressures on families. Moreover, the children were oblivious to the environmental impact of constantly buying and discarding new toys. So Phila and Kendra decided to do a series of activities about toys to encourage their children to reflect on what toys are, how they are made and used, and how they reflect cultures and personal histories.

Kendra and Phila started with a series of activities about the "life of a toy" to encourage the children to think about the environmental and emotional costs of constantly replacing old objects with new ones. Small groups of children each examined and wrote a dictated story about one classroom toy that was worn, and might be replaced. Working in their groups, the children had to figure out what materials and energy had gone into making that toy and trace them back to their origins as much as they could (e.g., a tree had to be cut down to provide the wood, plastic is made from oil). As children were investigating their toys, the teachers showed the children pictures of factories to help them imagine the natural resources, labor, and fuel that had gone into making their group's toy. After the groups had recorded their findings about the toys' origins, they then imagined and recorded all the ways that children in the classroom might have played with and felt about their particular toy over the years (e.g., feeding and dressing a doll, struggling with a challenging puzzle). In the final part of the story the children predicted what would happen to the toy when it was thrown away— where it would go and what it would look like in 100 years (e.g., would it have turned into dirt or would it still be intact and taking up space in a landfill). They then made a recommendation about whether or not the toy should be discarded or mended and kept.

As children were engaged in these investigations, they all dictated letters to their parents asking them about toys and games that they remembered from their childhoods and/or country of origin. Several families sent in descriptions of toys and games that they recalled. The teachers were able to gather stories from other parents through phone calls or community translators. Once all of the stories were collected, the children illustrated them and put them in a class book. The teachers also invited families to introduce their toys or games to the class. To encourage all the parents to participate, Phila and Kendra made sure that they had translators available for parents who needed them. Over several weeks a number of parents came and presented their toys or games, several of which became incorporated into ongoing classroom activities. The children were fascinated by the stories that families told about the games and toys. Their questions and comments suggested that they were learning and thinking a lot about each others' cultural and personal backgrounds. Kendra and Phila were gratified to notice that, at least for a while, conversations about the families' games and toys eclipsed the children's concerns about who owned the latest media-related fad.

# CHAPTER 7

# The Context of Gender and Sexual Orientation

## REFLECTIONS ON GENDER IDENTIFICATION AND ROLES

In your list of "Who am I?" you probably included gender, especially if you are a woman. In the United States (as in many countries) gender is often the first way we classify people, including ourselves. Since men are usually in more dominant roles, women tend to be more conscious of the effects of gender than men; but both may feel pressured by the expectations and limitations of gender-related roles. We need to be aware of our own biases and expectations in order to help children resist the pull of stereotypes and limited roles.

To consider how gender has influenced your identity and relationships with others, ask yourself:

- How has being a man or a woman influenced my life? How has it limited me? sustained me? opened up possibilities?
- If I had been a man instead of a woman or vice versa, how would my life have been different? How would that have changed my personal relationships? What jobs might I have had? Would I have occupied more/less powerful roles in my family? at work? in the world?
- On a day-to-day level as I go to work, do errands, spend time with my family and friends, would I be reacting to situations the same way if I were a woman instead of a man or vice versa? Would others be responding to me in the same way?
- What assumptions do I make about other people based on their gender? Would I be surprised if a woman made a daring rescue? the new teacher at the child-care center was a man? the newly appointed CEO of a company was a woman? and her administrative assistant was a man?
- For those in heterosexual relationships and/or in mixed-gender work places: How does my gender define my responsibilities at home? at

work? How would the dynamics change if I did all the jobs usually done by my opposite-sex partner or co-workers?

- When I am talking to someone, how would I be acting if the other person was a man instead of a woman (or vice versa)?

The way we interpret and react to children's behavior also reflects our gender-related assumptions. For example, loud, rambunctious boys are often tolerated more easily than girls with similar behavior. Likewise, we sometimes are more concerned about a quiet, shy boy than we are about a girl with the same behavioral profile. To examine your assumptions about and awareness of gender-related dynamics in the classroom, consider the following questions:

- Think of two classroom events: one that involved a girl and one a boy. Ask yourself, how would my interpretations and responses have differed if the first one had involved a boy instead of a girl and the second one a girl instead of a boy?
- When I put out art materials, which children do I expect will use them? What about blocks and trucks?
- When I select materials such as photographs, books, and puppets, how conscious am I of the images of males and females that are conveyed?
- What attributes of children do I praise? Are there gender differences (e.g., do I more often compliment girls on their appearance than boys)?
- How often do I notice whether children are playing in same-gender or mixed-gender groups? How aware am I of gender-related power differentials (e.g., boys intimidating the girls)?

## GROWING UP IN A GENDERED WORLD

Gender differentiation and roles emerge in almost all societies (Liben & Bigler, 2002; Whiting & Edwards, 1988) and are usually associated with inequities. In the United States, despite a great deal of legal and attitudinal change, girls and boys are still not treated equally in schools (see Sadker & Sadker, 1995). Girls are often overlooked by teachers and not encouraged to excel, particularly in math and science and in physically challenging activities. They do, however, learn to be nurturing and emotionally expressive and often are more skilled at maintaining personal relationships than boys are. Boys, on the other hand, are encouraged to be aggressive, to excel, to take physical risks, and to hide their emotions. They are both the best students and the worst troublemakers (Sadker & Sadker, 1995). Boys potentially grow up to be leaders and to earn more money than their female counterparts, but at the same time, they are more likely than girls to fail in school or to engage in violent and dangerous activities. Several recent books attest to the toll that the emotionally limited roles of traditional masculinity take on boys (e.g., Garbarino, 1999; Kindlon & Thompson, 1999; Kivel, 1999; Pollack, 1998). Thus, while girls have been more materially shortchanged in schools and workplaces, both sexes suffer from the effects of rigid gender-role expectations.

Gender roles are resistant to change and are re-created with each generation. One reason for this intransigence is the prevalent use of gender in our society to divide and differentiate people (Bem, 1981, 1983; Liben & Bigler, 2002). This pattern is exacerbated by the consumerist pressures that were discussed in Chapter 5. Walk into any toy or clothing store or those sections in a department store, and there will always be what I call the "pink aisles" (loaded with pink and purple outfits, sneakers, and toys—even Legos come in "girl colors" now) and the "grayish-brown aisles" (filled with darker-colored clothes—some imitating army camouflage—and action figures, vehicles, war toys, and guns).

Many television shows target either boys or girls and model gender-specific fantasies. Due to mergers, a decreasing number of corporations are defining the images that children are exposed to (Hughs & MacNaughton, 2001). As the same highly femininized and masculinized characters show up in movies, television, computer games, toys, and clothing, children have less access to counterstereoyped images. Ironically, some commercial attempts to challenge stereotypes actually reinforce them. For example, Barbie dolls of all skin tones now come in different career types, with the slogan "We Girls Can Do Anything" (Hughs & MacNaughton, 2001, p. 126). However, all the careers are lucrative and glamorous (will there ever by a "Custodian Barbie?") and are defined by elegant, sexy wardrobes that reinforce the image of women as sex objects. Moreover,

> no social and economic changes are required—Whites, men, and capitalism can each stay as they are. . . . Barbie rarely has to strive for anything. Each of her careers comes ready-made with its characteristic costume . . . reducing roles to costumes. (Hughs & MacNaughton, 2001, p. 126)

Racial and gender discrimination and unfair labor practices are obliterated; we will probably never see "Homeless Barbie" or "Laid-Off Barbie."

Gender differentiation and related inequities intersect with race, culture, and class. Stereotypes of males and females vary across race (e.g., Asian "China dolls," African American "Aunt Jemimas," "macho" Latino men), and the flexibility of gender roles varies considerably across cultural groups (Liben & Bigler, 2002; Whiting & Edwards, 1988). Economic status also affects gender inequities. For example, White, middle-class, college-educated women managers may enjoy a more equal relationship with male colleagues (at least officially) than Latina chambermaids or factory workers who are supervised by men. However, as with any generalization, we need to keep in mind that within groups, individual responses vary widely; some people conform willingly to prevailing gender roles, and others resist them (Liben & Bigler, 2002).

## CHILDREN'S RESPONSES TO GENDER DIFFERENCES

In contrast to discussions about race, one question that parents and teachers *never* ask is: "Do young children notice gender differences?" They don't need to. All of us who work or live with children in any capacity know that from an early age children identify and divide themselves by gender. Interestingly, some researchers have raised the question of whether or not gender differences are as biologically defined as we have assumed they are (Kessler & McKenna, 1978). Moreover, with new medical technologies, more individuals are physically changing their sex to become transgendered, further blurring the biological boundaries of males and females. However, in the lives and minds of children, gender differences are alive and well and *very* important. As Andrés announced one morning shortly after his fourth birthday, "I am a boy because I am 4 years old and I *hate* girls!"

As children grow up, they construct their gender identities and concepts from overt and covert messages in their environment. Many studies have shown that in preschool, children in the United States learn stereotypic beliefs and attitudes about gender roles that affect a wide range of behaviors, psychological constructs, and aspirations, including peer interactions, memory skills, self-identity, self-esteem, and social, educational, and vocational goals (Bigler, 1997). A full discussion of these implications is beyond the scope of this book, but I will talk about two that are particularly germane to multicultural education: gender stereotypes and gender segregation.

A number of researchers have proposed that gender stereotypes are developed and maintained by children's gender schema, a network of associations that organizes and guides children's perceptions of males and females (Bem, 1981, 1983; Martin & Halverson, 1981). These associations are complex and often contradictory. Liben and Bigler (2002) found that many children had different gender expectations for themselves than they did for others (e.g., a girl might think that both boys and girls could do carpentry, but she would not endorse that for herself). However, once they are established, gender stereotypes are self-perpetuating, and children often deny information that challenges them. One 4-year-old girl told me that her mother was a doctor (which was true), but later in the interview when I asked her what mommies did, she emphatically told me, "Mommies always stay home and take care of their babies and kids." Mapley and Kizer (1983) found that, when children were presented with information that violated their expectations of gender roles, they remembered it less well than information that was congruent with their stereotypes (e.g., several children insisted on calling a male nurse "Dr. Brown"). However, children may vary in the degree to which stereotypes influence their interpretations. As with racial stereotypes, children who in general use more flexible classification schemes are less likely to express gender stereotypes and can remember counterstereotypic information better than their peers who are more rigid classifiers (Bigler & Liben, 1992).

Children clearly prefer same-sex peers—all of their hypothetical and actual playmate choices demonstrate this over and over. One time in our school, we had the kindergarten boys and girls sit next to each other in circle time. The next day a mother called and said that her son was so upset about this arrangement that he was determined to quit school.

Gender segregation begins before preschool and becomes increasingly entrenched during the early childhood years. In a year-long study of the social dynamics of preschool classrooms (Ramsey, 1995), children in the younger groups (average age of 3) stated that they preferred same-sex playmates, but in the classroom they played in many mixed-sex groups throughout the year. However, in the 4-year-old groups, children's time in same-sex groups increased dramatically during the year, suggesting that the fourth year may mark the beginning of separate peer cultures and more rigid sex roles.

Gender segregation continues to increase during the elementary years and is reaffirmed by children's engagement in "borderwork" between the two groups (Thorne, 1986). These interactions include contests (e.g., boys' and girls' spelling bee teams), cross-sex chasing games that sometimes include a threat of kissing or pollution rituals (e.g., giving cooties to each other), and invasions in which one group (usually the boys) disrupts the play of the other.

Teachers and parents often ask why these gender divisions are so universal and intractable. After decades of research in this area, Maccoby (1986) concluded that, with early socialization, children learn to enjoy gender-typed activities and then are attracted to peers who share their preferences. Thus, preschool girls usually congregate in the art and housekeeping areas, and boys engage in more active play with blocks and trucks. In elementary school playgrounds, boys frequently play vigorous physical-contact games, whereas girls tend to have conversations and play games that require more precise physical skills and social coordination, such as jump rope. As children get to know their same-sex peers better, they become more confident of what to expect in terms of play and conversational styles and find same-gender groups more comfortable. When they get older, children also learn that peer acceptance depends on conforming to rigid gender-typed roles, which creates difficulties for children who do not fit the norms. Children who prefer cross-gender roles and activities (e.g., girls who like science and sports and, especially, boys who enjoy dressing up and playing with dolls) are often rejected and ridiculed by both children and adults, especially as they enter elementary school (e.g., Damon, 1977; MacNaughton, 2000; Sadker & Sadker, 1995). In short, as children spend more time in gender-typed activities and segregated playgroups, groups form their own connections, cultures, and rules, and the divisions become self-perpetuating.

As gender cleavage becomes more pronounced, children who enjoy playing with members of the opposite sex find it increasingly difficult to maintain these friendships. Peer pressure mounts against crossing the gender divide. Those who do are often accused of "liking" someone of the opposite sex or being a member of that group (Thorne, 1986), which are strong deterrents. Some children maintain old cross-gender friendships but often hide them from their same-gender peers.

Because children readily divide themselves by gender, teachers often unintentionally support and reinforce this segregation by using gender as a way of organizing their classes (e.g., seating, work groups) (Thorne, 1986). In a comparative study, Bigler (1995) found that in elementary classrooms explicitly organized by gender (such as boys' and girls' teams and lines), children developed more gender-stereotyped views of occupations and more rigid assumptions about the homogeneity of males and females than did their peers in classrooms where gender differences were not emphasized. The impact was particularly strong on children with less advanced cognitive skills, which underscores the need to avoid such practices in early childhood classrooms.

Breaking down the gender divide and, in particular, equalizing power between the two groups is difficult and requires active interventions (MacNaughton, 2000). Even when teachers do implement strategies to reduce gender segregation, they are not always successful. In a number of studies, children initially responded positively to rewards, praise, or new activities and played with more cross-sex peers. However, after the interventions were over, they reverted back to their same-sex classmates (e.g., Maccoby, 1986; Serbin, Tonick, & Sternglanz, 1977; Swadener & Johnson, 1989).

Some teachers have tried merging the block and housekeeping areas to encourage boys and girls to play together. However, these efforts often result in children simply avoiding the areas or playing in separate gender groups in the combined spaces (MacNaughton, 2000).

In our kindergarten, we went one step further by not only merging the block and role-play areas, but also removing most of the toys, clothes, and props that were associated with gender-specific play and turning the areas into an outer-space environment with materials designed to be equally appealing to boys and girls (Theokas, 1991). The teachers initially assigned groups to the combined area in order to establish the precedence of mixed-gender groups. Over the month-long curriculum, boys and girls began to play more cooperatively together and to develop themes that included both boys and girls. When the teachers stopped assigning groups, the children still chose to play in gender-mixed groups. Moreover, a few weeks after the project had ended, boys and girls were still playing together more than they had before it started. We felt that the success of this intervention relative to others was due to the fact that we did not simply rely on proximity or rewards but proactively helped girls and boys develop common interests. Despite the overall success of this project, however, we did not completely equalize the gender power differentials. A close reading the observations revealed that in many (not all) mixed-gender groups, the boys still played more dominant roles.

During the early childhood years children are forming their ideas about gender and the related power differentials and absorbing stereotypes that are portrayed in highly sex-differentiated media images. As they get older, many children divide themselves by gender and vigorously exclude the opposite sex. Moreover, power inequities often develop, with boys taking more dominant roles. However, with adult support, boys and girls can learn to work and play together and enact more flexible gender roles—at least some of the time.

## REFLECTIONS ON SEXUAL ORIENTATION

In answer to the question of "Who am I?" did you mention your sexual orientation? If you are gay, lesbian, bisexual, or transgendered, you may have. If you are heterosexual, you probably did not, because your sexual orientation is another invisible norm. Yet all of us have distinct sexual histories, preferences, and values that reflect our physiological and psychological traits, our culture, and our family situations. These perspectives in turn influence our responses to children's developing understanding of sexuality (Andrew et al., 2001).

The questions below are designed to help you to assess your knowledge and feelings related to sexual orientation. These questions are primarily directed to readers who are heterosexual because these concerns are probably all too familiar to most gay, lesbian, bisexual, and transgendered individuals.

- What images come to mind when I think of gay men? lesbian women? bisexual individuals? transgendered people? To what extent do my images fit prevailing stereotypes of these groups?
- What assumptions do I make about individuals whose sexual orientation is different from mine? Would it change my feelings about my child's teacher if I found out that she was lesbian? Would I still admire a particular athlete if I knew that he was gay? How would I react if I learned that the President of the United States was bisexual? if one of my co-workers was transgendered?
- As you walk around your community and watch television, imagine that you are gay, lesbian, bisexual, or transgendered, and ask yourself the following questions: Where and when do I feel safe? threatened? What images do I see that represent my life in store windows? movie advertisements? magazine covers? television shows?

As teachers, we often unwittingly support heterosexist perspectives because they are the invisible norm for us. Think about your teaching goals and practices and ask yourself the following:

- When I hear that a child is growing up in a gay- or lesbian-headed household, what questions, concerns, and expectations come to mind? What about a child whose father is having a sex-change operation?
- What assumptions about gender and families were woven into my courses in child development and early childhood education? To what extent was heterosexism the assumed norm? Were there exceptions?
- How do I react when I see children dressing in cross-gender clothes?
- What images of families are represented in classroom photographs, calendars, and storybooks? Are families with one male and one female parent the "norm"? Or are other family constellations, including ones with two mothers and two fathers, also visible?
- In the dollhouse and puppet collections are there multiple adults so that children can enact stories about a range of family constellations?
- How do I respond to children's questions about gay and lesbian families? Do I encourage or stifle discussions? What makes me anxious about the prospect of having these discussions in my class?

## GROWING UP IN A HETEROSEXIST WORLD

Most people in this country are not judged by their sexual practices, but lesbian, gay, bisexual, and transgendered individuals are often judged *exclusively* by their choice of sexual partners and by others' assumptions about their sexual practices. A person can go through life working and living alongside others, but as soon as colleagues find out that this person is gay or lesbian, they often begin to define him or her *only* in terms of sexuality.

Most politicians and community leaders, regardless of their true feelings, avoid making overt derogatory remarks about race and gender because they know that discrimination on those bases is illegal. In contrast, many religious, government, and community leaders vociferously denounce gay, lesbian, bisexual, and transgendered individuals and seek to exclude them from equal protection under the law. Although they often base their arguments on religious and/or moral beliefs, these condemnations create a climate of hatred in which homophobic insults and violence occur with frequency and impunity.

In our society, homophobia is often a measure of "masculinity" (Kokopeli & Lakey, 1983). Thus, antipathy toward gay, lesbian, bisexual, and transgendered individuals is further fueled by people's own sexual anxieties and the sexual contradictions that pervade our national culture. On one hand, heterosexual attraction and performance are graphically portrayed and glorified in movies, television shows, commercials, popular songs, magazines, and on the Internet. On the other hand, we cling to our myths of sexual propriety and prudishly condemn extramarital sex and, in particular, people who openly disclose that they are gay, lesbian, bisexual, or transgendered. Because we are a society titillated and amused by sexual innuendoes, jokes about gay, lesbian, transgendered, and bisexual people are often considered acceptable even by people who would never tell an ethnic joke (Smith, 1983).

In the United States different sexual orientations are now more openly acknowledged than they were two or three decades ago. A number of networks and publications for and by gay people currently exist in different occupations (Casper, Cuffaro, Schultz, Silin, & Wickens, 1996). Still, in most schools sexual orientation is rarely mentioned and often actively evaded. In a series of interviews, teachers who were recognized for their skills in working with young children around sensitive issues of race, class, and gender admitted that they generally avoided the topic of sexual orientation (Alvarado, Derman-Sparks, & Ramsey, 1999). Not only are teachers uncomfortable with this issue themselves, but they also worry about the reaction of parents, principals, and community members. Given the vitriolic response to even token efforts to incorporate these issues into classrooms (Casper & Schultz, 1999), these concerns are justified.

Sexual orientation intersects with race, culture, and class. For people of color, coming out as gay, lesbian, bisexual, or transgendered puts them in a doubly vulnerable position for employment and legal protection. In strongly homophobic cultures, gay, lesbian, bisexual, or transgendered individuals must go to great lengths to conceal their sexual orientation or make the painful choice to leave their home cultures. In terms of employment, individuals with secure professional jobs may be less vulnerable to discrimination than those who are marginally employed. However, even in the most open-minded settings, they are still at risk for discrimination (e.g., not considered "appropriate" for supervising others or taking on highly visible projects). Casper and Schultz (1999) describe several situations that illustrate how race, social class, job security, and community attitudes influence decisions about whether and when to disclose sexual orientation.

## DILEMMAS OF GAY AND LESBIAN PARENTS

Gay and lesbian parents face particular dilemmas about disclosing their family relationships to their children's teachers and parents of their classmates. Unlike race and gender, sexual orientation is not obvious at first sight. Also, while schools often ask for information about cultural and economic backgrounds (the latter for establishing fees or obtaining vouchers), rarely do applications and intake questionnaires include items about sexual orientation. Thus, many gay and lesbian parents have the option of not revealing the nature of their family relationships. They may use general terms such as *friend* or *housemate* or may present themselves as single parents. At the same time, *not* disclosing exacts a high price because they must always be on their guard and cannot engage openly with teachers and other parents. Casper and Schultz (1999) vividly describe how difficult, painful, and complicated these decisions are. Using numerous examples, the authors illustrate the many factors that parents and teachers need to consider, such as the parents' goals for their children, the attitudes of other parents, the comfort level of the teachers, and the support of the administration. Teachers, even when they are supportive or themselves are gay, lesbian, bisexual, or transgendered, must be careful not to push parents to disclose their sexual orientations before they are ready (Kroeger, 2001). Above all, teachers must ensure that these discussions with parents are treated with absolute confidentially (Andrew et al., 2001).

## CHILDREN'S UNDERSTANDING OF SEXUAL ORIENTATION

To prepare for writing this section, I did several computer searches for studies about young children's understanding of sexual orientation and attitudes toward homosexuality and heterosexuality. I came up with very little. As mentioned previously, many people are vehemently opposed to any mention of sexual orientation in schools, making it virtually impossible to conduct formal studies on this topic.

We do know, however, from informal observations that heterosexism is often embedded in children's definitions of themselves as members of their particular gender (and, in some cases, ethnic) groups. Children frequently use homophobic insults (which they may not even understand) to enforce gender-role conformity. Heterosexism and rigid gender roles mutually support each other. Thus, helping children to develop more flexible gender assumptions and roles may be one way to counteract heterosexist attitudes.

Casper and Schultz (1999) did one of the very few studies on children's ideas about sexual orientation. They conducted extensive observations in early childhood classrooms that contained a number of children from openly gay- and lesbian-headed families. Their findings may not generalize to more closed, heterosexist environments, but they do give us an idea of the questions and concerns children would express if they were encouraged to do so.

Most of the children's questions and comments focused on whether or not someone needed to have both a mother and a father to be born and on who could make up a family. In their play, the children often argued over who was the mommy or the daddy and whether or not there could be two (or more) mommies or daddies. Preschoolers still have a fairly flexible idea of family membership, but they quickly learn from parents, teachers, older peers, and the media that families can have only one mommy and one daddy (which of course eliminates lots of families beside gay and lesbian ones).

Casper and Schultz noted that children were most likely to bring up questions about family composition and reproduction when they had ample time to develop their fantasy play and access to toys that gave them the latitude to play out different family constellations (e.g., multiple adult puppets). Books and pictures that portrayed a range of families including those with two mothers and two fathers also stimulated their questions and comments. Under these conditions, children as young as kindergartners demonstrated a fairly sophisticated understanding of gay and lesbian relationships and other family constellations that differed from the "typical" heterosexual nuclear family.

Older children, when encouraged, are able to express and explore their feelings about sexual orientation, as is illustrated in Chasnoff and Cohen's

(1996) videotape entitled *It's Elementary: Talking about Gay Issues in School.*
The video shows conversations between teachers and students from six elementary and middle schools across the country. In each dialogue, concepts
and attitudes about homosexuality are explored as part of schoolwide curricula on social justice. Many of the children initially express anxiety and stereotypes about homosexuality and gay/lesbian life. However, as they talk
about these issues with reflective teachers, they begin to recognize that these
views are unfounded, unjust, and potentially harmful to gay and lesbian people.

Casper and Schultz (1999) also observed and interviewed teachers and
found that teachers' own levels of comfort (or discomfort) affected their
reactions to children's questions about sexual orientation. In the interviews,
teachers often disclosed that they worried about encouraging children to talk
about gay and lesbian families because they feared the reactions of parents
or school administrators. Casper and Schultz point out that working closely
with colleagues and parents helps to alleviate this anxiety. Teachers can
identify and work closely with individuals who are supportive and think
carefully about how to approach those who are resistant. Many teachers are
also afraid to raise these issues because they assume that discussing gay and
lesbian families means that they will have to talk about sexual practices.
However, just as conversations about heterosexual families do not include
this information, there is no reason to bring it into discussions about gay
and lesbian families.

Despite the challenges, teachers need to become comfortable talking
about gay and lesbian families. If teachers try to avoid or suppress children's
questions, then children from these families may feel marginalized and face
conflicts in loyalties similar to those of children who are crossing racial, cultural, and class boundaries between home and school. Moreover, children
from heterosexual families will have their misinformation and stereotypes tac-
itly confirmed. Ironically, well-intentioned efforts to close the gap between
home and school sometimes reinforce heterosexist assumptions and may need
to be modified. When talking about families, teachers should be sure to include examples with same-sex parents, even if there are no gay or lesbian
families in the classroom. Mother's and Father's Days might be recast as
"Family Days." In short, we need to constantly reinforce the notion that families are formed in many ways and that what really matters is love and caring.

## HOW TO LEARN WHAT CHILDREN KNOW, THINK,
## AND FEEL ABOUT GENDER AND SEXUAL ORIENTATION

Individual children are usually quite forthright about their views on gender
and often reveal their feelings in their selection and rejection of playmates

and dramatic play roles. However, the power dynamics between boys and girls are often less obvious, and identifying them requires close observation. Learning what children think and feel about sexual orientation is challenging and potentially controversial. Teachers need to find subtle ways to learn what heterosexist assumptions underlie children's peer interactions and role play. To learn about children's views about gender-related issues, try the following strategies.

1. Observe children's play groups for gender divisions. Where and when are the groups most gender-segregated? least segregated? What happens when you merge centers or create mixed-gender teams? Which children accept/resist these arrangements?

2. Take note of the power differentials in the classroom. Are some boys attacking, dominating, or intimidating the girls? Or is power fairly balanced among the groups?

3. Show children photographs of people who represent different ages and genders and ask them whom they would go to for help, to play a ball game, to get food.

4. When children are playing with puppets and dolls, observe the roles that children assign to male and female figures. Which children enact rigid gender roles? Which ones play out more flexible ones?

5. Show children photographs of men, women, girls, and boys in both stereotyped and counterstereotyped activities and see how they react. Encourage them to describe what they notice about the person in the photograph and/or tell stories about different people.

6. Show the children photographs of different families, including gay and lesbian ones. Listen to their questions and comments and try to hear their underlying assumptions about gender, sexual orientation, and family composition.

7. Set up a few "families" in the dollhouse that represent same-sex parents. How do children react when they see these arrangements. What questions or comments do they have? What assumptions do they reflect?

8. Observe children's fantasy roles. Are they usually based on sex stereotypes, or are they more flexible? In particular, what assumptions are expressed in their enactment of family roles—in terms of both composition of families and the gender roles within them? What happens when two girls or two boys want to play the parents?

9. Listen to children's insults to see if they reflect negative assumptions related to gender (e.g., boys derisively calling each other "woman") or sexual orientation (the derogatory use of the term *gay*).

## ACTIVITIES TO CHALLENGE CHILDREN'S ASSUMPTIONS
## ABOUT GENDER AND SEXUAL ORIENTATION

Teachers' observations of children's role play and friendship patterns may give them ideas for ways to counteract biases and to help children develop flexible views of gender roles and family constellations. The following examples illustrate some possibilities.

Doreen, an African American, and Carl, a European American, were co-teachers of a group of 4- to 5-year-old children in a middle-class, predominately White preschool. They were dismayed to see how the children, who had played together happily for the first few months of school, were beginning to separate into exclusive boy and girl groups. They realized that this separation commonly occurred during late preschool, but they wanted to try to maintain a stronger sense of community in the classroom. Carl and Doreen were also concerned about a few children who were still attached to their cross-gender friends and were feeling bereft at the new segregation that their classmates were vociferously enforcing. As they observed the children, they noticed that the gender split was most obvious and self-reinforcing outside on the playground. The children frequently played a chase game in which the boys, growling like monsters, chased after the girls, who screamed in "terror." Not only did this game codify the gender split, but it also reinforced gender power differentials and stereotypes of aggressive males and helpless, scared females.

Doreen and Carl realized that simply forbidding the chase game would be counterproductive. Instead, they decided to share their concerns with the children, to hear what they enjoyed about the game, and to work toward some modifications. They also wanted the children to hear how their classmates who did not usually participate felt about the game.

After the initial discussion, the teachers showed the children books and pictures that illustrated how "chasing" is a part of many sports, played by both females and males throughout the world. Over several days, the children talked about what was fun about chasing and made connections between their experiences and those portrayed in the pictures. At one point they began to talk about teams and came up with the idea of forming "chasing teams." Doreen and Carl quickly seized on this idea and assigned the children to two gender-mixed teams for the next day's chasing game. They each worked with a team to help them cooperatively decide on a team name and cheer.

The next day the teams took turns chasing and being chased. The activity did not have the same high energy that the boy–girl chasing did, and several boys complained that it was not as much fun. But most of the children enjoyed it, and some who had not been part of the earlier chasing game participated. As the team chasing games continued, children also became interested in timing themselves running and learning how to run faster, which led to a number of different gender-mixed physical activities besides chasing.

As they talked about different sports, children began to pay more attention to sports coverage on television. A few girls commented about how they saw many more men's sports than women's. This concern led to a class investigation of sports coverage, which involved parents and children keeping records for a few weeks. Through this activity, parents and children began to see that, besides differences in the *amount* of coverage, men's sports events were also advertised more prominently and aired during better time slots. Several children and their parents wrote letters to television producers pointing out these inequities.

Paul, a Chinese American second-grade teacher in a racially and economically mixed public school, was distressed to hear his students use the word *gay* for anything that they thought was negative (e.g., "Those pants are so gay—why'd you buy them?" "I hate this project—it's sooo gay!"). He suspected that some of them did not even know what the word meant but realized that they were absorbing prevalent homophobic attitudes.

Given the sensitivity of the issue, he knew that he needed to communicate with the parents before talking with the children. From his earlier conversations with parents, he predicted that some parents would be supportive and that others would be vehemently opposed. He wrote a carefully worded letter, telling the parents what he had heard the children say and pointing out that they were learning to be prejudiced. He realized that some of the parents who might be the most resistant had themselves suffered from discrimination. Thus, he explicitly pointed out the connection between prejudice against gay and lesbian people and biases related to race, ethnicity, gender, social class, and disabilities. He then invited the parents to a meeting to discuss this problem and explore possible solutions. Many parents were upset, and there were many tensions between those who supported and those who opposed talking about sexual orientation with the children. Paul opened the meeting by reading the following familiar passage: "First they came for the Communists, but I was not a Communist so I did not speak out. Then they came for the Socialists and the Trade Unionists, but I was neither, so I did not speak out. Then they came for the Jews, but I was not a Jew so I did not speak out. And when they came for me, there was no one left to speak out for me" (Niemoeller, quoted in Jewish Virtual Library, 2004). As he slowly read, the parents were quiet and thoughtful. Paul then started the discussion by having each person state their feelings with no discussion, so that everyone had a chance to be heard. Then he talked about possible strategies with the children, and the discussion opened up. It was often heated, but it was also productive, and, by the end, the parents agreed on some guidelines and strategies that they were all more or less comfortable with. They also formed a small committee made up of parents with different views to work more closely with Paul as he implemented the strategies.

After more planning and several discussions with the committee, Paul then introduced the topic to the children by telling them that he had often heard them use the word *gay* and asking them what they meant by it. As he had suspected, a number of them had only a vague idea of what it meant. However, others did know, and some embellished their responses with other words, such as *faggot*. Paul then talked about sexual orientation in terms of families with same-sex couples (he had agreed with the parents not to discuss sexual practices, bisexuality, or transgendered people with the children). He then organized several activities about name-calling, including ones in which children talked about names that they had been called and how they felt.

Over the next several weeks, Paul invited several gay and lesbian people to visit the classroom to talk about their lives and to share their work with the children (e.g., a gay coach showed the children some new basketball moves; a lesbian chef did a cooking project) so that children could see that gay and lesbian people had lives, jobs, and children just like other adults they knew. Each visit also included a discussion about discrimination that the guest had experienced and how derogatory terms hurt them. After each visit, Paul sent a newsletter home that included the children's descriptions of the visit and some of the comments that children had made during the discussion. After the first couple of visits, Paul began to invite a few parents at a time to come to meet the guests and listen to the discussion. He was thrilled when one of the parents who had been most opposed showed up for one of the visits. She sat and listened and later in a subdued voice thanked him.

Paul was never sure to what extent he had changed parents' thinking, but the children in his class no longer used the word *gay* pejoratively (at least not in his hearing), and he sometimes heard them on the playground telling children in other classes not to use the term. His biggest surprise came several months after the original parent meeting. A mother who had been very quiet during all of the discussions told him that she was a lesbian and that for the first time she felt comfortable disclosing that fact to her child's teacher.

# CHAPTER 8

# The Context of Abilities and Disabilities

## REFLECTIONS ON ABILITIES AND DISABILITIES

In response to the question of "Who am I?" did you include whether or not you had a disability? Because "ableness" is another social norm in our culture, most people without identified disabilities rarely include that in their list. However, *all* of us have a range of abilities and disabilities, some more visible in our culture than others. We need to recognize this continuum and avoid making a sharp distinction between "abled" and "disabled." To understand how your own abilities and disabilities have affected your lives, ask yourself:

- What activities or tasks make me feel confident? uncomfortable or incompetent?
- What skills have been hard for me to learn? When I have had to struggle to learn something, how have I felt about myself? about people who grasped it more easily than I did?
- How have my strengths and limitations affected my schooling? job choices? social life?

The following comments and questions are directed primarily to readers who do not identify themselves as disabled. However, even those who do so identify may harbor misconceptions and concerns about other types of impairments and find it useful to go through these exercises.

Many people have strong emotional reactions to disabilities; they may feel fear, pity, or revulsion (Palmer, 2001). These reactions are normal, but we need to recognize and resolve them in order to create inclusive classrooms where children of all abilities are equal members. To begin that process, think about the fact that most individuals go through life being judged for what they *can* do, whereas people with identified disabilities are usually seen through a lens of what they *cannot* do. Moreover, people often assume that limitations in one area mean that other functions are also affected (e.g., a person who is deaf is also cognitively impaired and/or socially isolated).

To reflect on your emotional reactions and your assumptions related to disabilities, ask yourself the following questions:

- How do I react when I meet an adult or child with a disability? Do I feel pity? respect? curiosity? revulsion? afraid that the same thing might happen to me or a member of my family? Since anyone can become disabled in a moment (e.g., car accident, bad fall), seeing someone with a disability often evokes this fear.
- What assumptions about the person's capabilities do I make on the basis of the disability? Are they warranted or not?
- Do I find myself immediately wanting to help or protect the person? Or do I wait for them to ask for assistance?
- How would I react if I learned that my new doctor used a wheelchair? my child's teacher for next year was blind? the person who had just moved in next door had been in a psychiatric hospital? the applicant for the school secretary job had severe facial scarring from burns?

As you think about these situations, note your initial reactions and then try to shift your focus away from what the individuals *cannot* do to what they *can* do. For example, a teacher who is blind may not be able to watch children with his eyes but may be sensitive to the emotional subtleties in children's voices that a sighted teacher might miss. Also, children in his class may have opportunities to learn nuances of sound, touch, smell, and taste that they might not experience with a sighted teacher.

## GROWING UP IN AN "ABLED" WORLD

How we define abilities and disabilities and respond to them is, to a large extent, culturally and economically determined. For example, in a society where livelihoods and social prestige depend on cooperating with other group members, a person lacking social skills may be seen as more disabled than someone who cannot read. In our society, where logical and analytical thinking is valued, people who hear voices are labeled as emotionally disturbed; in a spiritual and mystical society, these same people might be regarded as seers blessed by divine wisdom (Fadiman, 1997). Economic disadvantage and cultural discontinuities between schools and families often contribute to academic and social difficulties (as discussed in Chapters 5 and 6) that result in diagnoses of disability (Brown, 1998; M. E. Franklin,

1992; Odom et al., 1996). Thus, children from marginalized groups are often overrepresented in special education programs (Hilliard, 1992). Moreover, future prospects of children with disabilities are affected by the affluence of their families. Parents with more money and skills at working with bureaucracies are better positioned to get optimal equipment and services for their children than are those who are poor, new to this country, and/or intimidated by school personnel (Hanson, 2002).

In the United States, the approach to disabilities has changed over the past 30 years. Until the 1970s children with clearly identified disabilities (e.g., cerebral palsy, Down Syndrome) were usually placed in special classrooms and isolated from their "typical" peers. Children with milder or less identifiable disabilities, such as cognitive delays or attention-deficit disorder, usually remained undiagnosed and struggled to keep up in regular classrooms. After the 1970s, and particularly since the passage of PL 94-142 and PL 99-457, the principle of offering children services in the "least restricted environment" has guided efforts to ensure that "all children, no matter how diverse their needs, should expect to be served in the regular education setting that they would attend at any specific age" (Sheridan, Foley, & Radlinski, 1995, p. 42).

With the passage of the Americans with Disabilities Act in 1990, people with disabilities began to enter all institutions and organizations of our society. Yet fully integrating them into the society continues to be a challenge. The general public still tends to see children and adults with disabilities as second-class citizens, burdens, objects of pity, and incapable of making positive contributions. They are expected to accept their second-class-citizen status, have "realistic" (read "low") expectations, and be grateful for the few limited opportunities and rights they have been given (Turnball & Turnball, 1991). Despite some changes, there are still few images in the popular press that counteract this demeaning view by depicting people with disabilities as active, creative, and adventurous.

Efforts to include children with disabilities in regular classrooms (originally referred to as "mainstreaming") have followed a number of different models. In some cases, children go to special classrooms to get help in specific academic areas and spend the rest of their time in regular classrooms. This arrangement provides needed academic support but potentially disrupts the children's day and puts them at a disadvantage both socially and academically, as is illustrated by the following excerpt from Polakow's (1993) observations of Heather:

> Heather is taken out [of her class while they are working on math worksheets] and goes to the special education room for remedial reading. When she returns, math is over, and the children begin a social studies unit about Japan.

"Sit down and pay attention so you can make up what you missed," says Mrs. Mack. Heather stands looking lost next to her desk as the children are busy gathering papers. She has to miss recess so as to make up her lost social studies time, and never does get back to her math sheet that day. (p. 139)

Alternatively, specialists or aides come into the regular classroom and work with the students there. This arrangement smoothes the transitions for the children and keeps classroom teachers and specialists in closer contact. However, children with very extensive one-on-one assistance have almost a private class within the classroom and may be socially isolated because they are perceived as incompetent by their peers and do not participate in ongoing classroom activities (Siegel, 1996).

The movement to include children with disabilities into regular classrooms has been lauded by many but also has been controversial. The financial and time demands on schools and teachers have spawned some resistance. Teachers often feel overwhelmed trying to attend to a variety of "special needs" as well as the needs of the whole class, especially if they lack training in working with children with disabilities and do not have adequate support in their schools (Gemmell-Crosby & Hanzik, 1994). Without training (which should include opportunities for teachers to identify and challenge their assumptions about children with disabilities), teachers are vulnerable to seeing children with disabilities as objects of pity. They may overprotect them and/or lower their expectations and thereby unwittingly undermine the children's self-esteem and willingness to try hard in school (M. D. Clark, 1997). Even teachers who are knowledgeable about and embrace the principle of inclusion find that their implementation is constrained by time, lack of resources, space, staff, and materials (Odom, McConnell, & Chandler, 1993). Parents who support the concept of inclusion may have concerns when it involves their children (Diamond, Hestenes, & O'Connor, 1994). Those with "typical" children may worry that their children will be shortchanged because teachers are spending so much time with children with special needs. Parents of children with disabilities sometimes express fears that their children and they themselves will be socially excluded or that their children will not get needed services in a regular classroom.

Effective inclusion of children with disabilities requires a multifaceted approach including close coordination among parents, teachers, and specialists; careful scheduling of transportation, tutoring, and medications; and creative adaptations of curricula, classroom routines, and the physical environment. A full consideration of all of these aspects is beyond the scope of this book. Fortunately, a number of resources exist (e.g., Kemple, 2004; Kostelnick, Onaga, Rohde, & Whiren, 2002; Odom, 2002; Sheridan et al., 1995) that describe excellent strategies and examples of successful inclusive classrooms. In this chapter, I will focus on two aspects that are most germane to multicultural education: the social integration of children with special needs and children's ideas and feelings about disabilities.

## SOCIAL INTEGRATION OF CHILDREN WITH DISABILITIES

Despite many legal and educational reforms, children with disabilities are often socially and academically isolated from their peers (Diamond, Le Furgy, & Blass, 1993; Nabors, 1995; Pearl et al., 1998; Sheridan et al., 1995). In the United States, the emphases on individual achievement and high-stakes testing make authentic inclusion particularly difficult because children at an early age learn to judge themselves and others by what they can do and what they know. I vividly recall how, when my son Daniel walked through the door of his kindergarten on the first day of school, he was greeted by a child saying, "I can count up to 100, can you?"

Social inclusion in preschools is a little easier than it is in grade schools because teachers are not as bound by mandated curricula (although, unfortunately, this may change as high-stakes testing reaches into lower and lower grades). Also, preschoolers are rarely divided into ability groups, which highlight skill differences. Because most preschoolers have uneven developmental profiles, children with specific disabilities may not appear to be that different from their peers, and teachers are accustomed to adjusting activities to meet a wide range of skill levels. Moreover, the wide range of activities offered in preschool classrooms (art projects, block building, physical activities) means that children who have difficulty with one type of learning situation have alternatives (i.e., they do not have to sit at a desk the whole time).

Odom and colleagues (2002) did an extensive study of children's social inclusion in 16 preschool programs. They found that across all of them about one-third of the children with disabilities were rejected and one-third were well liked by their peers. The latter group tended to be easygoing and affectionate, to be socially and communicatively skilled, to behave in emotionally appropriate and positive ways, and to be willing to follow classroom routines and rules. Those disliked by their peers were aggressive, disruptive, withdrawn, lacked communication skills (i.e., had speech/language problems), and often engaged in conflicts with peers and adults (Odom et al., 2002). Interestingly, these behaviors are similar to those found in general populations of accepted and rejected children (Ramsey, 1991a). When asked how they feel about their classmates with disabilities, young children often say that they dislike them because they are disruptive and/or aggressive (Nabors & Keyes, 1995; Roberts & Zubrick, 1992). Thus, children with behavioral and emotional disabilities are particularly likely to be rejected by peers.

Furthermore, when these children are rejected by socially skilled classmates, they sometimes connect with classmates who, while not identified as disabled, are aggressive and defiant. These relationships, which in one sense are inclusive, often undermine, rather than support, children's social skill development and their full integration into the social mainstream (Pearl et al.,1998).

Unfortunately, some children with disabilities become more isolated during the schoolyear (Diamond et al., 1993; Guralnick & Groom, 1987), demonstrating that merely having contact with each other does not break down the barriers between children with and without disabilities. At the beginning of the year, children with disabilities may start to develop mutual friendships with their peers without disabilities. However, after a while, children with disabilities often get left behind when the play becomes more complex and requires more advanced social and cognitive skills (Guralnick, Connor, Hammond, Gottman, & Kinnish, 1996). Interestingly, children with disabilities do not always "see" their rejection, often telling teachers and interviewers that they have more friends than is evident from their classmates' comments about them (Helper, 1994).

The social impact of a disability can be affected by gender, race, culture, and social class. Girls with learning disabilities have the lowest status in classrooms (Helper, 1994; Juvonen & Bear, 1992). Juvonen and Bear speculate that, because girls are usually expected to be more academically and socially competent, those with learning disabilities are seen as especially deviant and therefore excluded. Boys, on the other hand, tend to be more inclusive because they play in larger groups that have more fluid boundaries than girls' smaller, more intimate groups do (Nabors, 1997). In some classrooms, the isolation of children with disabilities may be exacerbated if they are racially or culturally a minority in that setting. If they and their parents speak a language other than English, they may have difficulty communicating with teachers and other children; and their parents and teachers may not be able to form close partnerships to provide optimal support (Hanson, Gutierrez, Morgan, Brennan, & Zercher, 1997).

Social isolation, however, is not inevitable and may be overreported. Odom and colleagues (2002) found that one-third of the children with disabilities were accepted by their peers. Even children who are quite distant from the social mainstream often have one friend who serves as a social buffer and provides companionship (Juvonen & Bear, 1992). Social acceptance may also vary by the situation and the nature of the disability. For example, children are more likely to ignore or reject peers with orthopedic limitations when they are planning or doing physical activities (Harper, Wacker, & Cobb, 1986). On the other hand, children who are unable to hear can still engage in these activities and can use sign language, which their classmates often enjoy learning (Swadener & Johnson, 1989).

Successfully integrating children with disabilities requires hope, determination, flexibility, and creativity. Kostelnik and colleagues (2002) describe Rosie, who, due to severe cerebral palsy, was unable to use her arms or legs and could not speak or control her bladder. However, she became part of the social mainstream of her preschool classroom through the tireless efforts of her teacher, who carefully planned every detail of the classroom to best meet Rosie's needs and integrate her into the class (e.g., how to work with the parents and specialists, introduce Rosie to the other children, support her without overprotecting her, maintain age-appropriate expectations, get her physically closer to the other children). As the children got to know Rosie, they learned how to play with her (she communicated with her eyes) and even to tease and joke with her. At the end of the year, she was one of the most well-liked children in the class.

As this example illustrates, adults play a crucial role in the social inclusion of children with disabilities. A number of studies and reviews (Gonsier-Gerdin, 1995; Kemple, 2004; Kostelnik et al., 2002; Odom, 2002; Odom, Jenkins, Speltz, & DeKlyen, 1982; Odom et al., 1996; Sheridan et al., 1995; Swadener & Johnson, 1989) have identified specific ways in which teachers and parents can facilitate the integration of children with disabilities into social life both inside and outside of classrooms. A few of their points are summarized here:

1. Adults need to be determined and optimistic that children will be socially included.
2. Parents, teachers, and specialists must listen to each other and form mutual partnerships and collaborations.
3. Children with disabilities should be identified by everyone, including themselves, as full members of the group and an integral part of all activities.
4. Integration must go beyond the classroom to include outside play dates with classmates and participation in community events and activities (e.g., swimming lessons, library story hours).
5. When adults obviously enjoy interacting with children with disabilities and support interactions between them and their peers, children with disabilities participate more fully in classroom social life.
6. Adults can facilitate social interactions in a number of ways, including (but not limited to) the following:

   - Closely monitoring the social contacts of children with disabilities (how often and with whom they are interacting)
   - Providing activities to develop social skills and positive peer relations (e.g., stories and skits that address social situations)

- Explicitly instructing children who lack social skills how to enter groups, ask for materials, resolve conflicts, and so on
- Subtly supporting children as they play together (e.g., intervening before a conflict occurs; helping a child physically follow her friends as they move to a new area)
- Setting up a variety of activities in which children can interact at different levels (e.g., working side by side versus actively cooperating)
- Providing enough academic support so that children are not floundering and getting frustrated
- Organizing cooperative activities to encourage more participation

As we work with children of all abilities, we must constantly question our goals and assumptions. For example, in our enthusiasm for inclusion, we need to be sure that we are not forcing the one-way assimilation that has been experienced by many ethnic groups. Besides encouraging connections with peers with and without disabilities, programs should also include opportunities for children with disabilities to form friendships with each other and to enjoy being a member of those groups as well (Harry, Park, & Day, 1998). We also need to recognize that our goal of preparing all children to live as self-sufficient adults reflects the dominant cultural value of independence in the United States. This aspiration, however, may not mesh with the expectations of families who assume that their children with disabilities will be cared for by the extended family for the rest of their lives (Harry, 1998). We also need to continually and critically reflect on how an overemphasis on individual performance and competition hurts children of all abilities and undermines our efforts to create accepting and respectful communities. Finally, we have to challenge negative stereotypes of people with disabilities and the very notion that the world is divided into people with and without disabilities.

## CHILDREN'S KNOWLEDGE AND FEELINGS RELATED TO ABILITIES AND DISABILITIES

Knowing how children think and feel about disabilities can help teachers address children's concerns and misinformation and encourage more social inclusion. Many studies in the past two decades have contributed to our knowledge about children's awareness of and attitudes related to disabilities (for a comprehensive review, see Diamond & Innes, 2001).

Children's awareness and understanding varies across type of disability (Conant & Budoff, 1983; Diamond, 1993; Diamond & Hestenes, 1996).

Children often notice sensory and orthopedic disabilities first (DeGrella & Green, 1984; Diamond & Hestenes, 1996), because of the visibility of the associated equipment, such as crutches, wheelchairs or hearing aids, whereas they are least aware of cognitive or psychological disabilities. This variability is not surprising, because children also tend to interpret disabilities on the basis of their own experience (Diamond & Innes, 2001). For example, they can compare blindness with not being able to see in a dark room (Conant & Budoff, 1983), but they may not be conscious of how their cognitions and emotions function and therefore have difficulty understanding disabilities in those areas (Nabors & Keyes, 1995).

Many children have misconceptions about the causes of disabilities. They often explain disabilities by the equipment that children use (Diamond & Innes, 2001) (e.g., "He can't walk because he has a wheelchair"). Alternatively, they assume that disabilities are related to immaturity (e.g., "She hasn't learned to talk yet") or some kind of illness, injury, or other trauma (e.g.,"He had a really bad earache and now can't hear") (Diamond, 1993; Diamond & Hestenes, 1996; Sigelman, 1991).

Children's attitudes toward people with disabilities shift during their preschool and elementary school years. Preschoolers often state that they could be friends with peers with disabilities (Diamond & Hestenes, 1996). However, as they get older, children tend to develop more biases against persons with disabilities (DeGrella & Green, 1984; Goodman, 1989). In elementary school, children become more aware of specific peers and are often concerned about how their skills compare with those of others. Thus, classmates who cannot do the physical or academic activities that form the context of peer interactions may become less desirable. As they get older, children are also more likely to reject peers who are labeled and are treated in ways that make them stand out (Milich, McAnnich, & Harris, 1992), underscoring the need to avoid using labels and to administer medications and services in unobtrusive ways.

As interactions between children with and without disabilities decline, they have less common ground on which to build friendships, so that the children with disabilities may become increasingly isolated. Moreover, during the elementary school years, mutual friendships between peers with and without disabilities tend to shift to lopsided caretaking relationships. Often friends of children with disabilities are pushed into that role by teachers and peers who rely on them to communicate with and accompany children with disabilities (Grenot-Scheyer, Staub, Peck, & Schwartz, 1998; Salisbury & Palombar, 1998).

Children's attitudes vary across type of disability. As mentioned before, children are most likely to reject their peers with emotional and cognitive disabilities. Emotional disturbances that cause children to act unpredictably may lead their peers to distrust and avoid them. Likewise, impulsive behavior is often interpreted as misbehavior (Kostelnick et al., 2002). Because children do not usually understand the parameters of cognitive and language disabilities, they also tend to make more generalized negative assumptions about peers with cognitive and language delays than they do about peers with physical disabilities (Diamond, 1994). Children are also more accepting toward their peers who have disabilities that are clearly no fault of their own (e.g., blindness) than they are toward peers perceived as having more responsibility for their disability (e.g., obesity, poor impulse control) (Diamond & Innes, 2001).

Despite many challenges, integrating children with disabilities into regular classrooms clearly has advantages. Many studies show that children with disabilities thrive both socially and academically in inclusive settings (see Diamond & Innes, 2001; Odom, 2002). Moreover, children without disabilities also benefit; they become more sensitive to other people and more accepting of differences (Diamond, Hestenes, Carpenter, & Innes, 1997; Favazza & Odom, 1997). In some cases, they also develop more confidence by assisting peers with disabilities. The downside of these advantages, however, is the tendency for children without disabilities to treat their peers with disabilities as more helpless than they are and to "do things for [them] rather than with [them]" (Salisbury & Palombar, 1998). Teachers need to help children understand the nature and parameters of specific disabilities and to distinguish respectful and appropriate support from intrusive or demeaning services. Moreover, teachers should use every opportunity to emphasize the strengths of children with disabilities and the similarities between children with and without disabilities (Kostelnik et al., 2002; Palmer, 2001).

## HOW TO LEARN WHAT CHILDREN KNOW, THINK, AND FEEL ABOUT ABILITIES AND DISABILITIES

Classrooms where some children have obvious disabilities provide many opportunities to observe how children with and without impairments interact. In other cases, the disabilities may be more subtle and children may not be consciously aware of them, although they may react to behaviors that make them uncomfortable. In both situations, teachers need to be alert for signs that children with disabilities are becoming isolated. Teachers can also observe and listen for children's anxieties about their abilities (e.g., children who are scared to climb on the slide or who avoid all art projects). To get a sense of the classroom dynamics and to learn what individual children are thinking and feeling, teachers can do the following:

1. Observe interactions between children with and without disabilities. Are children with disabilities socially involved or are they on the periphery? What roles are children with and without disabilities playing in fantasy play? physical activities? academic tasks? Are there any signs of domination or overprotectiveness?

2. Show children dolls, puppets, and pictures that depict people with different types of disabilities. Ask them to describe the people in the pictures and see whether or not disabilities are salient. If they mention the disability, then ask them follow-up questions to see what they understand about the causes and effects of disabilities.

3. Put these dolls and puppets out in the classroom and see how the children play with them—what roles they assign them and the kinds of stories they create.

4. Show children counterstereotyped pictures of people with disabilities (e.g., blind skiers, wheelchair basketball players, amputee construction workers) and listen to their reactions.

5. Read stories or put on puppet shows about children and adults with disabilities. How do children respond? What are their assumptions? instances of misinformation?

6. Use sign language in storytelling and singing, and see how children react. Teach them how to use some sign language, and see if they can grasp the fact that for some people, sign language serves the same purpose as talking. For children who can read, do similar activities with Braille.

7. Have children go through a series of activities in which they briefly experience the effects of different disabilities. Listen to their questions and assumptions and help them empathize with (not pity!) people with these disabilities and see how they develop compensating skills. Be careful, however, that these exercises do not lead children to exaggerate the helplessness of people with specific disabilities or to enact negative stereotypes of them (Palmer, 2001).

8. Listen carefully for children using disability-related insults, such as *retard*, *spaz*, or *crip*. If you hear these words, talk to the children using them and try to find out what they understand about them and where they learned them.

## ACTIVITIES TO CHALLENGE CHILDREN'S ASSUMPTIONS ABOUT ABILITIES AND DISABILITIES

As teachers observe children with and without disabilities interacting with each other, they may identify social dynamics that they want to change in order to make the classroom more inclusive. Likewise, children's comments, questions, and concerns about disabilities may reveal fears and stereotypes that teachers can challenge through a variety of activities. For all children, with and without identified disabilities, the opportunity to talk about a range of similarities and differences may help to blur the distinctions between abled and disabled and alleviate their anxieties about their competence in different areas.

James, an African American, and Tara, a Chinese American, were teachers in a racially mixed Head Start classroom. They were frustrated by the constant conflicts between Bobby, a Japanese American who had been diagnosed with attention-deficit/hyperactivity disorder (ADHD), and the rest of his classmates. Bobby was bright and could be a lot of fun, but frequently he rushed into play spaces, destroying everything in his path. When he was frustrated, he would strike out either with words or fists. Not surprisingly, the other children avoided him, and the teachers frequently overheard comments about how "bad" Bobby was. A couple of children had made comments that suggested that they were beginning to associate Bobby's race with his behavior.

James and Tara decided to take turns watching Bobby and his interactions with both teachers and peers to get a better idea of what was happening. After a couple of days, they noticed that they themselves often publicly reprimanded Bobby and that rarely did they or anyone else in the classroom say anything positive to him. As they watched, it also became clear that many of the conflicts occurred when Bobby was trying to integrate himself into playgroups. They discussed their observations with Bobby's parents, who were very concerned and willing to help, as they were hoping to avoid using medication at this point. Together, the teachers and parents decided on the following plan, which would be followed at school and, as much as possible, at home: (1) engage in positive interactions with Bobby; (2) decrease the number of reprimands and avoid making them in public; (3) prevent conflicts by helping Bobby to both enter and stay in playgroups; (4) work with the other children to help them see Bobby's positive attributes and to be more patient and less judgmental; (5) increase the time that Bobby was able to do physical activities; and (6) help him learn ways of calming himself down (e.g., taking a few deep breaths).

They talked to Bobby, and together they implemented this plan. There were several rocky moments, but Tara and James learned to anticipate and prevent conflicts and slowly retrained themselves to stop making public reprimands. Most significantly, when they made a point of having positive contacts with Bobby, they found that they started enjoying their times with him and that the other children, noticing the fun, were often eager to join them.

They encouraged Bobby to spend time with a couple of children who were patient and calm and not bothered by his constant chatter and motion. As he became more confident in his peer interactions, he was less anxious and able to stay with a group for longer periods of time.

Bobby still had many conflicts, and his reputation did not die easily. Some of the children continued to talk about how "bad" he was and avoided or teased him. James and Tara read some books to the children and performed a few puppet shows that (often humorously) focused on the problems of judging people. They made sure that their examples would not single out Bobby but would encourage children to think a moment before making assumptions about their peers. Bobby continued to be a challenging child in the classroom, but the teachers felt that at least they had interrupted and maybe even reversed Bobby's slide into social isolation.

José, a Chilean American, taught in a economically and racially mixed school. He was disheartened by how often his third graders called each other *retard*—usually spoken with slurred speech and accompanied by flapping hands. Clearly, the children had learned and were busily reinforcing negative stereotypes of people with Down Syndrome. He decided to first learn what they knew about Down Syndrome. The children revealed lots of negative images and misinformation and were also worried that it might be contagious. As they spoke, he could also see how the emphasis on individual academic success had made this disability a particularly terrifying one for the children. He decided to try to challenge those values and the notion that you could divide up the world into abled and disabled people.

José made up a game called "What if you lived in _____ land?" which he played with the children a couple of days each week over the next month. Each time they played, he would present the children with a challenge such as seeing how long they could stand on one foot without falling, sing a tune perfectly after hearing it once, roll their tongues, and other tasks. He chose tasks that were nonthreatening and that required different types of skills so that all the children experienced more or less equal amounts of failure and success. After everyone had tried the challenge of the day, he would divide the class according to who could and could not do it. José then labeled the ones who could not do it (he always made sure that it was a fairly large group so no one felt singled out) by a derogatory-sounding term (e.g., "tuneless toners," "flat tongues") and had the successful group show off their skills. Then he encouraged the children to talk about how they felt being labeled in that fashion. When the children protested (e.g., "It's not fair to make fun of us because we can't roll our tongues!!"), José made the connection between their frustration and anger and the effects of calling people *retarded.* After several rounds of the game, the children began to "get it" and the use of *retard* as an insult diminished. In fact, a few children even told friends not in the class to stop using it on the playground.

However, José was still concerned that this insult had started to be used in the first place and (as he knew from friends and family) that all over the country children were using it. So he and the children tracked down images in the media—television, movies, video games, icons on the computer—that glorified "smart" people and derided "stupid" people. Then they began to write letters to producers and sponsors protesting the negative images.

José also consciously tried to avoid drawing attention to differences in children's academic performance in order to reduce children's concerns about who was "stupid" and "smart" (e.g., he shifted from ability-based reading groups to ones into which children self-selected every 2 weeks based on their interest in the stories being read by the different groups). Unfortunately, state tests, which dominated the spring and generated scores that rated children from "advanced" to "failing," undermined these efforts, but he tried as hard as he could to minimize those effects.

As he learned more about disability issues, José got in touch with some local activists, who visited the school and talked to the children about how they felt when people made fun of them. They also talked about what they were doing to change community and workplace policies, and they and the children generated ideas about how the children could be involved (e.g., the children made posters for a local rally for disability rights, and several participated in the rally with their families).

José suspected that a few children were still secretly calling each other *retard*, but felt that overall the peer culture had shifted from supporting stereotypes of people with disabilities to supporting the struggle for disability rights.

# PART III

# A Vision of the Future

To illustrate the issues, goals, and guidelines that I have described in the previous chapters, I am concluding this book by telling a story—a vision of what schools, families, and communities could accomplish by working together. It is unrealistic in many ways. Obstacles such as financial constraints, work schedules, and conflicts melt away more easily and quickly than they do in real life. Also, to provide as many examples as I could, I deliberately crammed more activities and reflections about them into the day than would be possible. Yet each incident and curriculum idea is based on real people and situations in many different schools. As you read it, you will see how the goals discussed in Chapter 1 can be implemented in many different ways.

This story is told from the vantage points of a female teacher and a father, both White, middle-class, able-bodied, and heterosexual. I chose these voices because they are the perspectives that I can represent most authentically. Also, people who are racially and economically privileged are often the most reluctant to critically examine societal inequities. I wanted to provide a counterexample of people who were able to see beyond their self-interest in preserving the status quo and open themselves up to new experiences and perspectives.

I enjoyed writing this story—imagining what it would be like if community people, teachers, administrators, and families truly collaborated to develop and support multicultural programs and more open and livable communities. I hope that you as a reader will find it a hopeful vision and a source of practical ideas.

# CHAPTER 9

# A Day at Wilson Street School

Laura hopped off the bus, hoisting her heavy backpack onto her shoulders, and walked briskly toward Wilson Street Elementary School. As she hurried along, she mentally reviewed the list of things she needed to do to prepare her kindergarten classroom for the day. Her shoulders ached a bit, and she regretted momentarily that today was one of her "no-car" days. A few months ago, the parents and staff of the school had come up with a novel idea to reduce their dependence on cars and to raise money for the special programs at the school. Each participating parent and staff member had asked friends and family members to pledge a donation to the school for every day that the parent or staff member did not use a car. It had been a big challenge, but everyone had come up with creative ways to transport themselves and their materials—using public transportation, bicycles, strollers, wagons, and wheeled suitcases. It had also inspired several classroom studies on transportation (e.g., learning about transportation in different parts of the world, analyzing current vehicles for their fuel consumption and pollution, and "inventing" new and more efficient ones). Still, "auto-independence" continued to be a challenge.

As Laura walked through the door of the school, she paused as usual to admire the displays of different school projects all over the lobby. She noticed a new poster of the third graders' investigations about the effects of a new power plant on local electricity rates (they went up) and on the wildlife on the banks of a local river. She recalled David, one of the third-grade teachers, describing how he and his students had spent several days camping on the banks of a local river observing wildlife habitats and experimenting with small erosion-control devices that the children had read about or invented. It had been a challenge, especially for students who had not spent much time in wilderness areas. However, after a few days, they had seemed to "connect" with their surroundings, and everyone had become involved in protecting the habitats along the shore line.

As she walked down the hall, Laura thought about how much the school had changed in the last 5 years after the arrival of their new principal, Gloria Robinson. A young, dynamic African American woman, Gloria was committed to multicultural, social justice, and environmental education. She had

come into a relatively well-run but complacent school and had—as they
say—shaken things up. Laura smiled and shook her head a little as she
recalled the turmoil. Gloria had started with a series of meetings with parents
and intensive in-service workshops with the teachers in which she explained
her goals and tried to get both parents and teachers involved in the process.
As the year went on, the workshops were opened to parents as well as
teachers because, as Gloria had said, "We are in this together—the school
can't change if the families don't change, and families can't change if the
school doesn't change; we need to support each other and learn together."

Gloria had realized that the teachers needed more support and that only
a few families (mostly White and affluent) and no community people were
involved in the school. She formed a committee of teachers and parents who
developed a program to encourage family members and retired people
(called community elders) to participate in school decision making and to
work in classrooms on a regular basis. Because the school was 80% White
and mostly middle and working class, Gloria had helped teachers find "partner schools" with different populations in other parts of the city and in other
countries with whom they could exchange visits—if possible—or videotapes,
letters, and e-mail.

Initially, Laura had been resistant to all these changes. A successful
kindergarten teacher at the school for 15 years, she had never seen any signs
of prejudice in her kindergartners and did not see the need for young children to learn about racism, poverty, or environmental degradation. Moreover, she knew that she wasn't a racist and resented the time these discussions took away from her own family. However, during parent conferences
that first February, Bernice and Shawn, the parents of one of the two African
American children in her class, mentioned how difficult it was for their
daughter to be in a virtually all-White classroom. Laura quickly reassured
them that Jeannette was doing fine and that they did not need to worry. As
she saw them exchange skeptical looks and heard them sigh, she suddenly
remembered a recent staff discussion about how White people often do not
see and therefore dismiss concerns about racism. She stopped talking, apologized, and asked the parents to tell her more. As they described subtle ways
in which their daughter felt excluded by peers and by the absence of images
and toys that reflected her background, Laura felt defensive and wanted to
prove to them that their daughter's interpretations were wrong. But again,
recalling the discussion, she remained quiet and listened carefully. At the
end, she thanked the parents and told them that they had given her a lot to
think about and that she would like to continue the conversation. During the
next few days Laura observed the children closely and noticed that the two
African American children were more on the periphery of groups than most
of the White children were. She also looked around and realized that there

were very few books or photographs that portrayed children of color and
that the Black dolls were often left in the housekeeping corner, while the
White dolls were in constant use. She was shocked that she had not noticed
these patterns before, and suddenly all of the discussions over the past few
months began to make sense. She also realized that the parents probably
would not have brought up their concerns had Gloria not encouraged families and staff to openly discuss these issues.

Over the next few years Laura had often felt angry, hurt, and discouraged as she had slowly and painfully recognized her privileges—as an able-
bodied, heterosexual, middle-class White—and challenged deeply held beliefs
and assumptions. She knew she still had a long way to go, but sometimes
she had moments of joy when she felt genuinely connected with people
whom she had not known or even thought about a few years ago. She was
beginning to see herself and the world in some new ways. It was scary but
exciting.

As she approached her classroom, Laura turned her attention to the
practicalities of her day in the kindergarten. She mentally reviewed which
adults would be in the classroom that day: two parents, Robert (European
American) and Susan (Korean American), and two community elders, Rose
(Irish American) and Herb (African American). She smiled as she thought
about Robert, the father of her student Alison. When his oldest son Jed had
been in her class 3 years ago, she had watched Robert, a widower and single
father, evolve from a skeptical workaholic software engineer to an enthusias-
tic classroom participant. Like Laura, he had initially rejected Gloria's ideas,
but after hearing his son's excitement about classroom projects and seeing
the children's performances and displays, he became more involved. With
considerable effort and anxiety, Robert had adjusted his work hours to do
more at home in the evenings and free up one day a week to work in the
school. With Laura's encouragement, Robert had also joined a family support group that she had helped to start. "Families For a Full Future"—the
4-F Club, as they jokingly referred to it—was a group of about 50 families—two-parent, single-parent, gay, lesbian, straight, blended, foster—from
a range of racial, cultural, and socioeconomic backgrounds. They supported
each other to bring their own lives into a better balance and to struggle for
a more equitable society. They participated in local and national social justice and environmental movements and supported the school in a variety of
ways (e.g., getting publicity for events and the children's projects). Group
members also provided alternative family activities to shopping, TV, and
fast food by organizing pot-luck suppers, hikes, workshops, and workdays
in various parts of the city.

Laura walked into her classroom, and soon Robert, Susan, Herb, and
Rose entered. While Robert and Susan's children played quietly in the block

area, Laura quickly briefed them on the day, and they all put out paints and other materials. The class was engaged in a complex study about food—how it is grown and prepared and why some people have more than they need and others do not have enough. The curriculum was evolving as children raised questions, and families and community people offered ideas and resources. Right now the children were learning about breads. Plastic replicas of different breads were in the housekeeping area, and the block area had become a "bakery"—a shift that had encouraged more girls to participate in the area. Today, Rose was going to make Irish soda bread, which she had learned to make as a child. She planned to tell stories about her childhood as the children ate the bread for snack. The class was also involved in an ongoing garden project. Last week Susan and Robert had helped the children dig up the soil of a small classroom garden, and today they were going to plant seeds. Herb, meanwhile, would help individual children record the changes in their "experimental" plants (being grown with various amounts of water and sunshine) that had occurred since his visit the week before.

The children began to arrive, and, as soon as everyone was there, Laura gathered them for the opening ritual of the day. As Robert watched, he recalled Laura's conversation with parents about rituals and how she tried to use them to build a sense of community not just within the classroom but with all people and the natural world. He remembered many intense discussions about rituals and holidays at the school. Some parents and teachers felt that it was safer not to observe any holidays, especially given the five Jehovah's Witness families in the school, whose religion forbids any participation in celebrations, including birthday parties. Others, however, felt that holidays and rituals were meaningful ways of noting the passage of time and building a sense of community. A committee of parents and teachers had been developing guidelines and related activities to incorporate holidays in ways that avoided stereotypical images of groups and fit the overall goals of the school. Recently there had been some discussions about the dilemmas inherent in state and national holidays such as Presidents' Day, the Fourth of July, Columbus Day, and Thanksgiving (e.g., many Native People regard Thanksgiving as the National Day of Mourning). The committee was gathering resources about national holidays (in other countries as well as the United States) that focus on struggles against oppression (e.g., Labor Day, Martin Luther King Day). They were discussing ways to encourage children to think critically about who is remembered and celebrated (e.g., we honor Abraham Lincoln—a White male—but not the African American slaves and freedmen who had resisted slavery for decades).

Meanwhile, Laura had invited parents and children to share rituals that they used at home—as long as they did not involve any specific religious practices or references to a particular deity. Often she and the children invented new ones that fit the interests and concerns of the classroom. Today, in keeping with the theme of food, Laura had the children close their eyes. In a soft, melodious voice, she told them to think about different parts of their bodies and how the food they eat keeps them strong. Then she asked them to imagine the garden they were planting that day and how it would look in a few weeks as the plants began to grow. After a few minutes of silence, the children sat up and together the class sang "Inch by Inch," a song about growing a garden.

As Laura moved into organizing the day, she reminded the children about the two parents and two elders who were in the class that day and made sure that everyone remembered each others' names. Then she mentioned a problem with the loft in the classroom, where recently there had been many conflicts, with children in the loft "shooting" at and otherwise repelling children who wanted to come in. Moreover, the girls complained that the boys said it was their clubhouse and that girls were not allowed. First, Laura asked the children what they liked and did not like about the loft. After several comments, Laura summarized their points and then suggested that everyone, including the parents and elders, brainstorm possible solutions. Ideas came rolling in, and Susan and Robert wrote them down on large pieces of news print. Laura read all the suggestions out loud, summarized them, and complimented everyone for their great ideas. Because the discussion had gone on for some time, Laura said, "I think that, for today, I will close the loft, and you can use this time when you can't play in the loft to think more about how we can make it work better for everyone. On Monday we will continue our discussion and decide on a plan to try out. Does that feel okay with all of you? Is there anyone who really disagrees?" A couple of boys muttered some complaints but agreed that "just today" without a loft was okay.

Laura then reviewed the procedure for planting the seeds in the garden. Near the beginning of the year, she had formed cooperative teams that were balanced (as much as possible) in terms of gender; ethnic, racial, and social-class backgrounds; and abilities. Throughout the year, these teams worked together on different projects, including the current one on planting. During the preceding days the teams had sorted their seeds, learned what different plants would need in terms of water and space, and diagrammed their part of the garden; now they were ready to put the seeds into the ground.

Laura asked if anyone wanted to say anything about the garden. One boy said, "What about all the people in the world who are hungry? I think we should give some of the food from the garden to them." The conversation continued for a few minutes about how they might donate some of their produce to a local shelter. Then Laura asked if anyone had any ideas about why some people did not have enough food. Rose talked about how her grandparents were forced off the land in Ireland by rich landowners who wanted all the land for themselves and that that was how she eventually came to live here in the United States. "Yeah, like the English grabbed all of the land from the Indians," chimed in one child, reflecting back on class discussions that had occurred in November.

One child, Sam, said angrily, "At my house we don't have any place to play outside—no yard and lots of broken glass all around. In the fancy houses, like where my mom works, kids have swings, slides, climbers, basketball hoops—all right there in their yard and all to themselves. It's not fair!" "You are right," said Laura and asked if other people had ideas about this situation and maybe what to do about it. Several children talked about other similar examples, and one child said that people with big houses and yards should let people with no yards play in their yards.

After the flurry of comments died down, Laura said, "There are a lot of unfair things in this world, and it's going to take a lot of people and a lot of work to change them. We need to keep noticing them and talking to each other and to other people about them. Next week we're going to visit the city manager at City Hall. Maybe we should talk about this particular problem—that in some neighborhoods in our city there are no places for kids to play." Several children suggested that they tell the city manager to make more parks. "Remember when we visited Sam's neighborhood," said one girl (at the beginning of the year, the class had visited all the neighborhoods of the children in the class), "we saw that empty lot and we talked about how it would make a great park if they got rid of the garbage and put in swings and stuff?" "Yeah, like that book we read about the kids and parents making a park," said one little boy. "That's right," said Laura. *The Streets Are Free* [Kurusa, 1985] is a good example of kids making a real difference. Let's be sure that we read that story again before we go visit City Hall. Also, it might be interesting to see how the City Hall and workers in our city are like and unlike those in the story, which, you remember, really happened in Caracas, Venezuela. Do you remember how we found it on our globe?"

The first team was ready to begin planting; they went to their cubbies got their sun hats and paraded back out decked out in a wonderful variety of hats of different shapes and materials, all colorfully decorated. One of the parents had done a sun-hat-making activity with the children. She had brought in books and magazines showing hats from different times and parts of the world, and she and the children had experimented with many materials, including old cereal boxes, plastic containers, leaves, twigs, and grasses. Despite many early failed attempts, the children had worked together to create the hats, and now everyone had a hat that was both beautiful and serviceable.

The first planting team worked well together, making rows and planting seeds. The children obviously knew each other well and were familiar with each others' strengths and vulnerabilities. Robert noticed how they accommodated Mariana's partial sightedness in a matter-of-fact, respectful way, showing neither pity nor resentment. He remembered a parent–teacher discussion group early in the year when Mariana's father had talked to the group about her loss of sight, what caused it, and the particular adaptations that she needed in the classroom. Robert had been impressed with how openly Mariana's father had answered the other parents' questions—such a change from the awkward "don't look/don't ask" response he had learned from his own parents whenever they had seen someone with a disability. Hearing Mariana's story, Robert learned more about the challenges of raising a partially sighted child in a world that runs on visual images and the written word. It had also made him rethink some of his opinions about too much money being spent on adapting classrooms, schools, and public buildings to accommodate children and adults with disabilities.

The second team also worked smoothly, but there was an incident that gave Robert a few minutes of uncertainty and panic. As the children made rows, their hands were getting caked with dirt. Brianna, a White girl, and Melissa, an African American child, were working together when suddenly Brianna held up her hands and said, "Look, Melissa, my hands look like yours now." Melissa looked up at Brianna, and a look of confusion crossed her face. She did not say anything but looked down again and went back to work. Robert heard and saw this exchange and felt his heart stop.

A year ago he would have dismissed Brianna's comment as just a well-meaning observation. But through some painful experiences he had come to understand how such "innocent" comments reflect unconscious racism and can hurt others. One time last year he had used the expression "the pot calling the kettle black" in a discussion, and one of the African American fathers told him that he found that expression offensive because it reflected a negative connotation with the word *black*. At first Robert had been furious—this oversensitivity every time the word *black* was mentioned. What was he supposed to do—stop and think for 5 minutes every time he opened his mouth? But after several conversations with Gloria and some African American parents about their painful childhood memories of always hearing the word *black* associated with something bad, he had realized how even small, unintentional comments could be hurtful. He had also become more aware that, despite his earlier denials, a lot of racist assumptions permeated his thoughts and speech and that, yes, he *did* have to stop and think about what he was saying.

So here he was faced with a situation that he knew was important but that he felt poorly equipped to handle. He considered telling Laura, so that she could talk to the two girls later in the day, but he realized that it would be too late to have much of an impact—they might not even remember exactly what had happened. It was up to him, and he was—yes—scared! As he cast about in his mind for what to say, he remembered that Laura, who often talked about her own uncertainties and mistakes, had once said that when she did not know what to do, she asked the children how they felt and/or what should be done. Often they came up with good ideas, and at the very least she gained a few minutes to come up with a strategy.

So, trying to sound more confident than he felt, Robert went over and sat down next to the girls. "I just heard what you said, Brianna, about how your hands looked like Melissa's because they were covered with dirt. I wonder, Melissa, how that made you feel?" Melissa said quietly, "I didn't like it. My hands aren't dirty, my skin is brown." "So it kind of hurt your feelings that Brianna said that," said Robert gently. "Brianna do you understand how that might have hurt Melissa?" "I didn't mean to hurt her," said Brianna in a defensive voice, "I just thought it was neat that my hands looked like hers." Robert held up a handful of dirt next to Melissa's skin and asked Brianna, "Do you really think that brown skin and dirt look the same?" Brianna looked and slowly shook her head. Robert pointed to a freckle on Brianna's arm and asked her, "How would you feel if someone pointed to your freckle and said 'Hey, look your arm is dirty'?" "Not good," Brianna replied softly and then added, "I'm sorry, Melissa." Robert turned to Melissa and asked, "How are you feeling, Melissa?" Melissa said, "Okay, I think. Just please don't tell me that my skin is dirty," she added, looking at Brianna, who nodded in agreement.

Robert, feeling relieved, decided to put this incident into a broader perspective. "We often say hurtful things without meaning to because we don't think about what we're saying. I'm learning to listen to what I say so that I don't hurt or insult people by mistake. We all need to do that," he said, looking at Brianna. "And," he went on looking at Melissa, "when you feel hurt try to say something—tell the person you don't like what they said. That way you aren't just sitting there and feeling bad, and also they learn that you don't like it and not to do it again. Okay?" he asked looking at both girls. They nodded solemnly. Robert smiled, "Okay, back to work!" and the girls continued on their row. Robert walked away, noticing how his heart was still pounding. "Phwew," he thought to himself. "I could never do this day after day . . . but," in a moment of self-congratulation, "I think I did okay!" He smiled.

After the second group had finished, it was time for snack. The children were arranged in snack groups, which Laura had formed after she had noticed that snack time was becoming a "popularity contest," with some children getting many invitations to sit next to someone and others getting none. Each group had five or six children—different from their cooperative teams and as balanced a mix as possible. Laura had encouraged the children to develop snack group identities by making placemats with the same theme or colors and deciding on group names. Each parent and elder sat with a group to encourage the children to talk to each other about what was happening that day and any major events in their lives.

After the third and fourth groups had finished their planting, Robert wandered around the classroom, noticing the photographs of different kinds of farms—rice paddies, orchards, huge agribusinesses, and small family farms—and pictures of people working on the land, some with tractors and others with hand hoes and sticks. He smiled at how Laura was putting the school photograph collection to good use. Every fall, parents were asked to donate photographs of people, animals, and landscapes. The school librarian would put the new pictures out on tables in the library for 2 weeks and invite parents and teachers to review them and to eliminate any that were stereotyped and/or misleading. At times there had been controversies about specific pictures, especially those depicting gay and lesbian families, which had given rise to a number of good discussions. After the review period, photographs that were acceptable were added to a comprehensive school picture file, organized into a number of categories, and cross-referenced.

In the art area, children were making mosaics and jewelry with seeds. Robert watched fascinated as children concentrated on the challenge of working with seeds of various sizes and tried different ways of attaching them to strings and pipe cleaners to make necklaces, bracelets, and anklets. He was impressed at how they helped each other solve various physical problems, such as measuring the string for a bracelet or figuring out how to attach a heavy chestnut to a string. Around this area were pictures of mosaics made from many different materials and pictures of people from many cultures wearing jewelry, much of it made from natural materials. Robert thought of Alison's Barbie doll collection, with its piles of plastic baubles, and inwardly groaned. "How is it that we have transformed these rich arts into commercialized junk—junk that our kids desperately want?" he asked himself. One child who had made a long heavy necklace with acorns and chestnuts was shaking her body to the sounds of drum music, obviously enjoying how her motions made the necklace move in different rhythms.

As he looked at the artwork displayed in the room and listened to the music, Robert thought about one of the workshops at the school last year that had helped him to see how much he (and most of the other participants) had always assumed that "art" referred to European and European American paintings, literature, and music. The workshop leader had pointed out that much of what we consider art was created for the pleasure or spiritual refreshment of the wealthy classes. She had shown them how popular folk art—songs, murals, plays, and dances—often expressed the pain and struggles of people overcoming adversity and injustice. After the workshop, a number of teachers and parents had searched music stores, libraries, bookstores, and the Internet for music, pictures, stories, and plays so as to include more voices and perspectives in the art programs.

By now it was time to clean up the classroom, during which time Laura encouraged children to work together as much as possible. Afterwards Laura read the children *Working Cotton* (Williams, 1992), a story about an African American migrant worker family who all—including the children—work throughout the day in the hot sun picking cotton. After she finished the book, the children talked about how they had gotten hot working in the garden but had been able to come in after a few minutes and get cooled off. Herb talked about his childhood memories of being a migrant worker during the Depression. He described how hard everyone in his family had worked and how after spending 12 hours a day harvesting bushels of food, they still went to bed hungry. Laura pointed to some photographs of contemporary migrant workers and their homes that were posted on the wall and reminded the children that many farm workers were still struggling to get decent wages and housing. Laura pointed to biographies of Cesar Chavez and Dolores Huerta that they had read a few days before and suggested that children might want to look at them again.

It was now time for lunch. In past years many staff and parents had been unhappy about the discipline problems, conflicts, and scapegoating that occurred in the big, noisy cafeteria. This year the school staff was experimenting with having the children eat lunch in their classrooms. The logistics were challenging, but overall the teachers felt that lunch was a calmer and more positive time and that the children were learning to be responsible for distributing food and cleaning up.

Gloria usually ate lunch with the parents and elders participating in the school that day. She had found that these conversations were a good way to hear about parent and community concerns, to air new ideas, and get advice about various issues facing the school. At first the teachers had been nervous about these lunches, fearing that parents might use this time to complain about individual teachers. However, Gloria had set specific guidelines about what could be discussed at these lunches (e.g., school, state, and national policies and issues) and what topics were off limits (e.g., specific teachers, children, families)—and these guidelines had reassured everyone. To meet with parents who could not participate during the schoolday, Gloria had parent breakfasts once a month in the different neighborhoods served by the school.

Today, Gloria and the parents and elders had an intense discussion about the recently instituted state tests that would ultimately determine who graduated from high school and which teachers and schools got merit raises and additional funding. Gloria talked about how the testing program was forcing the teachers to spend more time teaching specific skills and less time on larger questions and more innovative and conceptual teaching. Several parents described how their children were so nervous about the tests that they no longer wanted to come to school. Other people, however, argued that without the tests, schools and teachers could just ignore the children who were behind. A couple of parents mentioned that teachers, administrators, and parents all over the state were angry that they had had virtually no voice in the design and implementation of the testing program. They offered to get in touch with their local state representative and set up a schoolwide meeting with him and someone from the Department of Education to discuss their concerns. Gloria mentioned the names of a couple of websites that had more information about testing and alternative methods of assessments that she had found useful.

After lunch, the kindergartners had a quiet rest time, so Robert went up to visit his son Jed's third-grade class. They had been working on the theme of "water" all year. In the fall, Jed had come home armed with all kinds of statistics and water conservation techniques and had showed Robert and Alison how to wash dishes and brush their teeth in ways that could save water. He had prodded Robert to spend a weekend installing water conservation devices in the toilets and showers. Now the class was working on pollution.

When he entered, Robert noticed a large world map with different-colored pins stuck in it, each color signifying a different source of water pollution. Jed pointed out the large clusters of pins in poor countries. Robert also saw a partially completed class mural that was a biting commentary on the connection between pollution and wealth. There were images of bloated rich people sucking up the clean water with giant straws and menacing factories pouring vile potions into lakes and rivers surrounded by poor people and dying trees. Obviously Jed's teacher, James, was making good use of the workshop on popular and protest art. Under the map were several bound "reports" that children had written and illustrated on various kinds of water pollution and its effect on both the human and natural ecosystems. Robert read a couple of them and was impressed with the quality of the children's research and writing skills. He wondered if it would make sense to show them to their state representative and the Department of Education people as an alternative way to measure children's academic skills.

Robert then wandered over to where some students were working on inventing water purification machines with a variety of techniques and materials (e.g., filters made from a variety of natural and synthetic materials). James came over and thanked Robert for helping the class make their "Kids for Clean Water" website. They had already gotten "hits" from schools all over the world. James invited Robert to stay and watch a short video sent to them via e-mail by their partner third-grade class in Mexico, which was also working on water pollution. Narrated in English and Spanish, the video showed pictures of dry and flooded streams, and the children talked about the challenges of conserving water in a place where virtually all the rain falls during between June and October. They also acted out an Aztec legend about Tlalc the rain god and performed a short play about some local pollution problems. The class laughed heartily at the Mexican children's dramatic portrayals of choked-up streams and sick lakes and were roused by a rock-and-roll song at the end urging everyone to clean up the lakes and rivers. "Si! Si! Si! Podemos!" (Yes! Yes! Yes! We Can!).

As James and the class began to plan the next video that they would send to their partners in Mexico, Robert returned to Alison's class, where the kindergartners and the teacher and volunteers were starting their closing ritual during which everyone had a chance to say something about the day (e.g., issues that came up, compliments or thank-you's to other people). Afterwards Laura summed up the comments and thanked the parent and elder participants. Then everyone held hands and sang "De Colores," a Mexican folksong about the colors of spring and one of the songs sung by the Farm Workers Union when they picket fields to demand more rights for agricultural workers. Then children quickly got sweaters and backpacks and headed for either their bus line, their after-school program, or their walk home.

Robert, Susan, Herb, and Rose stayed behind for a short "debriefing" with Laura. She asked for feedback from them about the day and how they thought the class was doing in general. She asked if anyone had any questions or concerns. At the beginning of the year, Laura had explained that they could talk about incidents that had occurred but, because of confidentiality, they could not talk about ongoing problems of specific children or related family issues. Robert brought up the incident with Melissa and Brianna and was gratified that everyone thought that he had handled it well. Laura thanked him for letting her know so she could watch for derogatory comments about brown skin and do some other things with paints, photographs, and books to challenge children's association of brown skin and dirt.

Rose made them all laugh about some children's assumptions that that Irish soda bread had to be made with soda drinks. Laura pointed out how these moments of confusion are great opportunities because they force children to question their assumptions and think more flexibly. Rose then got serious and said, "Today I felt honored by the children and all of you—my family history, which has been a story of loss, struggle, and sadness, felt like a treasure today. Thank you." The five adults sat quietly, and then Susan said, "I think you have spoken for all of us. Thank *you!*"

# Suggested Books for Children

## RACE, CULTURE, AND CROSS-GROUP RELATIONSHIPS

Many books portray different groups and lifestyles and deal with racial and cultural identities; cross-group similarities and differences; and the experience of cultural discontinuity, prejudice, and stereotyping. The following examples are only a few of the many possibilities.

Ajmera, M., & Ivanko, J. D. (1999). *To be a kid.* Watertown, MA: Charlesbridge Publishing.

> Through photographs, this book shows how children all over the world do many of the same things—playing with friends, going to school, and spending time with families.

Angelou, M. (1994). Courtney-Clark, M. (Photos). *My painted house, my friendly chicken and me.* New York: Clarkson Potter.

> This book contains images of the contemporary Ndebele people in South Africa. Particularly striking is the contrast between the colorful houses and clothing of the Ndebele people in their community and the drab school uniforms that the children wear when they go to school.

Birdseye, D. H., & Birdseye, T. (1997). Crum, R. (Photos). *Under our skin: Kids talk about race.* New York: Holiday House.

> Six middle-school students from a range of ethnic backgrounds describe how ethnicity and race have affected their lives and relationships with others. They discuss their experiences with prejudice and share their views on racial relationships in the United States.

Carling, A. L. (1998). *Mama & papa have a store.* New York: Dial Books.

> This book is an account of a day in the life of the author when she was the young daughter of Chinese immigrants who ran a store in Guatemala City. As she and her parents and siblings go through the day, she hears Spanish, Mayan, and Chinese spoken and sees how the people from these different cultures are alike and different and how they connect with each other. Her parents' nostalgia for China, which they left because of the Japanese invasion in 1938, shows how many immigrants still miss their homelands, even when they have adapted to their new countries.

Castaneda, O. S. (1993). Sanches, E. O. (Illus.). *Abuela's weave.* New York: Lee & Low Books.

This book describes how a Guatemalan child and grandmother weave beautiful cloth and try to sell their work in competition with cheaper machine-made goods. Because they also worry that the grandmother's slight facial disfigurement will put off potential customers, the book can also stimulate discussion about how people react to disabilities and disfigurements.

Cowen-Fletcher, J. (1994). *It takes a village.* New York: Scholastic.

This story of how a young child in Benin, West Africa is cared for by many people as he wanders around the market in his village illustrates well the African proverb "It takes a village to raise a child."

Davol, M. W. (1993). Trivas, I. (Illus.). *Black, White, just right.* Morton Grove, IL: Albert Whitman.

In this story, a biracial child describes how her parents are different in appearance and in what they like (e.g., different foods). She sees how she is like them both and is at the same time her "just right" self.

Doherty, G., & Claybourne, A. (2002). *The Usborne book of peoples of the world: Internet-linked.* Tulsa, OK: Educational Development Corporation.

With vivid photographs and descriptions, this volume shows how different regions of the world are similar and different. The authors are quite forthright in their descriptions of past and present injustices in different countries. The book is a useful resource on its own, but, in addition, each section includes several Internet sites that readers can go to for more information about these regions.

Dorros, A. (1991). Kleven, E. (Illus.). *Abuela.* New York: Dutton.

This wonderful fantasy tells about a Puerto Rican American child and her grandmother flying with the birds above the city and seeing all the sights from a "bird's-eye" perspective. As she tells the story, the girl intersperses Spanish and English words in such a way that readers, even if they do not know any Spanish, can understand their meanings. The book also provides appealing visual examples of how the world looks from different physical as well as cultural vantage points.

Dorros, A. (1992). *This is my house.* New York: Scholastic.

This book develops the theme of similarities and differences by showing drawings of many kinds of houses, including the housing of the very poor and homeless. The book includes names for houses in different languages and explanations about how and why different types of houses are constructed.

Dr. Seuss (1961). *The Sneetches.* New York: Random House.

This humorous tale illustrates the costs and folly of one group setting itself above another one. It is very useful for raising these issues with younger children.

Gray, L. M. (1993). Rowland, J. (Illus.). *Miss Tizzy.* New York: Simon & Schuster.

This story tells about an elderly African American woman and the mostly White children in the neighborhood who adore her. Miss Tizzy wears green tennis shoes, likes to roller skate, and lets all her flowers grow any way they want. In contrast to the sterile overmanicured lawns on the street, hers is a riot of color and joy. When she gets sick, all the children in the neighborhood do things to make her feel better.

Isadora, R. (1991). *At the crossroads.* New York: Greenwillow Books.
   This book illustrates how family loyalty and joy still thrive despite the many hardships in a South African township. The scenes of children carrying water from a central faucet to their homes and using large tubs to bathe themselves is a good contrast to our expectations of running water in our houses.
Jenness, A. (1990). *Families: A celebration of diversity, commitment, and love.* Boston: Houghton Mifflin.
   This compilation of photographs and short autobiographies illustrates the many different lifestyles and family compositions in the United States. This book is one of the few written for children that openly discusses gay family life.
Joose, B. M. (1991). Lavallee, B. (Illus.). *Mama, do you love me?* San Francisco: Chronicle Books.
   This book is a conversation between an Inuit mother and her daughter, who is testing her mother's love for her by asking what she would do in response to many misbehaviors. The child's questions and the mother's sensitive responses reflect the universal theme that parents deeply and unconditionally love their children even at moments when they are angry with them.
Kindersley, B. A. (1995). *Children just like me.* New York: DK Publishing and UNICEF.
   This comprehensive volume contains hundreds of photographs of children from a wide range of countries all doing similar activities, such as going to school, playing with friends, and caring for pets. For each country there is a brief description of its history, geography, and cultures. Children are depicted in both traditional and contemporary clothing and settings, illustrating how many people merge these two influences in their lives.
Kroll, V. (1998). Cooper, F. (Illus.). *Faraway drums.* Boston, MA: Little Brown.
   Two African American sisters who are alone in their new apartment (while their mother is at work) reassure themselves that all the unfamiliar noises they hear are really the sounds of drums and animals in Africa, based on stories that their great-grandmother told them.
Kroll, V. (1992). Carpenter, N. (Illus.). *Masai and I.* New York: Four Winds Press.
   This is a young African American girl's vision about what her life would be like if she were growing up as a Masai—as she might have been had her ancestors not been kidnapped and enslaved.
Mason, O. (Ed.). (1997). *Atlas of threatened cultures.* Austin, TX: Raintree Steck-Vaughn Publishers.
   This volume contains case studies and photographs of 29 cultures that are threatened by loss of habitat and encroaching "development." For each group, there is a brief description of their history and culture and the specific threats to their way of life.
Morris, A. (1992). Heyman, K. (Photos). *Houses and homes.* New York: Lathrop, Lee & Shepard.
   Through photographs, this book illustrates the range of houses in many parts of the world and across social classes.

Nye, N. S. (1994). Carpenter, N. (Illus.). *Sitti's secrets.* New York: Four Winds Press.

In this story, a Palestinian American child visits her grandmother ("Sitti" in Arabic) in the Middle East and notices and appreciates many things that are different from her home in the United States. She comes home and writes a letter to the president of the United States about her grandmother and her desire for peace.

Onyefulu, I. (1993). *A is for Africa.* New York: Cobblehill Books (Dutton).

This volume illustrates how authors can provide information about particular cultures in appealing and meaningful ways. This book, which focuses primarily on the Igbo tribe in Nigeria, is especially informative because each photograph is accompanied by an explanation of the origin of the particular object or action shown and its significance.

Say, A. (1991). *A tree of cranes.* Boston: Houghton Mifflin.

Say, A. (1993). *Grandfather's journey.* Boston: Houghton Mifflin.

These two stories illustrate, through the experiences of different generations of a Japanese American family, both the richness and the sadness of living and belonging to two countries.

Schmidt, J., & Wood, T. (1995). *Two lands, one heart: An American boy's journey to his mother's Vietnam.* New York: Walker.

This photographic essay tells the story of a Vietnamese American family's visit to relatives in Vietnam. It is told from the perspective of T. J., the 7-year-old son of a woman who escaped from Vietnam at the age of 10, was raised by a family in the United States, and then married a European American.

Shanbe, N. (1997). Sporn, M. (Illus.). *White wash.* New York: Walker & Company.

An African American preschool girl and her big brother are attacked by a White supremacist gang, who spray her face with white paint. The story shows the girl's searing emotional pain and how she is able to gain strength and reenter the world with the support of her grandmother and her friends.

Stewart, M., & Kennedy, M., with Kalmanovitz, Spanish portions (2002). *Latino baseball's finest fielders.* Brookfield, CT: Millbrook Press.

This book, written in both English and Spanish, provides brief accounts of players' personal and professional accomplishments. It is a good resource for engaging young baseball fans in discussions about different cultures and languages.

Watkins, S. (1994). Doner, K. (Illus.). *White bead ceremony.* Tulsa, OK: Council Oak Books.

This book illustrates some of the tensions of cultural discontinuity but also ways in which people can blend their traditions with their contemporary circumstances. A Shawnee girl, living off the reservation, is resistant to learning the Shawnee language. Her parents and grandparents plan to give her a white bead ceremony at which she will receive her Shawnee name. The illustrations demonstrate how this ancient ceremony is still meaningful in a modern setting, with everyone dressed in current clothes and speaking English. A nice touch is that when the relatives who are supposed to be bringing the white bead necklace cannot come at the last minute, the grandmothers fashion a necklace out of white buttons and a piece of dental floss.

Wiles, D. (2001). *Freedom summer*. New York: Simon & Schuster.

Narrated by a young White boy, this book examines the complex relationships between Blacks and Whites in a small town during the civil rights movement. It personalizes the controversies of segregation and integration and the challenges yet possibilities in changing the hearts and minds of people with deeply entrenched racist beliefs.

## ECONOMIC CONTEXT

Some books can support efforts to help children become aware of economic disparities and detach themselves from the consumerist messages in their worlds. Here are a few examples.

Flourney, V. (1985). Pinkney, J. (Illus.). *The patchwork quilt*. New York: Dial Books for Young Children.

This book provides a good example of how something wonderful and useful can be made from old materials. It also portrays a loving African American family who help each other and find joy in making a patchwork quilt that contains many memories.

Gilman, P. (1992). *Something from nothing* New York: Scholastic.

This is an adaptation of a Jewish folktale about a boy's blanket made by his grandfather. As it wears out, the grandfather remakes it into smaller and smaller items (e.g., coat, vest, tie, handkerchief). As more material is cut off, the mouse family that lives downstairs decorates their house and themselves with the remnants. The story portrays the warm relationship between a grandfather and grandson in a small village and is a good counterexample to our society's obsession with buying new things.

McCourt, L. (1998). Ladwig, T. (Illus.). *The braids girl*. Deerfield Beach, FL: Health Communications.

Two young European American girls meet at a homeless shelter; Izzy is a volunteer and Susan is a resident. Izzy feels awkward and at first relates to Susan only by giving her used clothing and toys and is bewildered when Susan seems disappointed by her "gifts." With her grandfather's help, she comes to understand that friendship is a better gift than pity. This book raises good questions for children and teachers who are collecting money or items for homeless people. The one drawback is that, despite its critique of patronizing charity, the middle-class volunteers are still the central focus and are subtly portrayed as "rescuers."

Mitchell, M. K. (1993). Ransome, J. (Illus.). *Uncle Jed's barbershop*. New York: Simon & Schuster Books for Young Readers.

This book tells the story of an itinerant African American barber during the 1930s and 1940s who deferred his dream of owning his own barbershop in

order to help people in his family and community. His story personalizes the
effects of racial discrimination.

Williams, K. L. (1990). Stock, C. (Illus.). *Galimoto*. New York: Lothrop, Lee &
Shepard.

This is the story of a young boy who lives in Malawi and collects wire from
people in his village in order to make a galimoto, a car or truck made of wire
that can be pushed along with a long stick, a favorite toy in the village. The
persistence and creativity of the child and his pride in making his galimoto are
a useful antidote to children's assumptions that they need to buy the latest toy.

Williams, S. A. (1992). Byard, C. (Illus.). *Working cotton*. San Diego: Harcourt
Brace Jovanovich.

This portrayal of an African American family picking cotton together is told
from the perspective of the young daughter. The story conveys a strong sense
of family ties and mutual support yet also vividly illustrates the hardships of
migrant workers in general and child laborers in particular. It offers a compelling contrast to the cheery images of farm life depicted in many children's
books.

## THE NATURAL ENVIRONMENT

A number of books illustrate the dynamic relationships within the natural
environment, between people and nature, and how these connections are
interpreted through different cultural perspectives. The following examples
are only a few of the many possibilities.

Andrews, J., & Wallace, I. (1995). *Very last first time*. New York: Atheneum.

This book offers a fascinating look at the ocean bottom as seen by a young
Eskimo girl who goes under the frozen sea when the tide is out in order to
harvest mussels. The book is also a good example of children overcoming their
fears and contributing to their families' welfare

Asch, F. (1995). *Water*. San Diego: Harcourt Brace & Company.

This book about the different sources of water encourages children to think
about how crucial water is to our lives.

Cherry, L. (1992). *A river ran wild: An environmental history*. San Diego: Harcourt
Brace & Company.

In this book, the author traces the history of the Nashua River in New England
from the days when Native Americans fished and lived along its shores, to its
polluted state during and after the Industrial Revolution, to its recent cleanup
and reclamation and current recreational use.

Chinery, M. (2001). *Secrets of the rain forest: People and places*. New York: Crab-
tree.

With photographs and written descriptions, this volume shows the stunning
beauty of rain forests and describes the forces that are threatening their existence. It includes several accounts of the different groups who live in the rain

forests in South America and in Africa and shows how their cultures and livelihoods are entwined with the forest and are vulnerable to its destruction.

Fredericks, A. D. (2001). J. DiRubbio (Illus.). *Under one rock: Bugs, slugs and other ughs.* Nevada City, CA: Dawn Publications.

When we take time to observe carefully, we can see the rich variety of life-
forms that live in small places—in this case, under a single rock. This book
also encourages children to overcome their aversion to slugs, spiders, and other
animals and to rethink their initial negative responses to unfamiliar things.

Griese, A. (1995). Ragins, C. (Illus.). *Anna's Athbaskan summer.* Honesdale, PA: Boyds Mills Press.

This book illustrates how the native Athbaskans live in harmony with their
natural world and fish in ways that use the natural resources wisely and do not
exploit them. It also contains a number of examples of how contemporary
Athbaskans combine their traditions with current technology (e.g., motor boats
and life jackets).

Hesse, K. (1999). Muth, J. J. (Illus.). *Come on, rain!* New York: Scholastic Press.

This book, set in a multiracial city neighborhood, describes in detail a young
girl's anticipation of a summer rainstorm to break the oppressive heat. The
illustrations and words viscerally evoke the heat and the relief of the rain and
remind us of the timeless need for rain to refresh the Earth.

Hoyt-Goldsmith, D. (1993). Migdale, L. (Photos). *Cherokee summer.* New York: Holiday House.

This photographic essay of the summer activities of a young Cherokee girl and
her family illustrates how traditions and contemporary lifestyles are blended to
preserve their close community and unity with the natural environment.

James, B. (1994). Morin, P. (Illus.). *The mud family.* New York: G. P. Putnam's Sons.

This is a fictional story about the effects of a drought on an Anasazi family (a
very early people who inhabited the southwestern part of what is now the
United States) and how they both accommodate to the lack of water and try to
bring rain.

Myers, C. (2001). *Fly!* New York: Hyperion Books for Children.

A young boy becoming friends with an elderly man who takes care of pigeons
on the roof of an apartment building. This book portrays a warm relationship
between two generations of African American males and illustrates how the
rhythm, wonder, and companionship of nature is present everywhere, including
densely populated urban streets.

Nikolo-Lisa, W. (2002). Tate, D. (Illus.). *Summer sun risin'.* New York: Lee & Low Books.

This illustrated poem shows how a day on a farm is closely tied to the passage
of the sun from its rising to its setting. It also portrays rich and interdependent
relationships as members of this African American family collaborate to take
care of themselves and the animals and fields on the farm.

Orr, K. (1990). *My grandfather and the sea.* Minneapolis: Carolrhoda.

This book shows the connection between the exploitation of the environment
and of people. The narrator's grandfather, who lives on St. Lucia Island in the

Caribbean, can no longer fish as he had done for decades because larger mechanized ships have overfished the area. The book describes the dispiriting effects of unemployment and the devastation that results from disrupting the balance between people and their natural habitat.

Parsons, A. (1992). *Make it work! Earth.* New York: Thomson Learning.

This book contains a number of activities to demonstrate and explain some of the physical phenomena of weather, soil, and sun energy to help children understand these processes more concretely.

*Ranger Rick.* Vienna, VA: National Wildlife Foundation.

This popular children's magazine has articles and stories about different aspects of the environment and about environmental degradation, usually illustrated by photographs and/or first-person accounts. It has been used successfully in environmental education programs.

Reynolds, J. (1992). *Far north.* San Diego: Harcourt Brace Jovanovich.

This book describes the Sami (Lapland) lifestyle, which is tied to the reindeer herds that are now endangered by the contamination of the land and water and especially by the Chernobyl disaster.

## GENDER

Many of the books throughout this annotated list portray men and women in nontraditional gender roles. Here are a couple of the many books that specifically challenge gender stereotypes.

Ajmera, M., Omolodun, O., & Strunk, S. (1999). *Extraordinary girls.* Watertown, MA: Charlesbridge.

With photographs, biographical sketches, and brief commentaries, this volume illustrates how girls all over the world are engaged in education, sports, the arts, public service, and enjoying themselves and each other.

de Paola, T. (1979). *Oliver Button is a sissy.* New York: Harcourt Brace Jovanovich.

This book illustrates how children who do not conform to traditional gender roles are often scapegoated by their peers. Oliver prefers dancing school to football and is teased by his peers. However, after he demonstrates his dancing skills in a local talent show, his peers change their opinion of him.

## DIFFERENT ABILITIES

Several stories describe how different abilities can influence how people live and their relationships with others.

Cowen-Fletcher, J. (1993). *Mama zooms.* New York: Scholastic.

This book vividly portrays a European American mother who uses a wheelchair and her child "zooming" on various adventures.

Geheret, J. (1990). DePauw, S. A. (Illus.). *The don't-give-up kid and learning differ-ences.* Fairport, NY: Verbal Images Press.

Alex is struggling in school and feeling very discouraged. However, after mov-ing to a classroom with fewer children and more support, he begins to feel successful and realizes that lots of children and adults have learning differ-ences, including his hero Thomas Edison.

Heelan, J. R. (2002). Simmonds, N. (Illus.). *Can you hear a rainbow? The story of a deaf boy named Chris.* Atlanta, GA: Peachtree Publishers.

This book describes how Chris, who has been deaf since birth, has learned to use sign language, hearing aids, and lip reading to communicate. The book provides an optimistic picture of how children with disabilities can be inte-grated into regular classrooms and after-school activities and develop close friendships with peers of different abilities.

Lang, G. (2001). *Looking out for Sarah.* Watertown, MA: Talewinds.

Told from the perspective of Perry, a guide dog, this book describes a day in Perry and Sarah's life, which includes taking a train to go give a school con-cert, visiting with friends, and shopping. Both Perry and Sarah recall their 300-mile walk from Boston to New York, which they did to raise awareness about the value of guide dogs—a good example of creative activism.

## INJUSTICE AND RESISTANCE

Some books for children more directly address injustices and the accompa-nying emotional pain; in some cases, they offer hopeful visions of people resisting and trying to create a better world. The following are a few exam-ples.

Cherry, L. (1990). *The great kapok tree.* San Diego: Harcourt, Brace, Jovanovich.

This book combines the themes of activism and conservation of natural re-sources in a story of how the animals together convince the woodsman not to cut down their tree in the rain forest. The animals' arguments illustrate different facets of preserving the natural environment and could be used for organizing several activities around perserving ecosystems and rain forests in particular.

Hamanaka, S. (1995). *Peace crane.* New York: Morrow Junior Books.

In this fantasy poem, a young African American girl, inspired by the story of Sadako (the Japanese girl who made more than 1,000 paper cranes in her effort to overcome the leukemia she got as a result of the bombing of Hiroshima), makes a paper crane to bring peace to the inner city. In her fantasy, she flies with the crane all over the world and children everywhere join her quest for peace.

Harness, C. (2001). *Remember the ladies: 100 great American women.* New York: Harper Trophy.

Harness, C. (2003). *Rabble rousers: 20 women who made a difference.* New York: Dutton.

Both of these volumes contain short biographies and pictures that show how women from different ethnic and social class backgrounds and historical periods resisted racial, gender, economic, and political injustices and fought for change.

Heide, F. P., & Gilliland, J. H. (1992). Lewin, T. (Illus.). *Sami and the time of the troubles.* New York: Clarion Books.

This story of a family living with the day-to-day realities of civil war in Lebanon shows how family life is curtailed by the constant bombing. It is also a testament to human resilience as it also shows how children still find ways and places to play and continue to hope and struggle for better times.

Hopkinson, D. (2002). Ransome, J. E. (Illus.). *Under the quilt of night.* New York: Atheneum Books.

Based on fact and folklore, this story is told from the perspective of a young girl and vividly illustrates the dangers and hardships that runaway slaves faced. It also portrays the courage and perseverance of the runaways and of the people who ran the Underground Railroad.

Lasky, K. (2003). Lee, P. (Illus.). *A voice of her own: The story of Phillis Wheatley, slave poet.* Cambridge, MA: Candlewick Press.

This biography and picture book of Phillis Wheatley portrays the hardships of slave ships and indignities of being a slave. The story of how Phillis Wheatley overcame these disadvantages to become a recognized poet is inspiring.

Leoni, L. (1968). *Swimmy.* New York: Pantheon.

This classic story of how small fish work together to chase off larger predators provides an appealing example of how collaboration can make weaker and smaller beings strong and powerful.

Littlesugar, A. (2001). Cooper, F. (Illus.). *Freedom school, yes!* New York: Philomel Books.

Based on the 1964 Mississippi Freedom School Summer Project, this story tells of a young African American girl who overcomes her fears in the face of threats and a church burning to attend the Freedom School in her community. It also describes how the community comes together to rebuild the church and to construct a school. The relationship between the girl and the young White teacher at the Freedom School offers a positive example of Whites and Blacks working together for social justice.

McDonough, Y. Z. (2002). Zeldis, M. (Illus.). *Peaceful protest: The life of Nelson Mandela.* New York: Walker.

This biography of Nelson Mandela shows how his political activism was inspired by his father and developed through his years in college and law school, prison, and finally as the leader of the new South Africa. It is a powerful example of how people can persevere against enormous odds and still retain their dignity and hope and eventually prevail.

Rappaport, D. (2002). Evans, S. W. (Illus.). *No more! Stories and songs of slave resistance.* Cambridge, MA: Candlewick Press.

Based on true accounts, these stories document how African Americans courageously resisted the confinements and indignities of slavery with uprisings, escapes, education, religion, and music. These short stories and songs depict men, women, and children risking everything to help their families and to gain their freedom.

Wood, T., with Wanbli Numpa Afraid of Hawk. (1992). *A boy becomes a man at Wounded Knee.* New York: Walker.

This is a true account of an 8-year-old Lakota boy's grueling 6-day ride in −50°F weather to Wounded Knee, the place where many of his ancestors were massacred in 1890. This anniversary ride was done for 5 years by Lakotas to mend the sacred hoop of the Lakota people, which had been destroyed by the massacre. The fortitude of Wanbli Numpa Afraid of Hawk in the face of extreme cold, pain, and exhaustion is inspiring and a powerful message to children who may be unwilling or afraid to challenge themselves.

Wright, C. C. (1994). Griffith, G. (Illus.). *Journey to freedom.* New York: Holiday House.

This story of a group of slaves escaping with the help of Harriet Tubman is told from the perspective of a child who is part of the group.

Yolen, J. (1996). *Encounter.* San Diego: Harcourt Brace & Co.

This account tells of Columbus's arrival from the perspective of a young Taino boy. It vividly portrays the fear and devastation of the Taino people and the greed of the invading Spaniards.

# References

Aboud, F. E., & Amato, M. (2001). Developmental and socialization influences on intergroup bias. In R. Brown & S. L. Gaerther (Eds.), *Blackwell handbook of social psychology: Intergroup processes* (pp. 65–85). Oxford, UK: Blackwell.

Aboud, F. E., & Doyle, A. (1993). The early development of ethnic identity and attitudes. In M. E. Bernal & G. P. Knight (Eds.), *Ethnic identity: Formation and transmission among Hispanics and other minorities* (pp. 47–60). Albany: State University of New York Press.

Aboud, F. E., & Doyle, A. (1995). The development of in-group pride in Black Canadians. *Journal of Cross Cultural Psychology, 26*(3), 243–254.

Aboud, F. E., Mendelson, M. J., & Purdy, K. T. (2003). Cross-race relations and friendship quality. *International Journal of Behavioral Development, 27*(2), 165–173.

Adler, S. M. (2001). Racial and ethnic identity formation of midwestern Asian American children. *Contemporary Issues in Early Childhood, 2*(3). Online journal published by Triangle Journal: United Kingdom: www.triangle.co.uk/ciec.

Alejandro-Wright, M. N. (1985). The child's conception of racial classification: A socio-cognitive developmental model. In M. B. Spencer, G. K. Brookins, & W. R. Allen (Eds.), *Beginnings: The social and affective development of black children* (pp. 185–200). Hillsdale, NJ: Erlbaum.

Allen, P. G. (1992). *The sacred hoop: Recovering the feminine in American Indian traditions.* Boston: Beacon.

Allport, G. W. (1954). *The nature of prejudice.* Reading, MA: Addison-Wesley.

Alvarado, C., Derman-Sparks, L., & Ramsey, P. G. (1999). *In our own way: How anti-bias work shapes our lives.* St. Paul, MN: Redleaf.

Andrew, Y., Baird, J., Benjamin, R., Dean, S., Holmes, R., MacNaughton, G., Newman, B., & Payne, C. (2001). Mother Goose meets Mardi Gras: Lesbian and gay issues in early childhood. In E. Dau (Ed.), *The anti-bias approach in early childhood* (2nd ed.; pp. 63–81). Frenchs Forest, New South Whales, Australia: Pearson Education Australia.

Anzaldúa, G. (1987). *Borderlands/La frontera: The new Mestiza.* San Francisco: Aunt Lute Books.

Aptheker, H. (1993). *Anti-racism in U.S. history: The first two hundred years.* Westport, CT: Praeger.

Asher, S. R., Singleton, L. C., & Taylor, A. R. (1982, April). *Acceptance versus friendship: A longitudinal study of racial integration.* Paper presented at the annual meeting of the American Educational Research Association, New York.

Averhart, C. J., & Bigler, R. S. (1999). Shades of meaning: Skin tone, racial attitudes, and constructive memory in African-American children. *Journal of Experimental Child Psychology, 67,* 363–388.

Ayvazian, A. (1997). Barriers to effective mentoring across racial lines. *Multicultural Education, 4*(4), 13–17.

Banks, J. A. (1995). Multicultural education: Historical development, dimensions, and practice. In J. A. Banks & C. A. M. Banks (Eds.), *Handbook of research on multicultural education* (pp. 3–24). New York: Simon & Schuster/Macmillan.

Banks, J. A. (1997). *Educating citizens in a multicultural society.* New York: Teachers College Press.

Banks, J. A. (1999). *Introduction to multicultural education* (2nd ed.). Boston: Allyn & Bacon.

Banks, J. A., & Banks, C. A. M. (Eds.). (1995). *Handbook of research on multicultural education.* New York: Simon & Schuster/Macmillan.

Bem, S. L. (1981). Gender schema theory: A cognitive account of sex typing. *Psychological Review, 88,* 354–364.

Bem, S. L. (1983). Gender schema theory and its implications for child development: Raising gender-aschematic children in a gender-schematic society. *Journal of Women in Culture and Society, 8,* 597–616.

Berti, A. E., & Bombi, A. S. (1981). The development of the concept of money and its value: A longitudinal study. *Child Development, 52,* 1179–1182.

Bigelow, B. (1995). Dumb kids, smart kids, and social class. *Rethinking Schools, 10*(2), 12–13.

Bigler, R. S. (1995). The role of classification skill in moderating environmental influences on children's gender stereotyping: A study of the functional use of gender in the classroom. *Child Development, 66,* 1072–1087.

Bigler, R. S. (1997). Conceptual and methodological issues in the measurement of children's sex-typing. *Psychology of Women Quarterly, 21,* 53–69.

Bigler, R. S., Jones, L. C., & Lobliner, D. B. (1997). Social categorization and the formation of intergroup attitudes in children. *Child Development, 68*(3), 530–543.

Bigler, R. S., & Liben, L. S. (1992). Cognitive mechanisms in children's gender stereotyping: Theoretical and educational implications of a cognitive-based intervention. *Child Development, 63,* 1351–1363.

Bigler, R. S., & Liben, L. S. (1993). A cognitive-developmental approach to racial stereotyping and reconstructive memory in Euro-American children. *Child Development, 64,* 1507–1518.

Bisson, J. (1997). *Celebrate!: An anti-bias guide to enjoying holidays.* St. Paul, MN: Redleaf Press.

Bolger, K. E., Patterson, C. J., Thompson, W. W., & Kupersmidt, J. B. (1995). Psychological adjustment among children experiencing persistent and intermittent family economic hardship. *Child Development, 66,* 1107–1129.

Bowers, C. A. (1995). *Educating for an ecologically sustainable culture.* Albany: State of University of New York Press.

Bowers, C. A. (2001). *Educating for eco-justice and community.* Athens, GA: Thue.

Bowman, B. T., & Stott, F. M. (1994). Understanding development in a cultural context. In B. L. Mallory & R. S. New (Eds.), *Diversity and developmentally appropriate practices: Challenges for early childhood education* (pp. 119–133). New York: Teachers College Press.

Bronfenbrenner, U. (1979). *The ecology of human development.* Cambridge, MA: Harvard University Press.

Bronfenbrenner, U. (1986). Ecology of the family as context for human development. *Developmental Psychology, 22,* 723–742.

Brooks-Gunn, J., Duncan, G. J., & Maritato, N. (1997). Poor families, poor outcomes: The well-being of children and youth. In G. J. Duncan & J. Brooks-Gunn (Eds.), *Consequences of growing up poor* (pp. 1–17). New York: Russell Sage.

Brown, C. S. (2002). *Refusing racism.* New York: Teachers College Press.

Brown, N. (1998, August). *The impact of culture on the education of young children with special needs.* Paper presented at the biennial meeting of Organization Mondiale de l'Education Preescolaire, Copenhagen, Denmark.

Burnett, M. N., & Sisson, K. (1995). Doll studies revisited: A question of validity. *Journal of Black Psychology, 21*(1), 19–29.

Burton, V. (1939). *Mike Mulligan and his steam shovel.* Boston: Houghton Mifflin.

Cadwell, L. B. (1997). *Bringing Reggio Emilia home: An innovative approach to early childhood education.* New York: Teachers College Press.

Cadwell, L. B. (2003). *Bringing learning to life: The Reggio approach to early childhood education.* New York: Teachers College Press.

Carlsson-Paige, N., & Levin, D. E. (1990). *Who's calling the shots? How to respond effectively to children's fascination with war play and war toys?* Philadelphia: New Society Publishers.

Carter, D. B., & Patterson, C. J. (1982). Sex roles as social conventions: The development of children's conceptions of sex-role stereotypes. *Developmental Psychology, 18,* 812–824.

Casper, V., Cuffaro, H. K., Schultz, S., Silin, J. G., & Wickens, E. (1996). Toward a most thorough understanding of the world: Sexual orientation and early childhood education. *Harvard Educational Review, 66*(2), 271–293.

Casper, B., & Schultz, S. B. (1999). *Gay parents, straight schools: Building communication and trust.* New York: Teachers College Press.

Chafel, J. A. (1997). Children's views of poverty: A review of research and implications for teaching. *The Educational Forum, 61,* 360–371.

Chang, H. N., Muckelroy, A., Pulido-Tobiassen, D., & Dowell, C. (2000). Redefining child care and early education in a diverse society: Dialogue and reflection. In L. D. Soto (Ed.), *The politics of early childhood* (pp. 142–164). New York: Peter Lang.

Chasnoff, D., & Cohen, H. (1996). *It's elementary: Talking about gay issues in school* [Video]. San Francisco, CA: Women's Educational Media.

*Child Development.* (1990). Special Issue on Minority Children, *61*(5).

*Child Development.* (1994). Special Issue: Children and Poverty, *65*(2).

Children's Defense Fund. (2003). 2002 Facts on Child Poverty in America. Available: www.children'sdefense.org/familyincome/childpoverty/ basicfacts.asp

Clark, A., Hocevar, D., & Dembo, M. H. (1980). The role of cognitive development in children's explanations and preferences for skin color. *Developmental Psychology, 16*, 332–339.

Clark, K. B., & Clark, M. P. (1947). Racial identification and preference in Negro children. In T. M. Newcomb & E. L. Hartley (Eds.), *Readings in social psychology* (pp. 169–178). New York: Holt, Rinehart & Winston.

Clark, M. D. (1997). Teacher response to learning disability: A test of attributional principles. *Journal of Learning Disabilities, 30*(1), 69–79.

Cochran-Smith, M. (2000). Blind vision: Unlearning racism in teacher education. *Harvard Educational Review, 70*(2), 157–190.

Colby, A., & Damon, W. (1992). *Some do care: Contemporary lives of moral commitment.* New York: Free Press.

Coles, R. (1996). *The moral life of children.* Boston: Atlantic Monthly Press.

Conant, S., & Budoff, M. (1983). Patterns of awareness in children's understanding of disabilities. *Mental Retardation, 21*(3), 119–125.

Conger, R. D., Ge, X., Elder, G. H., Lorenz, F. O., & Simons, R. L. (1994). Economic stress, coercive family process, and developmental problems of adolescents. *Child Development, 65*, 541–561.

Cook, D. A., & Fine, M. (1995). "Motherwit": Childrearing lessons from African American mothers of low income. In B. B. Swadener & S. Lubeck (Eds.), *Children and families "at promise": Deconstructing the discourse of risk* (pp. 118–142). Albany: State University of New York Press.

Corenblum, B., & Annis, R. C. (1993). Development of racial identity in minority and majority children: An affect discrepancy model. *Canadian Journal of Behavioural Science, 25*(4), 499–521.

Cose, E. (1993). *The rage of a privileged class.* New York: HarperPerennial.

Cottle, T. J. (1974). *Black children, White dreams.* New York: Dell.

Crawford, J. (1999). *Bilingual education: History, politics, theory, and practice* (4th ed.). Los Angeles: Bilingual Education Services.

Cross, W. E. (1985). Black identity: Rediscovering the distinction between personal identity and reference group orientation. In M. B. Spencer, G. K. Brookins, & W. R. Allen (Eds.), *Beginnings: The social and affective development of Black children* (pp. 155–171). Hillsdale, NJ: Erlbaum.

Cross, W. E. (1987). A two-factor theory of Black identity: Implications for the study of identity development in minority children. In J. Phinney & M. J. Rotheram (Eds.), *Children's ethnic socialization* (pp. 117–133). Beverly Hills: Sage.

Cross, W. E. (1991). *Shades of black.* Philadelphia: Temple University Press.

Csikszentmihalyi, M. (1999). If we are so rich, why aren't we happy? *American Psychologist, 54*, 821–827.

Csikszentmihalyi, M., & Schneider, B. (2000). *Becoming adults: How teenagers prepare for the world of work.* New York: Basic Books.

Damon, W. (1977). *The social world of the child.* San Francisco: Jossey-Bass.

Damon, W. (1980). Patterns of change in children's social reasoning: A two-year longitudinal study. *Child Development, 51,* 1010–1017.

Daniel, G. R. (1996). Black and White identity in the new millennium. In M. Root (Ed.), *The multiracial experience: Racial borders as the frontier* (pp. 121–139). Thousand Oaks, CA: Sage.

Darder, A. (1991). *Culture and power in the classroom: A critical foundation for bicultural education.* New York: Bergin & Garvey.

De Brunhoff, J. (1984). *The story of Babar.* New York: Random House.

De Gaetano, Y., Williams, L. R., & Volk, D. (1998). *Kaleidoscope: A multicultural approach for the primary school classroom.* Columbus, OH: Merrill.

DeGrella, L. H., & Green, V. P. (1984). Young children's attitudes toward orthopedic and sensory disabilities. *Education of the Visually Handicapped, 16*(1), 3–11.

Delgado-Gaitan, C., & Trueba, H. (1991). *Crossing cultural borders.* New York: Falmer.

DeLone, R. H. (1979). *Small futures.* New York: Harcourt Brace Jovanovich.

Delpit, L. (1995). *Other people's children: Cultural conflict in the classroom.* New York: New Press.

Derman-Sparks, L., & the A. B. C. Task Force. (1989). *Anti-bias curriculum: Tools for empowering young children.* Washington, D.C.: National Association for the Education of Young Children.

Derman-Sparks, L., Higa, C. T., & Sparks, B. (1980). Children, race and racism: How race awareness develops. *Interracial Books for Children Bulletin, 11,* 3–9.

Derman-Sparks, L., & Phillips, C. B. (1997). *Teaching/learning anti-racism: A developmental approach.* New York: Teachers College Press.

Devine, P. G., Plant, E. A., & Buswell, B. N. (2000). Breaking the prejudice habit: Progress and obstacles. In S. Okamp (Ed.), *Reducing prejudice and discrimination* (pp. 185–208). Mahwah, NJ: Erlbaum.

DeVries, R., & Zan, B. (1994). *Moral classrooms, moral children: Creating a constructivist atmosphere in early education.* New York: Teachers College Press.

Diamond, K. E. (1993). Preschool children's concepts of disability in their peers. *Early Education and Development, 4*(2), 123–129.

Diamond, K. E. (1994). Evaluating preschool children's sensitivity to developmental differences in their peers. *Topics in Early Childhood Special Education, 14*(1), 49–62.

Diamond, K. E., & Hestenes, L. L. (1996). Preschool children's conceptions of disabilities: The salience of disability in children's ideas about others. *Topics in Early Childhood Special Education, 16,* 458–475.

Diamond, K. E., Hestenes, L. L., Carpenter, E. S., & Innes, F. K. (1997). Relationships between enrollment in an inclusive class and preschool children's ideas about people with disabilities. *Topics in Early Childhood Special Education, 17*(4), 520–536.

Diamond, K. E., Hestenes, L. L., & O'Connor, C. E. (1994). Integrating young children with disabilities in preschool: Problems and promise. *Young Children, 49*(2), 69–75.

Diamond, K. E., & Innes, F. K. (2001). The origins of young children's attitudes toward peers with disabilities. In M. J. Guralnick (Ed.), *Early Childhood Inclusion: Focus on Change* (pp. 159–178). Baltimore, MD: Brooks.

Diamond, K., Le Furgy, W., & Blass, S. (1993). Attitudes of preschool children toward their peers with disabilities: A year-long investigation in integrated classrooms. *Journal of Genetic Psychology, 154*, 215–221.

Dovidio, J. F., Kawakami, K., & Gaertner, S. L. (2000). Reducing contemporary prejudice: Combating explicit and implicit bias at the individual and intergroup level. In S. Okamp (Ed.), *Reducing prejudice and discrimination* (pp. 137–163). Mahwah, NJ: Erlbaum.

Doyle, A. (1982). Friends, acquaintances, and strangers. In K. H. Rubin & H. S. Ross (Eds.), *Peer relationships and social skills in childhood* (pp. 229–252). New York: Springer-Verlag.

Doyle, A., & Aboud, F. E. (1993). Social and cognitive determinants of prejudice in children. In K. A. McLeod (Ed.), *Multicultural education: The state of the art* (pp. 28–33). Toronto: University of Toronto Press.

Dressner, M., & Gill, M. (1994). Environmental education at summer nature camp. *Journal of Environmental Education, 25*(3), 35–41.

Edwards, C. (1986). *Promoting social and moral development in young children: Creative approaches for the classroom.* New York: Teachers College Press.

Fadiman, A. (1997). *The spirit catches you and you fall down.* New York: Farrar, Strauss, & Giroux.

Farrell, W. C., & Olson, J. (1982, April). *Kenneth Clark revisited: Racial identification in light-skinned and dark-skinned Black children.* Paper presented at the annual meeting of the American Educational Research Association, New York.

Farver, J. M., Kim, Y. K., & Lee, Y. (1995). Cultural differences in Korean- and Anglo-American preschoolers' social interaction and play behaviors. *Child Development, 66*, 1088–1099.

Farver, J. M., & Shin, Y. L. (1997). Social pretend play in Korean- and Anglo-American preschoolers. *Child Development, 68*(3), 544–556.

Farver, J. M., Welles-Nystrom, B., Frosch, D. L., Wimbarti, S., & Hoppe-Graff, S. (1997). Toy stories: Aggression in children's narratives in the United States, Sweden, Germany, and Indonesia. *Journal of Cross-Cultural Psychology, 28*(4), 393–420.

Favazza, P., & Odom, S. L. (1997). Promoting positive attitudes of kindergarten-age children toward people with disabilities. *Exceptional Children, 63*, 405–418.

Feagin, J. R., & Sikes, M. P. (1994). *Living with racism: The Black middle-class experience.* Boston: Beacon.

Finkelstein, N. W., & Haskins, R. (1983). Kindergarten children prefer same-color peers. *Child Development, 54*, 502–508.

Fishbein, H. D., & Imai, S. (1993). Preschoolers select playmates on the basis of gender and race. *Journal of Applied Developmental Psychology, 14*, 303–316.

Fox, D. J., & Jordan, V. B. (1973). Racial preference and identification of Black, American Chinese, and White children. *Genetic Psychology Monographs, 88*, 229–286.

Franklin, K. L., & McGirr, N. (Eds.). (1995). *Out of the dump: Writings and photographs by children from Guatemala.* New York: Lothrop, Lee & Shepard.

Franklin, M. E. (1992). Culturally sensitive instructional practices for African-American learners with disabilities. *Exceptional Children, 59*(2), 115–122.

Fruchter, J. (1999). Linking social justice concerns with environmental issues. *ZPG Recorder* (Special Issue on Kid-Friendly Cities), *31*(4), 10–11.

Furby, L. (1979). Inequalities in personal possessions: Explanations for and judgments about unequal distribution. *Human Development, 22,* 180–202.

Furnham, A., & Stacey, B. (1991). *Young people's understanding of society.* New York: Routledge.

Furth, H. (1980). *The world of grown-ups: Children's conceptions of society.* New York: Elsevier.

Garbarino, J. (1999). *Lost boys: Why our sons turn violent and how we can save them.* New York: Free Press.

Garbarino, J., Dubrow, N., Kostelny, K., & Pardo, C. (1992). *Children in danger: Coping with the consequences of community violence.* San Francisco: Jossey-Bass.

Garcia, R. L. (1990). *Teaching in a pluralistic society: Concepts, models, and strategies* (2nd ed.). New York: HarperCollins.

Garcia Coll, C., Lamberty, C., Jenkins, R., McAdoo, H. P., Crnic, K., Wasik, B. H., & Vazquez Garcia, H. (1996). An integrative model for the study of developmental competencies in minority children. *Child Development, 67,* 1891–1914.

Gay, G. (1995). Mirror images on common issues: Parallels between multicultural education and critical pedagogy. In C. E. Sleeter & P. L. McLaren (Eds.), *Multicultural education, critical pedagogy, and the politics of difference* (pp. 155–189). Albany: State University of New York Press.

Gay, G. (2000). *Culturally responsive teaching: Theory, research & practice.* New York: Teachers College Press.

Gemmell-Crosby, S., & Hanzik, J. R. (1994). Preschool teachers' perceptions of including children with disabilities. *Education and Training in Mental Retardation and Developmental Disabilities, 29*(4), 279–290.

Gibbs, J. T., Huang, L. N., & Associates. (1989). *Children of color: Psychological interventions with minority youths.* San Francisco: Jossey-Bass.

Gollnick, D. M., & Chin, P. C. (1983). *Multicultural education in a pluralistic society.* St. Louis: Mosby.

Gollnick, D. M., & Chin, P. C. (1998). *Multicultural education in a pluralistic society* (5th ed.). Columbus, OH: Merrill.

Gonsier-Gerdin, J. (1995, March–April). *An ethnographic case study of children's social relationships in a full inclusion elementary school.* Poster presented at the biennial meeting of the Society for Research in Child Development, Indianapolis.

Gonzalez-Mena, J. (1992). Taking a culturally sensitive approach in infant–toddler programs. *Young Children, 47*(2), 4–9.

Gonzalez-Ramos, G., Zayas, L. H., & Cohen, E. V. (1998). Child-rearing values of low-income, urban Puerto Rican Mothers of preschool children. *Developmental Psychology, 29*(4), 377–382.

Goodman, J. E. (1989). Does retardation mean dumb? Children's perceptions of the nature, cause, and course of mental retardation. *The Journal of Special Education, 23,* 313–329.

Goodman, M. (1952). *Race awareness in young children.* Cambridge, MA: Addison-Wesley.

Gottfried, A. W., Gottfried, A. E., Bathurst, K., Guerin, D. W., & Parramore, M. M. (2003). Socioeconomic status in children's development and family environment: Infancy through adolescence. In M. Bornstein (Ed.), *Socioeconomic status, parenting, and child development* (pp. 189–207). Mahwah, NJ: Erlbaum.

Gramezy, N. (1992). Resiliency and vulnerability to adverse developmental outcomes associated with poverty. In T. Thompson & S. C. Hupp (Eds.), *Saving children at risk: Poverty and disabilities* (pp. 45–60). Newbury Park, CA: Sage.

Grenot-Scheyer, M., Staub, D., Peck, C. A., & Schwartz, I. S. (1998). Reciprocity and friendships: Listening to the voices of children and youth with and without disabilities. In L. H. Meyer, H.-S. Park, M. Grenot-Scheyer, I. S. Schwarz, & B. Harry (Eds.), *Making friends: The influences of culture and development* (pp. 149–167). Baltimore, MD: Brooks.

Gruenewald, D. A. (2003). The best of both worlds: A critical pedagogy of place. *Educational Researcher, 32*(4), 3–12.

Guralnick, M. J., Connor, R. T., Hammond, M. A., Gottman, J. M., & Kinnish, K. (1996). The peer relations of preschool children with communication disorders. *Child Development, 67,* 471–489.

Guralnick, M. J., & Groom, J. M. (1987). The peer relations of mildly delayed and nonhandicapped preschool children in mainstreamed playgroups. *Child Development, 58,* 1556–1572.

Hallinan, M. T., & Teixeira, R. A. (1987). Opportunities and constraints: Black–White differences in the formation of interracial friendships. *Child Development, 58,* 1358–1371.

Hanson, M. J. (2002). Cultural and linguistic diversity: Influences on preschool inclusion. In S. L. Odom (Ed.), *Widening the circle: Including children with disabilities in preschool programs* (pp. 137–153). New York: Teachers College Press.

Hanson, M. J., Gutierrez, S., Morgan, M., Brennan, E. L., & Zercher, C. (1997). Language, culture, and disability: Interacting influences on preschool inclusion. *Topics in Early Childhood Special Education, 17*(3), 307–336.

Harper, D. C., Wacker, D. P., & Cobb, L. S. (1986). Children's social preferences toward peers with visible physical differences. *Journal of Pediatric Psychology, 11*(3), 323–342.

Harrah, J., & Friedman, M. (1990). Economic socialization in children in a midwestern American community. *Journal of Economic Psychology, 11,* 495–513.

Harry, B. (1998). Parental visions of "una vida normal/a normal life": Cultural variations on a theme. In L. H. Meyer, H.-S. Park, M. Grenot-Scheyer, I. S. Schwarz, & B. Harry (Eds.), *Making friends: The influences of culture and development* (pp. 47–62). Baltimore, MD: Brooks.

Harry, B., Park, H.-S., & Day, M. (1998). Friendships of many kinds: Valuing the choice of children and youth with disabilities. In L. H. Meyer, H.-S. Park, M. Grenot-Scheyer, I. S. Schwarz, & B. Harry, *Making friends: The influences of culture and development* (pp. 393–402). Baltimore, MD: Brooks.

Harvey, M. R. (1980). Public school treatment of low-income children: Education for passivity. *Urban Education, 15,* 279–323.

Haymes, S. N. (1995). *Race, culture, and the city: A pedagogy for Black urban struggle.* Albany: State University of New York Press.

Helm, J. H., & Beneke, S. (Eds.). (2003). *The power of projects: Meeting contemporary challenges in early childhood classrooms—strategies and solutions.* New York: Teachers College Press.

Helms, J. (1990). *Black and White racial identity: Theory, research, and practice.* New York: Greenwood.

Helper, J. B. (1994). Mainstreaming children with learning disabilities: Have we improved their social environments? *Social Work in Education, 16*(3), 143–154.

Hertz-Lazarowitz, R., & Miller, N. (Eds.). (1992). *Interaction in cooperative groups.* Cambridge, UK: Cambridge University Press.

Hill, L. D. (2001). *Connecting kids: Exploring diversity together.* Gabriola Island, British Columbia, Canada: New Society Publishers.

Hilliard, A. G. (1992). The pitfalls and promises of special education practice. *Exceptional Children, 59*(2), 168–172.

Hirschfield, L. A. (1995). Do children have a theory of race? *Cognition, 54,* 209–252.

Hoffman, M. (2000). *Empathy and moral development: Implications for caring and justice.* Cambridge, UK: Cambridge University Press.

Holmes, R. (1995). *How young children perceive race.* New York: Sage.

hooks, b. (1990). *Yearning: Race, gender, and cultural politics.* Boston: South End Press.

Howard, G. R. (1999). *We can't teach what we don't know.* New York: Teachers College Press.

Howes, C., & Ritchie, S. (2002). *A matter of trust: Connecting teachers and learners in early childhood classrooms.* New York: Teachers College Press.

Howes, C., & Wu, F. (1990). Peer interactions and friendships in an ethnically diverse school setting. *Child Development, 61,* 537–541.

Hughes, P., & MacNaughton, G. (2001). Fractured or manufactured: Gendered identities and culture in the early years. In S. Grieshaber & G. S. Cannella (Eds.), *Embracing identities in early childhood education: Diversity and possibilities* (pp. 114–130). New York: Teachers College Press.

Huston, A. C. (1991). Children in poverty: Developmental and policy issues. In A. C. Huston (Ed.), *Children in poverty: Child development and public policy* (pp. 1–22). Cambridge, UK: Cambridge University Press.

Igoa, C. (1995). *The inner world of the immigrant child.* New York: St. Martin's Press.

Jewish Virtual Library. (2004). *Martin Niemoeller.* Available: www.us-israel.org/jsource/biography/niemoeller

Jackson, A., Brooks-Gunn, J., Huang, C., & Glassman, M. (2000). Single mothers in low-wage jobs: Financial strain, parenting, and preschoolers' outcomes. *Child Development, 71*, 1409–1423.

Jackson, J. F. (1999). What are the real risk factors for African American children? *Phi Delta Kappan, 81*(4), 308–312.

Johnson, D. W., & Johnson, R. T. (2000). The three Cs of reducing prejudice and discrimination. In S. Okamp (Ed.), *Reducing prejudice and discrimination* (pp. 239–268). Mahwah, NJ: Erlbaum.

Juvonen, J., & Bear, G. (1992). Social adjustment of children with and without learning disabilities in integrated classrooms. *Journal of Educational Psychology, 84*, 322–330.

Kahn, P. H., & Friedman, B. (1995). Environmental views and values of children in an inner-city Black community. *Child Development, 66*, 1403–1417.

Kang, B., & Ramsey, P. G. (1993, April). *The effects of gender, race, and social class differences on children's friendships*. Paper presented at the annual meeting of the American Educational Research Association, Atlanta.

Katz, P. A. (1973). Perception of racial cues in preschool children. *Developmental Psychology, 8*, 295–299.

Katz, P. A. (1976). The acquisition of racial attitudes in children. In P. A. Katz (Ed.), *Towards the elimination of racism* (pp. 125–154). New York: Pergamon.

Katz, P. A. (1982). Development of children's racial awareness and intergroup attitudes. In L. G. Katz (Ed.), *Current topics in early childhood education* (pp. 17–54). Norwood, NJ: Ablex.

Katz, P. A., & Kofkin, J. A. (1997). Race, gender, and young children. In S. Luthar, J. Burack, D. Cicchetti, & J. Weisz (Eds.), *Developmental perspectives on risk and pathology* (pp. 51–74). New York: Cambridge University Press.

Kemple, K. M. (2004). *Let's be friends: Peer competence and social inclusion in early childhood classrooms*. New York: Teachers College Press.

Kendall, F. (1996). *Diversity in the classroom: New approaches to the education of young children* (2nd ed.). New York: Teachers College Press.

Kessler, S. J., & McKenna, W. (1978). *Gender: An ethnomethodological approach*. New York: Wiley.

Kich, G. K. (1992). The developmental process of asserting a biracial, bicultural identity. In M. P. P. Root (Ed.), *Racially mixed people in America* (pp. 304–317). Newbury Park, CA: Sage.

Kincheloe, J. L. (1993). *Toward a critical politics of teacher thinking: Mapping the postmodern*. Westport, CT: Bergin & Garvey.

Kindlon, D., & Thompson, M. (1999). *Raising Cain: Protecting the emotional lives of boys*. New York: Ballantine Books.

Kirchner, G. (2000). *Children's games from around the world* (2nd ed.). Boston: Allyn and Bacon.

Kivel, P. (1999). *Boys will be men: Raising our sons for courage, caring, and community*. Gabriola Island, British Columbia, Canada: New Society Publishers.

Kivel, P. (2002). *Uprooting racism: How white people can work for racial justice*. Gabriola Island, British Columbia, Canada: New Society Publishers.

Kline, S. (1993). *Out of the garden: Toys and children's culture in the age of TV marketing*. London: Verso.

Kobayashi-Winata, H., & Power, T. G. (1989). Child rearing and compliance: Japanese and American families in Houston. *Journal of Cross-Cultural Psychology, 20*(4), 333–356.

Kohen, D. E., Brooks-Gunn, J., Leventhal, T., & Hertzman, C. (2002). Neighborhood income and physical and social disorders in Canada: Associations with young children's competencies. *Child Development, 73*(6), 1844–1860.

Kokopeli, B., & Lakey, G. (1983). *Off our backs . . . and on our own two feet*. Philadelphia: New Society Publishers.

Kostelnik, M. J., Onaga, E., Rohde, B., & Whiren, A. (2002). *Children with special needs: Lessons for early childhood professionals*. New York: Teachers College Press.

Kozleski, E. B., & Jackson, L. (1993). Taylor's story: Full inclusion in her neighborhood elementary school. *Exceptionality, 4*(3), 153–175.

Kozol, J. (1991). *Savage inequalities*. New York: Crown.

Kroeger, J. (2001). A reconstructed tale of inclusion for a lesbian family in an early childhood classroom. In S. Grieshaber & G. S. Cannella (Eds.), *Embracing identities in early childhood education: Diversity and possibilities* (pp. 73–86). New York: Teachers College Press.

Kurusa. (1985). Doppert, L. M. (Illus.). Englander, K. (Trans.). *The streets are free*. Copenhagen, Denmark: Annick Press.

Lambert, W. E., & Klineberg, O. (1967). *Children's views of foreign peoples*. New York: Appleton-Century-Crofts.

Leahy, R. (1983). The development of the conception of social class. In R. Leahy (Ed.), *The child's construction of inequality* (pp. 79–107). New York: Academic Press.

Leahy, R. (1990). The development of concepts of economic and social inequality. *New Directions for Child Development, 46*, 107–120.

Lebra, T. S. (1994). Mother and child in Japanese socialization: A Japan–U.S. comparison. In P. M. Greenfield & R. R. Cocking (Eds.), *Cross-cultural roots of minority child development* (pp. 259–274). Hillsdale, NJ: Erlbaum.

Levine, J. (1994, March–April). White like me: When privilege is written on your skin. *Ms.*, pp. 22–24.

Liben, L. S., & Bigler, R. S. (2002). The developmental course of gender differentiation: Conceptualizing, measuring, and evaluating constructs and pathways. *Monographs of the Society for Research in Child Development, 67*(2, Serial No. 269).

Longstreet, W. S. (1978). *Aspects of ethnicity*. New York: Teachers College Press.

Lott, B. (2002). Cognitive and behavioral distancing from the poor. *American Psychologist, 57*(2), 100–110.

Luthar, S. S., & Becker, B. E. (2002). Privileged but pressured? A study of affluent youth. *Child Development, 73*(5), 1593–1610.

MacNaughton, G. (2000). *Rethinking gender in early childhood education*. Thousand Oaks, CA: Sage.

Maccoby, E. E. (1986). Social groupings in childhood: Their relationship to prosocial and antisocial behavior in boys and girls. In D. Olewus, J. Block, & M.
Radke-Yarrow (Eds.), *Development of antisocial and prosocial behavior* (pp.
263–284). New York: Academic Press.

Mapley, C. E., & Kizer, J. B. (1983, April). *Children's process of sex-role incongruent information: "The nurse's name was Dr. Brown."* Paper presented at the
biennial meeting of the Society for Research in Child Development, Detroit.

Mapp, K. L. (2002, April). *Having their say: Parents describe how and why they are
involved in their children's education.* Paper presented at the annual meeting of
the American Educational Research Association, New Orleans.

Martin, C. L., & Halverson, C. (1981). A schematic processing model of sex typing
and stereotyping in children. *Child Development, 52,* 1119–1134.

McAdoo, H. P. (1993). *Family ethnicity: Strength in diversity.* Beverly Hills: Sage.

McIntosh, P. (1995). White privilege and male privilege: A personal account of
coming to see correspondences through work in women's studies. In M. L.
Anderson & P. H. Collins (Eds.), *Race, class, and gender: An anthology* (pp.
76–87). Belmont, CA: Wadsworth.

McIntyre, A. (1997). *Making meaning of Whiteness: Exploring racial identity with
White teachers.* Albany: State University of New York Press.

McLaren, P. (1994). White terror and oppositional agency: Towards a critical multiculturalism. In D. T. Goldbert (Ed.), *Multiculturalism: A critical reader* (pp.
45–74). Cambridge, MA: Blackwell.

McLoyd, V. C. (1998a). Socioeconomic disadvantage and child development. *American Psychologist, 53,* 185–204.

McLoyd, V. C. (1998b). Socioeconomic hardship on Black families and children:
Psychological distress, parenting, and socioemotional development. *Child Development, 61,* 311–346.

McLoyd, V. C., & Ceballo, R. (1998). Conceptualizing and assessing the economic
context: Issues in the study of race and child development. In V. C. McLoyd
& L. Steinberg (Eds.), *Studying minority adolescents: Conceptual, methodological, and theoretical issues* (pp. 251–278). Mahwah, NJ: Erlbaum.

McLoyd, V. C., & Wilson, L. (1992). The strain of living poor: Parenting, social
support, and child mental health. In A. C. Huston (Ed.), *Children in poverty:
Child development and public policy* (pp. 105–135). New York: Cambridge
University Press.

Meltzer, M. (1996). The role of Whites in combating racism. *Rethinking Schools,
10*(4), 4–5.

Menchu, R. (1983). *I, Rigoberta Menchu: An Indian woman in Guatemala.* London:
Verso.

Menzel, P. (1994). *Material world: A global family portrait.* San Francisco: Sierra
Club Books.

Miles, M. (1971). *Annie and the old one.* Boston: Little Brown.

Milich, R., McAnnich, C. B., & Harris, M. J. (1992). Effects of stigmatizing information on children's peer relations: Believing is seeing. *School Psychology
Review, 21*(3), 400–409.

Milton, B., Cleveland, E., & Bennett-Gates, D. (1995). Changing perceptions of nature, self, and others: A report on a park/school program. *Journal of Environmental Education, 26*(3), 32–39.

Minami, M., & Ovando, C. J. (1995). Language issues in multicultural contexts. In J. A. Banks & C. A. M. Banks (Eds.), *Handbook of research on multicultural education* (pp. 427–444). New York: Simon & Schuster/Macmillan.

Molnar, J. M., Rath, W. R., & Klein, T. P. (1990). Constantly compromised: The impact of homelessness on children. *Journal of Social Issues, 46,* 109–124.

Moran, C. E., & Hakuta, K. (1995). Bilingual education: Broadening research perspectives. In J. A. Banks & C. A. M. Banks (Eds.), *Handbook of research on multicultural education* (pp. 445–462). New York: Simon & Schuster/Macmillan.

Morland, J. K. (1962). Racial acceptance and preference of nursery school children in a southern city. *Merrill-Palmer Quarterly, 8,* 271–280.

Nabors, L. (1995, March). *Attitudes, friendship ratings, and behaviors for typically developing preschoolers interacting with peers with disabilities.* Paper presented at the biennial meeting of the Society for Research in Child Development, Indianapolis.

Nabors, L. (1997). Social interaction among preschool children in inclusive child care centers. *Applied Developmental Science, 1*(4), 162–167.

Nabors, L., & Keyes, L. (1995). Preschoolers' reasons for accepting peers with and without disabilities. *Journal of Developmental and Physical Disabilities, 7*(4), 335–355.

Naimark, H. (1983, April). *Children's understanding of social class differences.* Paper presented at the biennial meeting of the Society for Research in Child Development, Detroit.

Newman, M. A., Liss, M. B., & Sherman, F. (1983). Ethnic awareness in children: Not a unitary concept. *The Journal of Genetic Psychology, 143,* 103–112.

Nieto, S. (2004). *Affirming diversity: The sociopolitical context of multicultural education* (4th ed.). Boston: Allyn & Bacon.

Nightingale, C. H. (1993). *On the edge: A history of poor Black children and their American Dreams.* New York: Basic Books.

Noddings, N. (1992). *The challenge to care in schools: An alternative approach to education.* New York: Teachers College Press.

Noddings, N. (2002). *Educating moral people: A caring alternative to character education.* New York: Teachers College Press.

Ocampo, K. A., Bernal, M. E., & Knight, G. P. (1993). Gender, race, and ethnicity: The sequencing of social constancies. In M. E. Bernal & G. P. Knight (Eds.), *Ethnic identity: Formation and transmission among Hispanics and other minorities* (pp. 11–30). Albany: State University of New York Press.

Odom, S. L. (2002). *Widening the circle: Including children with disabilities in preschool programs.* New York: Teachers College Press.

Odom, S. L., Jenkins, J. R., Speltz, M. L., & DeKlyen, M. (1982). Promoting social interaction of young children at risk for learning disabilities. *Learning Disability Quarterly, 5,* 379–387.

Odom, S. L., McConnell, S. R., & Chandler, L. K. (1993). Acceptability and feasi-bility of classroom-based social interaction interventions for young children with disabilities. *Exceptional Children, 60*(3), 226–236.

Odom, S. L., Peck, C. A., Hanson, M., Beckman, P. J., Kaiser, A. P., Lieber, J., Brown, W. H., Horn, E. M., & Schwartz, I. S. (1996). Inclusion at the pre-school level: An ecological systems analysis. *Social Policy Report of the Soci-ety for Research in Child Development, 10*(2 & 3), 18–30.

Odom, S. L., Zercher, C., Marquart, J., Li, S., Sandall, S. R., & Wolfberg, P. (2002). Social relationships of children with disabilities and their peers in inclusive classrooms. In S. L. Odom (Ed.), *Widening the circle: Including children with disabilities in preschool programs* (pp. 61–80). New York: Teachers College Press.

Orellana, M. F. (1994). Appropriating the voice of the superheroes: Three preschool-ers' bilingual language uses in play. *Early Childhood Research Quarterly, 9*, 171–193.

Orlick, T. (1978). *The cooperative sports and games book: Challenge without com-petition.* New York: Pantheon.

Orlick, T. (1982). *The second cooperative sports and games book: Over 200 brand-new cooperative games for kids and adults and both.* Ann Arbor, MI: North American Students of Cooperation.

Paley, V. G. (1992). *You can't say you can't play.* Cambridge, MA: Harvard Univer-sity Press.

Palmer, A. (2001). Responding to special needs. In E. Dau (Ed.), *The anti-bias approach in early childhood* (2nd ed.; pp. 83–94). Frenchs Forest, New South Wales, Australia: Pearson Education Australia.

Pang, V. O. (2001). *Multicultural education: A caring-centered, reflective approach.* Boston: McGraw-Hill.

Pang, V. O., & Park, C. D. (2002, April). *Self regulation: Using strategic questions to engage pre-service teachers in reflection and writing about prejudicial atti-tudes and beliefs.* Paper presented at the annual meeting of the American Edu-cational Research Association, New Orleans.

Patchen, M. (1982). *Black–White contact in schools: Its social and academic effects.* West Lafayette, IN: Purdue University Press.

Pearl, R., Farmer, T. W., Van Acker, R., Rodkin, P. C., Bost, K. K., Coe, M., & Henley, W. (1998). The social integration of students with mild disabilities in general education classrooms: Peer group membership and peer-assessed social behavior. *The Elementary School Journal, 99*(2), 167–185.

Pellegrini, A. D. (1995). *School recess and playground behaviors: Educational and developmental roles.* Albany: State University of New York Press.

Peters, M. F. (2002). Racial socialization of young Black children. In H. P. McAdoo & J. L. McAdoo (Eds.), *Black children: Social, educational, and parental envi-ronment* (pp. 57–72). Newbury Park, CA: Sage.

Phelan, P., & Davidson, A. L. (1993). *Renegotiating cultural diversity in American schools.* New York: Teachers College Press.

Phillips, C. B. (1994). The movement of African-American children through sociocultural contexts: A case of conflict resolution. In B. L. Mallory & R. S. New (Eds.), *Diversity and developmentally appropriate practice* (pp. 137–154). New York: Teachers College Press.

Piaget, J. (1951). *The child's conception of the world.* New York: Humanities Press.

Piaget, J., & Inhelder, B. (1968). *The psychology of the child.* New York: Basic Books.

Piaget, J., & Weil, A. M. (1951). The development in children of the idea of the homeland and of relations to other countries. *International Social Science Journal, 3,* 561–578.

Pina, J. (2002). *Identifying and challenging children's aversions and fears of elements in the natural environment using a classroom intervention.* Unpublished honors thesis, Mount Holyoke College, South Hadley, MA.

Polakow, V. (1993). *Lives on the edge.* Chicago: University of Chicago Press.

Polakow, V. (2000). Savage policies: Systemic violence in the lives of children. In V. Polakow (Ed.), *The public assault on America's children: Poverty, violence and juvenile justice* (pp. 1–18). New York: Teachers College Press.

Pollack, W. (1998). *Real boys: Rescuing our sons from the myths of boyhood.* New York: Random House.

Porter, C. P. (1991). Social reasons for skin tone preferences of Black school-age children. *American Journal of Orthopsychiatry, 6*(1), 149–154.

Porter, J. D. (1971). *Black child, White child: The development of racial attitudes.* Cambridge, MA: Harvard University Press.

Putallaz, M., & Wasserman, A. (1990). Children's entry behavior. In S. R. Asher & J. D. Coie (Eds.), *Peer rejection in childhood* (pp. 60–89). New York: Cambridge University Press.

Radke, M., & Trager, H. G. (1950). Children's perceptions of the social roles of Negroes and Whites. *Journal of Psychology, 29,* 3–33.

Ramirez, D. A. (1996). Multiracial identity in a color-conscious world. In M. Root (Ed.), *The multiracial experience: Racial borders as the new frontier* (pp. 49–62). Thousand Oaks, CA: Sage.

Ramsey, P. G. (1982, August). *Racial differences in children's contacts and comments about others.* Paper presented at the annual meeting of the American Psychological Association, Washington, DC.

Ramsey, P. G. (1983, April). *Young children's responses to racial differences: Sociocultural perspectives.* Paper presented at the biennial meeting of the Society for Research in Child Development, Detroit.

Ramsey, P. G. (1986a). Possession disputes in preschool classrooms. *Child Study Journal, 16,* 173–181.

Ramsey, P. G. (1986b). Racial and cultural categories. In C. P. Edwards with P. G. Ramsey, *Promoting social and moral development in young children: Creative approaches for the classroom* (pp. 78–101). New York: Teachers College Press.

Ramsey, P. G. (1987). Young children's thinking about ethnic differences. In J. Phinney & M. Rotheram (Eds.), *Children's ethnic socialization: Pluralism and development* (pp. 56–72). Beverly Hills, CA: Sage.

Ramsey, P. G. (1991a). *Making friends in school: Promoting peer relationships in early childhood.* New York: Teachers College Press.

Ramsey, P. G. (1991b). The salience of race in young children growing up in an all-White community. *Journal of Educational Psychology, 83,* 28–34.

Ramsey, P. G. (1991c). Young children's awareness and understanding of social class differences. *Journal of Genetic Psychology, 152,* 71–82.

Ramsey, P. G. (1995). Changing social dynamics of early childhood classrooms. *Child Development, 66,* 764–773.

Ramsey, P. G. (1996). Successful and unsuccessful entries in pre-schools. *Journal of Applied Developmental Psychology, 17,* 135–150.

Ramsey, P. G., & Myers, L. C. (1990). Salience of race in young children's cognitive, affective and behavioral responses to social environments. *Journal of Applied Developmental Psychology, 11,* 49–67.

Ramsey, P. G., & Williams, L. R., with Vold, E. B. (2003). *Multicultural education: A source book* (2nd ed.). New York: RoutledgeFalmer.

Rist, R. C. (1970). Student social class and teacher expectations: The self-fulfilling prophecy in ghetto education. *Harvard Educational Review, 40,* 411–451.

Ritchie, J. (2001). Reflections on collectivism in early childhood teaching in Aotearoa/New Zealand. In S. Grieshaber & G. S. Cannella (Eds.), *Embracing identities in early childhood education: Diversity and possibilities* (pp. 133–147). New York: Teachers College Press.

Roberts, C., & Zubrick, S. (1992). Factors influencing the social status of children with mild academic disabilities in regular classrooms. *Exceptional Children, 59*(3), 192–202.

Rodriguez, R. (1981). *Hunger of memory: The education of Richard Rodriguez.* Boston: Godine.

Roopnarine, J. L., Lasker, J., Sacks, M., & Stores, M. (1998). The cultural contexts of children's play. In O. Saracho & B. Spodek (Eds.), *Play in Early Childhood* (pp. 194–219). Albany: State University of New York Press.

Root, M. P. P. (Ed.). (1992). *Racially mixed people in America.* Newbury Park, CA: Sage.

Root, M. P. P. (Ed.). (1996). *The multiracial experience: Racial borders as the new frontier.* Thousand Oaks, CA: Sage.

Rosenfield, D., & Stephan, W. G. (1981). Intergroup relations among children. In S. S. Brehm, S. M. Kassin, & F. X. Gibbons (Eds.), *Developmental social psychology* (pp. 271–297). New York: Oxford University Press.

Rosman, E. A., Yoshikawa, H., & Knitzer, J. (2002). Towards an understanding of the impact of welfare reform on children with disabilities and their families: Setting a research and policy agenda. *Social Policy Report of the Society for Research in Child Development, 16*(4), 3–15.

Running-Grass. (1994). Towards a multicultural environmental education. *Multicultural Education, 2*(1), 4–6.

Sadker, M., & Sadker, D. (1995). *Failing at fairness: How our schools cheat girls.* New York: Simon & Schuster.

Salisbury, C. L., & Palombar, M. M. (1998). In L. H. Meyer, H.-S. Park, M. Grenot-

Scheyer, I. S. Schwarz, & B. Harry, *Making friends: The influences of culture and development* (pp. 81–104). Baltimore, MD: Brooks.

Schaffer, M., & Sinicrope, P. (1983, June). *Promoting the growth of moral judgment: An inservice teacher training model.* Paper presented at the annual meeting of the Jean Piaget Society, Philadelphia.

Schofield, J. W. (1989). *Black and White in school: Trust, tension, or tolerance.* New York: Teachers College Press.

Scholl, L. (2002, April). *Hybridity in (multicultural) education.* Paper presented at the annual meeting of the American Educational Research Association, New Orleans.

Serbin, L. A., Tonick, I. J., & Sternglanz, S. H. (1977). Shaping cooperative cross-sex play. *Child Development, 48,* 924–929.

Sheridan, M. K., Foley, G. M., & Radlinski, S. H. (1995). *Using the supportive play model: Individualized intervention in early childhood practice.* New York: Teachers College Press.

Shils, E. (1981). *Tradition.* Chicago: University of Chicago Press.

Siegel, B. (1996). Is the emperor wearing clothes? Social policy and the empirical support for full inclusion of children with disabilities in the preschool and early elementary grades. *Social Policy Report of the Society for Research in Child Development, 10*(2 & 3), 2–17.

Sigelman, C. K. (1991). The effect of causal information on peer perceptions of children with physical problems. *Journal of Applied Developmental Psychology, 12,* 237–253.

Sigelman, C. K., & Singleton, L. C. (1986). Stigmatization in childhood: A survey of developmental trends and issues. In G. Becker, L. M. Colema, & S. Ainley (Eds.), *The dilemma of difference: A multidisciplinary view of stigma* (pp. 185–208). New York: Plenum.

Silin, J. G. (1995). *Sex, death, and the education of children: Our passion for ignorance in the age of AIDS.* New York: Teachers College Press.

Silverstein, S. (1964). *The giving tree.* New York: Harper & Row.

Simmons, D. A. (1994). Urban children's preferences for nature: Lessons for environmental education. *Children's Environments, 11*(3), 194–203.

Sims, R. (1982). *Shadow and substance: Afro-American experience in contemporary children's fiction.* Chicago: American Library Association.

Singleton, L. C., & Asher, S. R. (1977). Peer preferences and social interaction among third-grade children in an integrated school district. *Journal of Educational Psychology, 69,* 330–336.

Slavin, R. E. (1995). Cooperative learning and intergroup relations. In J. A. Banks & C. A. M. Banks (Eds.), *Handbook of research on multicultural education* (pp. 628–634). New York: Simon & Schuster/Macmillan.

Sleeter, C. E. (1992). *Keepers of the American Dream: A study of staff development and multicultural education.* Bristol, PA: Taylor & Francis.

Sleeter, C. E. (1993, April). *This curriculum is multicultural . . . isn't it?* Paper presented at the annual meeting of the American Educational Research Association, Atlanta.

Sleeter, C. E. (1994). White racism. *Multicultural Education, 1*, 5–8, 39.

Sleeter, C. E., & Grant, C. A. (1988). *Making choices for multicultural education: Five approaches to race, class, and gender.* New York: Macmillan.

Smith, B. (1983). Homophobia: Why bring it up? *Interracial Books for Children Bulletin, 14*, 112–113.

Snell, M. B. (2003). Neighborhood watch: A Texas twosome takes on polluters and wins. *Sierra, 88*(5), 12–16.

Sobel, D. (1996). *Beyond ecophobia: Reclaiming the heart in nature education.* Great Barrington, MA: The Orion Society and the Myrin Institute.

Spencer, M. B., Brookins, G. K., & Allen, W. R. (1985). *Beginnings: The social and affective development of Black children.* Hillsdale, NJ: Erlbaum.

Spencer, M. B., & Markstrom-Adams, C. (1990). Identity processes among racial and ethnic minority children in America. *Child Development, 61*, 290–310.

Stabler, J. R., Zeig, J. A., & Johnson, E. E. (1982). Perceptions of racially related stimuli by young children. *Perceptual and Motor Skills, 54*(1), 71–77.

Stalvey, L. M. (1989). *The education of a WASP.* Madison: University of Wisconsin Press.

Stipek, D. J., & Ryan, R. H. (1997). Economically disadvantaged preschoolers: Ready to learn but further to go. *Developmental Psychology, 33*(4) 711–723.

Stott, F., & Bowman, B. (1996). Child development knowledge: A slippery base for practice. *Early Childhood Research Quarterly, 11*, 169–183.

Stronge, J. H. (Ed.). (1992). *Educating homeless children and adolescents: Evaluating policy and practice.* Newbury Park, CA: Sage.

Sutherland, D. S., & Ham, S. H. (1992). Child-to-parent transfer of environmental ideology in Costa Rican families: An ethnographic case study. *Journal of Environmental Education, 23*(3), 9–16.

Swadener, E. B. (2000). "At risk" or "at promise"? From deficit constructions of the "other childhood" to possibilities for authentic alliances with children and families. In L. D. Soto (Ed.), *The politics of early childhood education* (pp. 117–134). New York: Peter Lang.

Swadener, E. B., & Johnson, J. E. (1989). Play in diverse social contexts: Parent and teacher roles. In M. N. Bloch & A. D. Pellegrini (Eds.), *The ecological context of children's play* (pp. 214–244). Norwood, NJ: Ablex.

Tajfel, H. (1973). The roots of prejudice: Cognitive aspects. In P. Watson (Ed.), *Psychology and race* (pp. 76–95). Chicago: Aldine.

Takaki, R. (1993). *A different mirror: A history of multicultural America.* Boston: Little, Brown.

Tatum, B. D. (1992). Talking about race, learning about racism: The application of racial identity development theory in the classroom. *Harvard Educational Review, 62*(1), 1–24.

Tatum, B. D. (1994). Teaching White students about racism: The search for White allies and the restoration of hope. *Teachers College Record, 95*, 462–476.

Tatum, B. D. (1997). *"Why are all the Black kids sitting together in the cafeteria?" and other conversations about race.* New York: Basic Books.

Tharp, R. G. (1989). Psychological variables and constants: Effects on teaching and learning in schools. *American Psychologist, 44*, 349–359.

Tharp, R. G., & Gallimore, R. (1988). *Rousing minds to life: Teaching, learning, and schooling in social context.* Cambridge, UK: Cambridge University Press.

Theokas, C. (1991). *Modifying sex-typed behavior and contact patterns in a kindergarten classroom with an outer space intervention curriculum.* Unpublished master's thesis, Mount Holyoke College, South Hadley, MA.

Thompson, A. (1998). Not the color purple: Black feminist lessons for educational caring. *Harvard Educational Review, 68*(4), 522–554.

Thompson, T. (1992). For the sake of our children: Poverty and disabilities. In T. Thompson & S. C. Hupp (Eds.), *Saving children at risk: Poverty and disabilities* (pp. 3–10). Newbury Park, CA: Sage.

Thompson, T., & Hupp, S. C. (Eds.). (1992). *Saving children at risk: Poverty and disabilities.* Newbury Park, CA: Sage.

Thorne, B. (1986). Girls and boys together . . . but mostly apart: Gender arrangements in elementary schools. In W. W. Hartup & Z. Rubin (Eds.), *Relationships and development* (pp. 167–184). Hillsdale, NJ: Erlbaum.

Tobin, J. J., Wu, D. Y., & Davidson, D. H. (1989). *Preschool in three cultures: Japan, China, and the United States.* New Haven, CT: Yale University Press.

Turnball, R., & Turnball, A. (1991). Including all children. *Children Today, 20*(3), 3–5.

Ulichny, P. (1994, April). *Cultures in conflict.* Paper presented at the annual meeting of the American Educational Research Association, New Orleans.

Urberg, K. A., & Kaplan, M. G. (1989). An observational study of race-, age-, and sex-heterogeneous interaction in preschoolers. *Journal of Applied Developmental Psychology, 10*, 299–311.

Valdés, G. (1996). *Con respeto: Bridging the distances between culturally diverse families and schools.* New York: Teachers College Press.

Van Ausdale, D., & Feagin, J. R. (2001). *The first R: How children learn race and racism.* Lanham, MD: Rowman & Littlefield.

Vasquez, O. A., Pease-Alvarez, L., & Shannon, S. M. (1994). *Pushing boundaries: Language and culture in a Mexican community.* Cambridge, UK: Cambridge University Press.

Vorrasi, J. A., & Gabarino, J. (2000). Poverty and youth violence: Not all risk factors are created equal. In V. Polakow (Ed.), *The public assault on America's children: Poverty, violence and juvenile injustice* (pp. 59–77). New York: Teachers College Press.

Vygotsky, L. S. (1978). *Mind in society: The development of higher psychological processes.* Cambridge, MA: Harvard University Press.

Wals, A. E. J. (1994). "Nobody planted it, it just grew!" Young adolescents' perceptions and experiences of nature in the context of urban environmental education. *Children's Environments, 11*(3), 177–193.

Wardle, F. (1996). Multicultural education. In M. Root (Ed.), *The multiracial experience: Racial borders as the new frontier* (pp. 380–391). Thousand Oaks, CA: Sage.

Werner, E. E. (1989). High-risk children in young adulthood: A longitudinal study from birth to 32 years. *American Journal of Orthopsychiatry, 59*, 72–81.

West, C. (1993). *Race matters.* Boston: Beacon.

Westridge Young Writers Workshop. (1992). *Kids explore America's Hispanic heritage*. Santa Fe, NM: John Muir Publications.

Westridge Young Writers Workshop. (1993). *Kids explore America's African American heritage*. Santa Fe, NM: John Muir Publications.

Whiting, B. B., & Edwards, C. P. (1988). *Children of different worlds: The formation of social behavior*. Cambridge, MA: Harvard University Press.

Whiting, B. B., & Whiting, J. W. M. (1975). *Children of six cultures: A psychocultural analysis*. Cambridge, MA: Harvard University Press.

Williams, J. E., & Morland, J. K. (1976). *Race, color and the young child*. Chapel Hill: University of North Carolina Press.

Williams, S. A. (1992). Byard, C. (Illus.). *Working cotton*. San Diego: Harcourt Brace Jovanovich.

Wilson, C. (2000). *Telling a different story: Teaching and literacy in an urban preschool*. New York: Teachers College Press.

Wilson, R. A. (1993). Educators for Earth: A guide for early childhood instruction. *Journal of Environmental Education, 24*(2), 15–21.

Wilson, R. A. (1995). Nature and young children: A natural connection. *Young Children, 50*(6), 4–11.

Wong-Filmore, L. (1991). When learning a second language means losing the first. *Early Childhood Research Quarterly, 6*(3), 323–346.

Yeung, W. J., Linver, M. R., & Brooks-Gunn, J. (2002). How money matters for young children's development: Parental investment and family processes. *Child Development, 73*(6), 1861–1879.

# Index

# About the Author

**Patricia G. Ramsey** is Professor of Psychology and Education and Director of Gorse Child Study Center at Mount Holyoke College in South Hadley, Massachusetts. Formerly, she taught in the Early Childhood Education Departments at Wheelock College, Indiana University, and the University of Massachusetts. She holds a master's degree from California State University in San Francisco and a doctorate in early childhood education from the University of Massachusetts in Amherst. She is a former preschool and kindergarten teacher.